The Argentine Generation of 1880

The Argentine Generation of 1880

Ideology and Cultural Texts

David William Foster

University of Missouri Press
Columbia and London

University of Missouri Press, Columbia, Missouri 65211
Printed and bound in the United States of America

5 4 3 2 1 94 93 92 91 90

Library of Congress Cataloging-in-Publication Data

Foster, David William.
The Argentine generation of 1880 : ideology and cultural texts / David William Foster.
p. cm.
Includes bibliographical references and index.
ISBN 0-8262-0732-4 (alk. paper)
1. Argentine literature—19th century—History and criticism.
2. Argentina—Civilization—19th century. 3. Literature and society—Argentina—History—19th century. I. Title.
PQ7650.F67 1990
860.9′982—dc20 89-29204
CIP

This paper meets the requirements of the American National Standard for Permanence of Paper for Printed Library Materials, Z39.48, 1984.

Designer: Liz Fett
Typesetter: Connell-Zeko Type & Graphics
Printer: Thomson-Shore, Inc.
Binder: Thomson-Shore, Inc.
Typeface: Garamond No. 3

To the artists, writers, and intellectuals of the current Argentine generation of the 80s

Contents

Acknowledgments ix

Introduction 1

1. Textual Powers: Reading the Social Text 15

2. Rewriting National History 68

3. Writing the Tensions of Transition 91

4. The Failure of Control: The Limits of Power and Knowledge 128

5. Rural Culture Revisited 151

Conclusion 178

Appendix: Chronology 183

Bibliography 187

Index 201

Acknowledgments

The research for this project was conducted pursuant to grants from the American Philosophical Society and various programs of Arizona State University. I wish to express my gratitude to these agencies and to my research associates: Zoila Gamero de Tovar, Virginia Shen, Daniel Altamiranda, and Juliette Spence. Katharine Kaiper Phillips provided me with invaluable editorial assistance.

Several fragments of this study have appeared in scholarly journals and are incorporated here with the permission of the editors: *Symposium* for the section on Cané; *Romance Notes* for the sections on *¿Inocentes o culpables?* and on the dramatic version of *Juan Moreira; Bulletin of Hispanic Studies* for the section on Eduardo Gutiérrez's *Juan Manuel de Rosas: los dramas del terror; Revista hispánica moderna* for the section on Mansilla; and *Hispanic Review* for the section on López's *La gran aldea.*

All translations from the Spanish in this study are my own.

The Argentine Generation of 1880

Introduction

> That the artist is the more or less active reproducer of social meaning, a maker as well as a product of social influences, is a view current in much modern sociological criticism.[1]

> There is an obvious need for a general term to describe not only the products but the processes of all signification, including the signification of values. It is interesting that 'ideology' and 'ideological' have been widely used in this sense. . . . For the practical links between 'ideas[']' and 'theories' and the 'production of real life' are all in this material social process of signification itself.[2]

Within just two decades after gaining its final independence from Spain in 1816, Argentina fell under the tyrannical leadership of Juan Manuel Rosas, a wealthy landowner and cattleman dedicated to affirming his power by repudiating the Enlightenment and Romantic principles of the independence leaders in order to restore the primacy of Hispanic traditions. The Rosas regime has cast a long shadow over the entire social, political, and cultural history of Argentina. For Rosas was in many ways a symbol of the struggle in Argentina, a struggle that was certainly occurring elsewhere, regarding what a national life independent of Spanish colonial rule was to be.

If independence from Spain meant the culmination of the sympathy of influential leaders toward the currents of the eighteenth century, the rise of a reactionary force like Rosas underscored the intense internecine fighting over who would control the economic wealth of the country (whether as a centralized union or a loose confederation), as well as the ideological structures elaborated to account for that control. The complexity of the issues associated with Rosas and the way in which his administration between 1829 (the year he became governor of the province of Buenos Aires) and 1852 is returned to over and over again in the analysis of Argentine culture attest to the crucial defining power of his figure:

1. Priscilla B. P. Clark, "Literature and Sociology," 114.
2. Raymond Williams, *Marxism and Literature,* 70.

> La caída de Rosas—3 de febrero de 1852—tiene una primera significación indudable: se rompe un sistema en el cual un hombre—su principal protagonista—, y detrás de él un grupo que por el momento representa irónicamente las fuerzas productivas de la Provincia de Buenos Aires, trata de modelar la fisonomía del país entero. Años de una conducción por lo menos sibilina aunque también violenta habían dado por resultado una cierta homogeneidad política (el generalizado caudillismo que de una manera u otra era autorizado por Rosas o desembocaba en él) y un tono económico (aislamiento y proteccionismo) que podían hacer sentir el futuro como invariable. . . .
>
> Por lo tanto: 1880 empieza a cobrar sentido en tanto cierre de este período que parte de Caseros y, fundamentalmente, porque ofrece soluciones concretas a los problemas que se debaten en esos 30 años y que nacieron con la Revolución de Mayo si no antes.[3]
>
> (Rosas's fall on February 3, 1852, has as its undoubted primary importance the destruction of a system in which one man—its principal protagonist—and behind him a group that for the moment ironically represents the productive forces of the Province of Buenos Aires attempts to mold the physiognomy of the entire country. Years of a leadership that was at least sybilline, although it was also violent, had resulted in a certain political homogeneity [the generalized caudillismo that in one way or another was authorized by Rosas or flowed toward him] and an economic tone [isolationism and protectionism] that could make the future appear to be invariable. . . .
>
> Therefore, 1880 began to take on meaning as the closure of this period that stems from Caseros and, fundamentally, because it offered concrete solutions to the problems being debated in those thirty years that dated from the May Revolution if not before.)

Many of the constants of Argentine social history are associated with Rosas: the landowning oligarchy versus Liberal capitalism, countryside versus city, Hispanic legacy versus modern European concepts of progress, authoritarianism versus relative individualism, regionalism versus centralism, to name only the most recurring oppositions. That these disjunctions become rather tenuous upon close scrutiny and often break down in their application to historical data does not invalidate them as constants attendant upon Rosas as a symbol of ideological struggle. And rather than merely confirming the difficulties of reducing historical data to facile semantic oppositions, their essentially amorphous quality is perhaps best seen as a form of "poetic eloquence" with respect to the entire agenda of definitions confronting thinkers and actors in this ini-

3. Noé Jitrik, *El 80 y su mundo,* 23–24. See also E. Bradford Burns, *The Poverty of Progress: Latin America in the Nineteenth Century,* 68–69.

tial stage of Argentine national history. A scientific historiography may wish to define these oppositions in a precise manner and to correlate them securely with facts and events. However, from the point of view of the cultural texts, particularly the especially dense ones we associate with literature, such vague oppositions merely serve to alert one to the possible parameters of meaning organized in a specific text.

When Rosas was forced to relinquish power in 1852, the architects of a new society dedicated themselves with equal fervor to establishing Liberal institutions that would free Argentina from its (for them, benighted) Hispanic past and place that country in the mainstream of Western European values. If Rosas's program was reactionary not so much in the popular political sense of the term as in the fact that it "reacted" to the sociopolitical themes that had led up to independence, the post-Caseros project as it evolves toward the Liberal hegemony of 1880 and after has generally been credited with well-defined goals and the capacity to execute these goals efficiently. Certainly, the dynamic of social engineering, the convictions about political and economic operativity, and the unwavering dedication to the pursuit of beliefs that were thought to be scientifically derived and confirmed account in large measure for the inexorable changes in Argentine society wrought by the group of individuals who had fashioned power in their own image by 1880.[4]

Rosas had been quite successful in pursuing his goals, and the vivid memory of how he had pursued them provided, in the first place, a convenient terminus a quo for changes in Argentine society in a way that its past could be confidently left behind. The Liberal model provided by the dominant European nations and the success of its emergence in the United States provided the men of 1880 with examples of how to construct a new society. The result was a national order that, despite internal conflicts that led eventually to the woes Argentina has experienced in the twentieth century, held together for a remarkably long period of time, and provided Argentina with one of that country's high points of self-esteem:

> The liberal Argentina planned in the 1850s by Alberdi and Urquiza, put into practical working order by Mitre, Sarmiento, Avellaneda, and Roca, and brought safely through its crisis of development by Pellegrini lasted until the great world depression of 1929. . . .
>
> The age of gold did glow indeed, but no one must be blinded by the dazzle. The old liberal Argentina depended on a great many political and

4. The enormous changes of this period are designated under the rubric of "the alluvial era" by José Luis Romero, "La era aluvial."

economic relations which were destroyed or profoundly changed by the Great Depression. Furthermore the dynamics and the stability of the liberal order were related to a set of internal circumstances which were bound sooner or later to reach a limit, and inevitably would present the community with a problem of transcending those limits or falling back into stagnation and conflict.[5]

Perhaps there has been a tendency to exaggerate the efficacy of the policies of 1880: Human life goes on in its own complex, chaotic, and ultimately irreducible fashion despite whatever public ideology prevails.[6] Certainly, Burns's research has underscored the reverse side of the myths of progress in Latin America,[7] and Biagini attempts to correct the balance of the customary insistence on the Europeanizing elitism of this group and to show that their interests may be considered rather more diverse.[8] The literature at the beginnings of the economic and social failures of 1890, stepping back from the exuberance of the 1880 high point,[9] transmits to a large degree such a perception of the uncontained flux of existence. But whatever the real structural changes brought about by the consolidation of power of the Generation of 1880 (and when one considers what Buenos Aires, at least, was able to stand for in Latin America by this time, they were not inconsiderable), the characterization of that group of leaders in virtually all spheres of public life constitutes a compact network of ideas that cannot be eluded in understanding the general ideology of Argentine society at this juncture or in reading the cultural texts that interrelate with society and its dominant ideology.[10] David Viñas, who has written some of the most lucid pages on the tensions between ideology and social reality in Argentine culture, underscores the intellectual and artistic practices of these leaders:

5. H. S. Ferns, *Argentina,* 121.

6. Certainly, this is the sense of comments by Ezequiel de Olaso, "Notas para una discusión sobre la cultura de ochenta"; and Mauricio Lebedinsky, *La década del 80: una encrucijada histórica.*

7. Burns, *The Poverty of Progress.*

8. Hugo Edgardo Biagini, *Cómo fue la generación del 80.*

9. Alberto Oscar Blasi, "Las crisis del noventa y sus imágenes en la narrativa argentina"; Luis Arturo Castellanos, "Situaciones conflictivas en la historia y literatura argentina entre 1880 y 1910"; and Jorge M. Scalavini, "La literatura crítica del Unicato. 1880–1890."

10. "In general, by ideology one understands an ordered cluster of ideas (that is, general affirmations that describe, interpret, and provide value for reality, as well as the guidelines for the action resulting from those ideas). These ideas are found to be in conformance with the conscious or unconscious needs and interests of a specific social group, and ideology is in the last instance reducible to the standing as social class of that group" (Henry Markiewicz, "Ideología y obra literaria," 33).

> Para ellos el quehacer literario es excursión, *causerie,* impresiones y ráfagas: "colocaban una frase" como quien toma un potich para depositarlo sobre un estante o "tenían salidas" cuando empezaban a presentir que el uso de las palabras acorrala. Tomar las palabras con las puntas de los dedos, picar una comida, afilar un cigarro, palmear una yegua de raza. Todo venía a ser lo mismo: al fin de cuentas la literatura no era oficio sino privilegio de la renta. Eran, pues, *gentlemen*-escritores y su estilo "daba tono y sello" por más espectacular y por conjugarse con un ocio mayor articulado en su prestigio y en el control de las estructuras de difusión.[11]

> (Literary activity for them is an excursion, a *causerie,* impressions and flashes of insight: they "put down" a sentence as though they were taking a potiche in hand to set it on a shelf or they "had bright ideas" when they began to sense that the use of words is intimidating. Picking up words with the tips of the fingers, chopping a meal, rolling a cigarette, patting a purebred mare. It was all part of the same thing: in the final analysis literature was not a profession but the privilege of an income. They were, then, gentlemen writers, and their style "provided class and a hallmark" because it was the most outstanding and because it matched a greater leisure articulated by their prestige and in the control they exercised over the structures of its diffusion.)

For many Viñas's characterizations are petulant and willfully tendentious. Nevertheless, they possess the exceptional merit of deconstructing the most venerable myths of Argentine culture, most notably in this case, that of the sophisticated writer in full possession of the most advanced levels of knowledge and artistic forms to be had from the prestigious European centers.

As a consequence of the effective execution of prevalent notions of political, intellectual, and literary accomplishment, no matter how arrogantly patriarchal and self-satisfied its leaders may have been, we may agree that the social and cultural project referred to as the Generation of 1880 was singularly successful from the point of view of what emerged as the dominant financial and political class. Indeed, by the end of the century Argentina had attained prominent international economic status. In some interpretations (for example, that of Ferns), it was to become the fourth economic power in the world by the time of the First World War, in great part because of the foreign investments that were aggressively sought in order to wed Argentina to an international economy conceived of as self-sustaining. Concomitantly, Argentina assumed a significant inter-American political role, spearheading the founding of the Pan

11. David Viñas, *Literatura argentina y realidad política: apogeo de la oligarquía,* 100.

American Union, the forerunner of the Organization of American States. These activities, which must be viewed as major fragments in a mosaic of ever-expanding but overlapping interests, contributed to the image of the Argentine public man making his own fortune and, in the process, that of his country.

Much has been written about the multifaceted career of such important figures as Lucio V. Mansilla, Miguel Cané, and Eduardo Wilde. These were individuals who combined an intense private life with extensive public service, who were able to bridge disciplines subsequently conceived of as antagonistic, and who as dynamic personalities cemented what were still inevitably fragmentary realms of Argentine social life. The nineteenth-century ideal of the dynamic personality has understandably contributed to the lionization of these men, and the accomplishments attributed to them abet the appreciation of their generation as particularly productive. We cannot concern ourselves so much with confirming this productivity or questioning how much there in fact was and whom it affected. It is sufficient to contemplate its sustained evocation in Argentine social history as an index of the defining role played by whatever did, in fact, get done.

As far as literature and culture were concerned, there can be little doubt that they viewed this "high" human activity, at least in the terms in which artistic and intellectual creativity was viewed during the period, as a highly specialized domain, as of central importance in formulating a critical and ameliorative posture toward a society being forged with iron determination:

> ¿Qué es la literatura para los hombres de esta generación? Ante todo, y de acuerdo con lo visto, una entre las múltiples actividades enumeradas, actividad que, como las otras, es ejercida únicamente por ellos. Todos los representantes significativos de esta generación se han expresado a nivel literario, lo que demuestra que esta actividad tiene para ellos una importancia singular. Es que la literatura les permite canalizar la necesidad de emitir juicios y opiniones que fundamenten su posición frente a la realidad circundante. Ninguna de las otras actividades desarrolladas por ellos puede cumplir acabadamente este requisito.[12]

> (What is literature for the men of this generation? Above all, in accord with what is apparent, it is one among the multiple activities that have been enumerated, an activity that, like the others, is exercised only by them. All of the important representatives of this generation have expressed themselves literarily, which demonstrates that this activity has a

12. *El 80,* 1:7–8.

singular importance for them. The fact is that literature allows them to channel the need to pass judgment and give opinions that support their position in the face of the reality around them. None of the other activities they pursued can adequately fulfill this requirement.)

A recurrent issue in the analyses of texts that make up this study will be the specific ways in which literature provides the opportunity for and permits a highly ideologized reading of Argentine society during the period 1880–1900.

The political interests, the intellectual forces, and the attendant cultural activities associated with this project of providing Argentina with a specifically nineteenth-century Liberal identity are thus customarily identified with the Generation of 1880. That is the year that Julio A. Roca, one of the leading spokesmen of dominant economic interests with extensive foreign ties, assumed the presidency, and it is the year that the city of Buenos Aires was federalized. These individuals, both in the public arenas of politics and economic venture and in the private spheres of intellectual and artistic activity, laid the groundwork for the Liberal ideology in Argentina. This ideology provided Argentina with a basic national and sociocultural identity that, despite enormous subsequent political transformations, continues to characterize that nation's abiding self-image (at least from the optic of Buenos Aires) as a progressive, sophisticated, and essentially European people. Although Latin America in general was turning in this period to Western European models of social and economic organization as part of the attempt to free itself from its Hispanic past (compare the so-called *científicos*—men of science—engaged in a massive project in Mexico), it is Argentina where one finds the greatest implementation of a coherent program of nation building around these principles. Nearly overnight, it seems, Argentina assimilated the constellation of ideologemes known as positivism, a scientific codification of attitudes that supported the Liberal economic program. This occurrence resulted from two forces: Argentina's need to free itself from Rosas's attempts to reinstitute a Hispanic influence and the complementary need to establish cultural independence and set aside colonial margination and stagnation.

The consequences of the assimilation of positivism are abundantly clear in the case of Argentina's subsequent social evolution. Not only did it mean the general repudiation of whatever could be considered "Hispanic" in terms of a notion of a premodern society to be transcended, but it had immediate consequences for social and cultural programs that are interpreted by the cultural texts of the period. The most famous of these consequences involved the "whitening" of Argentina. If the small black population, where it had not melded with indigenous elements, was tending to die out for a variety of health reasons, Argentina's fabled promotion of immigration from select areas of Europe was intended, with no apologies, to supplant both the old Hispanic roots and the scattered native groups (at least in the central area of demographic expansion) with what it was hoped (rather jejunely, it turned out) would be vigorous strains of hard-working peasants. Although these immigrants did turn out to be industrious in the almost scandalous way they took over vast sectors of Buenos Aires, their principal whitening influence was to bring with them a whole range of European social problems amply ventilated in the literature of Naturalism examined in Chapter 3. The leaders of the Generation of 1880, in their zeal to create a European nation that would essentially, if not definitively, reject its Hispanic past, introduced into Argentina a complex of social factors that provide the nucleus of the themes—national history, class conflict, rural versus urban priorities, individual self-identity—dealt with by the texts examined in this study.

These efforts produced an explosion of publications unheard of in a Latin American society. This study will examine a central core of texts that may be considered (with some flexible inclusions) to constitute a representative canon of the period. However, it must be borne in mind that the creation of a unifying ideological project and its inevitable counterpoints can only occur under the aegis of an enormous textual production, which meant, in the age of print that the late nineteenth century had become, a staggering array of publications in the form of books, monographs, pamphlets, magazines, reviews, newspapers, and the like. Pérez Amuchástegui, with visible sarcasm, comments on the outpouring of publications that is one of the truly impressive correlatives of the cultural self-image propagated at this time:

> Entre escritores de verdadero valor, circulaban muchísimos que ni siquiera llegaban a mediocres aunque llenaran cuartillas y más cuartillas colmadas de sandías disquisiciones. Y esto no solo ocurría en la cosmopolitizada metrópolis; en el interior la cosa era aún más grave. La mala literatura invadía, osada, los campos de la filosofía y, por supuesto, de la historia; pero no se detenía allí, sino que aventuraba temerarias incursiones en los peligrosos territorios de la medicina y la psicología. Y el grueso de la oligarquía paternalista absorbía con deleite esos audaces abortos del pensamiento, a través de periódicos 'sociales' que por entonces circulaban con bastante profusión al módico precio de cuarenta centavos equivalentes a unos cinco pesos de hoy, al cambio internacional de la libra.[13]

(Among writers of true value were there to be found very many who

13. A. J. Pérez Amuchástegui, *Mentalidades argentinas (1860–1930)*, 71.

could not even be considered mediocre, no matter how many reams of paper they filled with stupid disquisitions. And this was true not only in the cosmopolitanized metropolis—matters were even worse in the interior. Bad literature daringly invaded the fields of philosophy and, of course, history. But it did not stop there, but undertook fearless incursions in the dangerous territories of medicine and psychology. And the bulk of the patriarchal oligarchy absorbed enthusiastically those audacious abortions of thought in the form of "social" newspapers that circulated at that time with considerable profusion at the modest price of forty cents—some five pesos in today's money—at the international exchange rate of the pound sterling.)

As a consequence of the importance of the Generation of 1880, there has been considerable historiographic writing about the period, which may be easily considered the "classic" era of Argentine history. But concomitantly there is a notable lack of contemporary criticism dealing with the artistic production of the major intellectual and literary figures responsible for the writings that constitute the primary cultural documents of the period. While one finds a sporadic output of writing about major texts, such criticism tends to be confined to narrow thematic studies or broad life-and-works inventories. Both approaches are reasonable and are easily understood as consistent with the historical role of the Generation of 1880.

Thematic studies correlate, on the basis of a metaphor of semantic echoing, the public issues of the day with their "fictional" and "narrative" treatment in literature. Whether literature is viewed as simply an artful form of the rhetoric of debate or whether it is acknowledged to permit a heightened representation of the texture of social existence, if read thematically it is approached against a standard inventory of "real-life" topics to be discovered and gauged for their relative accuracy. As a consequence, it is no surprise to find that principal texts of the Generation of 1880 are customarily viewed as primary historical sources and are cited as such. This is quite obvious in the case of the so-called Stock Market Cycle, a group of a half-dozen novels that appeared in rapid succession to comment fictively on the 1890 financial crisis. This crisis scarred the insouciant facade of the economic boom of 1880 and inaugurated a specifically jaundiced view of where the national commonwealth was headed. As such, it is no surprise to find an unusual attention toward these cultural texts by historians and by literary scholars who appreciate the sociohistorical value of such documents.

In a corollary fashion, a preoccupation with the continuities between the life and works of these writers can be comprehended most immediately on the basis of the public roles most of them played, whereby writing was both a public activity by extension and whereby the concerns they wrote about were public issues. Here, perhaps, one might begin to explain why no significant "psychological" novel emerges from this appreciable production of texts. The writer as a prominent public figure invites a reading of his work as a function of biographical interpretation. The specific semiotic features of the work may fade or even vanish in such a reading, but it does serve to remind us both of the ways in which literature was conceived of during the period when these texts were produced and of the paraliterary historical importance of the names involved.

By contrast to either a thematic or a biographical approach, this study involves an adherence to the critical premise that one may view literary works as particular versions of "(re)writings" of the ideological patterns of a society. That is, from this point of view, literary narratives (whether in the form of fictional tales, dramatic texts, or the essay in its many guises) constitute semiotic transformations of the ideological and sociocultural structures of a society. Moreover, they are both reflexes of those structures and persuasive articulations of values and beliefs that contribute to a society's evolving formulation of its guiding ideologies.

Such a view of the cultural texts is less interested in the necessary ways in which novels and other works of literature "treat" themes of prominent public concern as may be identified from other sources. Rather, an ideological approach necessarily stresses the manner in which topics are dealt with, how they are framed, how they are defined, how they are interpreted as a part of the structure of human society.

Viewed in this fashion, literature is neither a reflection nor a portrait of society: metaphors of representation are set aside as promoting a conception of literature as transparent and easily accessible information about life and society. By contrast, the problematic nature of literature (indeed, of all cultural production) is addressed by an ideological criticism out of attention to an imperative to investigate the processes whereby literature becomes a reading or interpretation of personal and social life. The larger questions relate to why life requires interpretation at all and why something we call art/literature/narrative can pretend to satisfy the impetus to provide interpretations in the first place. Viewed from the more narrow confines of the literary text, the ponderables involve how the semiotic structure of the cultural text moves between reinscribing the ideological conflicts of human existence and articulating in a putatively coherent fashion an interpretation of those conflicts. Our prevailing view of literary texts continues to be that they should be coherent in a way life is not usually sensed to be, with the result that one characterization of literature is that it "imposes" meaning through a gesture of coherency as much as it restages the complex ambiguities of life.

There is no reason to feel uncomfortable with the impositions of art if we can be sensitive to how the semiotics of meaning work and to all of the decisions that must be made in the construction of literary texts in order to achieve any measure of apparent coherency. It has become a commonplace to say that what a text does not explicate is as important as what it chooses to deal with, and a deconstructive reading of the gaps, the silences, the ruptures, and, finally, the failed coherency has come to be considered an integral part of a criticism that is both ideological and semiotic at the same time:

> We are then not only concerned with the restoration of social content in its full sense, that of a generative immediacy. The idea of a structure of feeling can be specifically related to the evidence of forms and conventions—semantic figures—which, in art and literature, are often forming. . . . As a matter of cultural theory this is a way of defining forms and conventions in art and literature as inalienable elements of a social material process: not by derivation from other social forms and pre-forms, but as social formation of a specific kind which may in turn be seen as the articulation (often the only fully available articulation) of structures of feeling which as living processes are much more widely experienced.[14]

The present exploration from an ideological point of view of the literature produced by members of the Generation of 1880 has involved the identification of a canon of essential texts, with a specification of their major literary works (because of the cultural priorities of the period, basically narratives, although some attention is paid to drama and the essay), and with a comparative analysis of the literary works in detail in terms of the textual strategies for structuring a characteristically literary response (within the parameters of what the period considered to be literature) to sociocultural circumstances, paradigms, and concerns.

No attempt is made to discover figures hitherto unjustly overlooked or poorly assessed or to construct a revised hierarchy of relative importance for the names most commonly evoked. No new themes are identified, and an evaluation of the styles and techniques of the writers has not been a preoccupation. Rather, the readings presented here conform essentially to the principles of an ideological criticism in that they propose to explore the semiotic organization of the texts as interpretations within the conventions recognized by literature of general ideological

14. Williams, *Marxism and Literature,* 133.

issues. What the writer views the literary text as able to do, how he sees the function of character (so essential to nineteenth-century fiction) as an embodiment of particular views and experiences, how he makes use of a specific narrative consciousness as a central axis for his text, how he metaphorizes the details of life in accord with the privileged status assigned to art as a separate and formal domain are all issues that permit access to a literary text as a form of semiotic transformation of social and political ideologies and, by the recursive nature of meaning, as a form of inscribing ideology to begin with.

We can no longer view literature as an interpretation of "reality" that exists in a precultural or neutral state: "Semiotic analysis does not dissolve the difference between literature and reality so much as alert us to social reality as an already-constituted field of symbolic meaning."[15] Rather, what we perceive as immediate reality is, in fact, a symbolic realm that we have been taught to read in certain ways because of the semiotic systems we have internalized. Literature is one way of reading this symbolic realm, and yet it is at the same time one of the cultural instruments that teach us how to read the symbolic realm(s) within which we live and which we wish to interpret. This explains how literature both assists us in reading our sociocultural experience (the demythificational gesture of art) and induces us to see it in particularly ideologized ways (the mythificational gesture of art).

The analysis of the literary texts must necessarily seek to do more than engage in historical analysis simply to confirm the recurrence in fiction of motifs that can be described in general terms as "historical" or "sociopolitical." Rather, the concern must be to address questions of literary structure and language from the perspective of the dominant query of the ideological critic: What are the ways in which a literary text reflects in its structural organization the ideological system of writers and their various audiences? Of interest, therefore, are the sort of characters chosen, the plot configurations elaborated, the dynamics of the relationship established between narrator and reader, the self-image of the narrators in terms of the conventions of their discourse as against the conventions of the discourse of the characters in the novel, the modes of addressing the reader utilized by the narrator, the implications of these details for an understanding of the evolution of a norm of educated and literary writing in Argentina during the formative period of the Generation of 1880, and the continuities between fictional writing and other

15. William C. Dowling, *Jameson, Althusser, Marx: An Introduction to the Political Unconscious*, 88.

protocols of writing during the period. In the case of the latter issue, of interest is the framing of narrative vis-à-vis journalism, the essay, and the burgeoning historical writing of the period. And, finally, such a study involves the very image of the role of literature in the Argentine Liberal society projected by authors and their strategies for providing their writing with sociocultural contextualizations through the aforementioned details of textual production.

In the final analysis, the prominent texts of the Generation of 1880 are not just rewritings of a period of complex evolution in Argentina; they play an important part in the process of defining that evolution by giving it meaning, in the form of literary texts in particular and cultural writing in general. Rather than mere reflexes of change, they are programmatic inscriptions of the forms of that change, which is, after all, why this group of writings can continue to be viewed as so integral to the global project of the Generation of 1880.

* * *

The chapters that follow are not intended to represent a coherent literary history of the writing of the Argentine Generation of 1880. In the first place, a reasonable review in depth of that writing would require a monograph of many hundreds of pages. The conjunction of three factors result in the Generation of 1880 being bibliographically one of the most productive in Argentine cultural history: a way of life that permitted the considerable leisure necessary for sustained writing; an overall economy that stimulated the interrelated practices of writing, publishing, bookselling, reviewing, and reading; and the simple fact that the vast changes taking place in society were enough to stimulate an outpouring of literary and paraliterary production.

Furthermore, my interest has not been in using written documents as sources to provide a coherent portrait of Argentine society during the period of this seminal boom, although my readers most assuredly will learn about the goals and failures of that society as seen by some of its most important writers. Rather, my purpose is to use the ideological reading of cultural (basically, literary) texts as one reasonable way of showing the interface between these cultural texts and the larger societal issues to which they respond.

As a consequence of this approach, this study is organized into five rather generally defined sections. Since cultural texts may, among other axes, be distributed between those texts that serve to define and confirm a society's self-image and those texts that undertake to critique and "deconstruct" it, this division has served as one way of dividing up the works that are discussed (see, specifically, Chapters 1, 3, and 4). In a completely different register, the need for the Generation of 1880 to address itself to the projection of a specific social program that would both incorporate the past into an overarching master plan and set the boundaries accounting for contemporary views of national culture accounts for another order of significant texts (Chapters 1 and 2). Finally, as the Generation of 1880 was principally interested in confirming a modern urban culture that would bring all of society under its tutelage, it necessarily involved a reconsideration of rural culture that, after its autonomy and even primacy with Romanticism, needed to be homogenized, or at least made continuous, with the dominant urban (that is, Buenos Aires) dynamic (Chapter 5 versus 1–4). This ordering of the sections that focus in detail on major texts is perhaps more fragmentary than cultural and literary histories are wont to be, but it does have the virtue of defining each text, in addition to a major intrinsic feature, in terms of one dominant contextual framework that gives it ideological meaning. Such a heterogeneous ensemble is proposed as a particularly effective way of exploring in some detail significant documents, while at the same time respecting the need to insert them into controlling sociohistoric contexts.

CHAPTER 1

Textual Powers
Reading the Social Text

The four texts examined in this chapter, in addition to being classics of Argentine literature written by members of the Generation of 1880, represent various analyses of Argentine society in terms of the values and convictions of those members. Lucio V. Mansilla addresses the possibility of knowing indigenous culture and coming to terms with it within the frame of reference of an educated man like himself. Miguel Cané, by evoking nostalgically the formative years of his youth at the Colegio Nacional, defends the program of liberal education established by his generation. José Sixto Alvarez, while providing a series of sketches about the emerging criminal class in Buenos Aires, details the story of a poor provincial integrated into the new, professionalized system of law and order in modern Buenos Aires. Joaquín V. González evokes the provincial setting of his youth and, in the process, engages in a nativist paean to a poeticized landscape that serves as a refuge from the turmoil of the ever-more complex metropolis. All four of these texts constitute ideologies of the Generation of 1880 in the sense of articulating accepted values to which their society will adhere unquestioningly: formal knowledge, liberal education, law and order, and a mythified countryside.

Knowledge in Mansilla's *Una excursión a los indios ranqueles*

> Creerán algunos que a medida que corre la pluma voy fraguando cosas imaginarias, por llenar papel y aumentar el efecto artificial de estas mal zurcidas cartas.
>
> Y sin embargo todo es cierto.[1]
>
> Yo no soy más que un simple cronista, ¡felizmente! (157)

(There are those who will believe that I am making imaginary things up as my pen flies, just to fill the page and enhance the artificial effect of these poorly joined letters.

1. Lucio V. Mansilla, *Una excursión a los indios ranqueles,* 29. Hereafter cited parenthetically in the text by page number.

Yet nevertheless all this is true.

I am nothing more than a simple chronicler, alas!)

Lucio V. Mansilla's *Una excursión a los indios ranqueles* (An excursion to the Ranqueles Indian nation; 1870) is the most famous, and undoubtedly the most accomplished, of the frontier writings of the fourth quarter of nineteenth-century Argentine literature. Written on the edge, so to speak, of the Generation of 1880, for whose figures Mansilla served as a sort of patriarchal presence, *Excursión* is a key document in the accounts of the encounter between the indigenous population and an expanding Buenos Aires society that required the pacification of the Indians in order to pursue its goals of economic expansionism.

Mansilla (1831–1913) was a maternal nephew of Juan Manuel Rosas, and his family suffered upon the fall of the dictator in 1852.[2] By 1858, nevertheless, Mansilla, who had distinguished himself militarily, had been named a frontier commander in the area occupied by the Ranqueles Indians, a post he held until 1870. During this tenure, Mansilla was called upon to negotiate with the Indians, and his book is both a record of the frustratingly complex and eventually futile attempts to negotiate peaceful relations between the central government and the indigenous population and his personal reactions to his official mission.[3]

Ultimately marked by a notable sensitivity toward a culture radically different from his own and convinced that the Indians were victims of Buenos Aires and its army, Mansilla chose to write *Excursión* as an appeal for a measure of awareness by the urban elite toward the realities of the frontier. Julio A. Roca's *Expedición al Desierto* was still a decade away when Mansilla wrote his memoir, and the apparent curiosity toward the Indians his text reveals was still a sociocultural possibility. After 1879, when Indian resistance had been wiped out and close to nine million *hectáreas* of "liberated" land passed into the hands of the less than four hundred individuals who had financed Roca's blitzkrieg-like expedition, indigenous culture was left to be forgotten by the general populace and studied by only the professional anthropologists.

Thus, Mansilla's *Excursión,* as a personal memoir underlain by an individual commitment to life on the frontier between European and Indian societies, stands both as a closing sign for a period of national culture (the period prior to the definitive conquest of the open desert)

2. General biographical and historical information on Mansilla may be consulted in the studies by Enrique Popolizio, *Vida de Lucio V. Mansilla,* and José Luis Lanuza, *Genio y figura de Lucio V. Mansilla.*

3. Carlos Orlando Nallim, "La visión del indio en Lucio V. Mansilla: testimonio y literatura en *Una excursión a los indios ranqueles.*"

and as a symptom of the intellectual scrutiny of sociocultural issues that would later characterize the Generation of 1880. The period of the 1870s included a considerable range of writing about the "Indian problem," and many subsequent texts will be produced both to justify Roca's expedition and to laud this important facet of the forging of a unified Argentine republic.[4] However, no text equals *Excursión* in the dynamic presence of its narrator and the subtle range of considerations raised with respect to indigenous culture and the relationships between it and that of the representatives of a self-styled modern central government. As a probing and sensitive treatment of the Other and of the culture of a society radically different from one's own, Mansilla's memoir is a harbinger of the attention to the complex patterns of culture that concerned the writers of the generation that saw him as a guiding spirit.[5]

As in the case of so many popular classics, any detailed analysis of *Excursión* must strip away accrued commonplaces. The most important one that must be questioned here is that of its charming "transparency." Because it is so filled with information about indigenous society, complemented by the personal adventures of the narrator and sundry tales he repeats as told to him, *Excursión* has come to be remembered in terms of certain particularly notable episodes referred to over and over again in history books, manuals of literature, and the recollections of other authors.[6] The result is the image of a book that provides a reliable and

4. David Viñas, *Indios, ejército y frontera,* focuses specifically on the Roca expedition and writings subsequent to it. For an analysis of Viñas's interpretive strategies of these writings and his attempt to deconstruct the ideological bases of them, see David William Foster, "David Viñas: lecturas reconstructivistas de la historia nacional." Viñas discusses the historical precedent of *Excursión* in "Mansilla, arquetipo," underscoring the disabling conversion of *Excursión* into "a book read by children and adolescents" (p. 149) and Mansilla's reduction to being little more than a venerated gentleman. A more extensive analysis by Viñas of Mansilla's "clubman mentality" is found in "Mansilla: clase, público y clientela."

5. Mansilla's other best known text is the famous collection of sketches that are at the center of his fame as a gentleman intellect, *Entre-nos: causeries del jueves* (1889–1890). See the introduction by Juan Carlos Ghiano, "Estudio preliminar." The major importance of *Entre-nos,* in addition to the wealth of material it contains concerning the *mentalidad* of the Argentine clubmen of the period, is the strong projection of Mansilla's personality as a discourse presence, which only serves to confirm the well-defined image of his narrative voice in *Excursión.* Concerning the fragmentary style associated with this type of writing by members of the Generation of 1880, see Graciela de Solá, "El fragmentarismo en los escritores del 80: 'Entre-nos' de Lucio V. Mansilla."

6. The interest inherent in these anecdotes, quite apart from their insertion within the general narrative framework of *Excursión,* is evident in the independent publication of the most famous: *Narraciones de un porteño.* I do not know why this ad hoc collection underscores the Porteño nature of these anecdotes, although it would be in the spirit of

straightforward guide to the curiosities of frontier life during a moment of important conflict between an expanding central government and its Indian subjects. While it may be important and culturally symptomatic for classics to be remembered in this fashion, it usually means a significant distraction from the total dynamics of a text as one salient example of socially symbolic writing.

The idea of *Excursión* as a charmingly transparent memoir necessarily obscures what a moment's reflection might suggest as complicating factors concerning both its composition and its incorporation into the social context of which Argentine literature is a component.[7] First, *Excursión* is marked by the sign of curiosity: Mansilla makes it abundantly clear on repeated occasions that the excursion he describes was undertaken by his own initiative and in order to gain useful information about the Ranqueles. But, also, Mansilla insists that he was motivated by a profound personal interest beyond the strict discharge of his official duties. Thus, he is able to correlate the useful information he wishes to record with considerations about the wisdom of his personal initiative: "En efecto, querido Santiago, mirando con sangre fría mi viaje a los toldos, ¿no te parece que ha sido perder tiempo?" (In effect, dear Santiago, looking in cold hard terms upon my trip to the tents, doesn't it seem to you that I wasted my time? 145). The tension between personal goals, which may or may not have been satisfied at specific junctures of his expedition, and the need to justify in a utilitarian fashion the official nature of his adventures are two characteristics that provide for important textual divergences in *Excursión,* the major one being the foregrounding of Mansilla's insistent vindication of cultural differences.

Written as a series of letters addressed to a friend identified as Santiago,[8] Mansilla's text foregrounds its features as a personal narrative colored incessantly by the structure of the narrator's own personal convictions as regards human society and cultural values. Mansilla accords to himself as narrator the right to speak exclusively qua Mansilla, and there is virtually no intrusion in the text of the official policies that Mansilla, as a colonel in the Argentine army and frontier commander,

---

Viñas's much later deconstructive reading to focus on the contradictions of an urban reading of the frontier. Another such collection is *Cuentos del fogón (Excursión a los indios ranqueles).*

7. Sylvia Molloy, "Imagen de Mansilla."

8. The Santiago whom Mansilla addresses directly as the narratee of his text is Santiago Arcos, a Chilean who had published a tract in favor of an offensive war against the Indians, *Cuestión de los indios: la frontera y los indios en 1860,* according to Biagini, *Cómo fue la generación del 80,* 64–65.

ought to have represented in his dealings with the Ranqueles Indians. This personalization of an important fragment of Argentine political history provides both for the outstandingly "novelistic" nature of *Excursión* and for the density of its treatment of events as personal rather than official history.

Mansilla's personal commitment toward what he is describing and his understanding of individual motivations and the contradictions of human destiny necessitate a text that constantly turns in upon itself in the examination of the many constituents of its narrative: the personality of the narrator; the details of Argentine history; the features of life on the frontier far from a highly codified polite society; the disjunctions between immediate reality and reported versions of it; the gap between what is known about the Indians and all that remains to be known; the contradictions between an imposed social order and the flux of individual human lives. Rather than being a single-minded, day-by-day account of a military expedition, *Excursión* is, in fact, a highly convoluted text. This is a consequence of the narrator's decision to attempt to fit within the confines of a single discourse a rich counterpoint of details and thoughts about the aforementioned and other constituent elements of interest to him. Far from being the discourse of a narrator who finds it difficult to settle on a principal line of exposition, *Excursión* emerges as a complex text that attempts to fuse all of these considerations as pertinent to an adequate account of what Mansilla—from the vantage point of the as yet unconquered frontier—perceived to be the issues facing Argentine society.

The "liminalness" of this vantage point stimulates or provokes the narrator's evocation of all of these issues as correlatives of his perception that, far from being peripheral matters for a man of his education and class, they are essential to a consideration of the sociocultural processes Argentina is undergoing. Thus, Mansilla views himself implicitly as avatar for a process of cultural discovery, interpretation, and synthesis that explains and legitimizes his excursion to the frontier of civilized society.[9] More than the delightful chronicle of a personal adventure, it is the complex analysis of matters central to a nation still in the process of

9. *Excursión* is the most significant example of the motif of the *viaje* in Mansilla. "In general, criticism does not classify *Una excursión a los indios ranqueles* as a travel book. But its central narrative axis rests on the round-trip expedition undertaken by Mansilla to the Ranqueles settlement on the frontier. Although the trip in question is not that period's consecrated European tour, or one to another distant continent, its content is nevertheless no less exotic for the citizens of Buenos Aires" (George D. Schade, "Los viajeros argentinos del ochenta," 87).

defining its controlling ideologies. Mansilla's text is both an examination of that process and a major contribution to the self-definition that exists at this time. To the extent that Argentina's dominant ideologies become invested in cultural figures who personify an intellectual elite, the organization of *Excursión* in terms of a narrative that promotes a controlling or screening consciousness is one of the prime features that have confirmed its status as a classic. And, as an implied dialogue with the Santiago to whom the text is explicitly addressed, the image is confirmed of *Excursión* as primarily a dialogue between two members of an educated elite. The professional historiography that emerged later in Argentine culture as an echo of the protocols of European social sciences eschewed, of course, the sort of centrifugal narrator (and narratee) that characterizes *Excursión.* Yet this assertive narrative presence (and, to be sure, the full range of interests it manifests) is what makes Mansilla's text such an imposing cultural document.

It is difficult to know which one of the salient textual features of *Excursión* to focus on first, by way of initiating an explication of its complexity. But let us begin with one that does relate directly to the justification of Mansilla's undertaking, both his expedition and his written description of it. This feature involves the need to "know." Certainly, the primary need to know for Mansilla as a military officer and designated commander of an army fortification relates to the urgency of acquiring information about the Indian adversary (253). Although technically a part of the Argentine nation, the Ranqueles comply with a structure of power that is internal to their society and antedates the attempts to impose authority from Buenos Aires. By the same token, while acknowledging some commitment to this authority, their dealings with its delegates demonstrate that they live in fact fundamentally beyond its control. Consequently, the most immediate imperative for knowledge is the necessity to control these aliens, who are viewed as posing a real threat to the security of the frontier.

Yet, Mansilla avoids appealing to this utilitarian justification. Indeed, his first reference to Santiago to whom his text is addressed in the form of letters numbered as chapters, alludes only to a general curiosity and, moreover, one that is circumscribed only by its direct personal reference:

> Hacía ya mucho tiempo que yo rumiaba el pensamiento de ir a Tierra Adentro.
>
> El trato con los indios que iban y venían al Río Cuarto, con motivo de las negociaciones de paz entabladas, había despertado en mí una indecible curiosidad. (6)

(I had been turning over in my head a long time the idea of going to the Outback.

Dealings with the Indians that came back and forth to Río Cuarto, with the motive of the peace negotiations that had been undertaken, had awakened in me an unspeakable curiosity.)

It is important to underscore two elements of this statement: the transition from official responsibility to personal interest and the recourse to a hyperbolic characterization of the intensity of curiosity provoked by the unknown. Moreover, it is at this early point that the narrator emphasizes the intriguingly hypostatized entity of the Tierra Adentro. This phenomenon, which to a modern reader is so immediately evocative of the Lacanian concept of the Other, assumes the category of a controlling presence throughout *Excursión.* It is, to be sure, all that is unknown about the Ranqueles, all that the narrator must discover in his expedition into their realm and that he must accurately report to his reader. It is, in a recurring bundle of disjunctive features, the binary opposition of the cultural frame of reference out of which Mansilla has stepped in his incursion into the other side, into which he leads his reader through the artifice of his memoir. If it is both the unknown and the antithesis of what is known, it is also the undefined. The fundamental challenge to the effort of discursive explanation is to construct a definition for all of the data that have yet to be accounted for by the Spanish language and the Argentine national sociocultural reality which it has hitherto been adequate enough to account for. Thus, almost in the tradition of the medieval Bestiary, *Excursión* is obliged to tame the strange and the forbidding by assimilating it to the language of its exposition and to the quadrants of knowledge of its audience.

A great measure of the fascination for the reader of a document like *Excursión,* which, to be sure, belongs to an extensive inventory of the paraliterature of anthropological discovery in Western culture since the eighteenth century, is the sense of total ignorance about a realm like the Tierra Adentro. Were the narrator to have prior knowledge about what he is soon to experience, were the reader to possess already information concerning the adventures to be described, the rhetorical effect of the hypostatized Tierra Adentro would be considerably attenuated. The starkness of the disjunction implied by the term is what compels the interlocking interest of the first-person narrator and his reader and what provides the opportunity for the text to be propelled by the amassing of details and their explanation as a confirmation of the importance of having crossed over the line into this realm.

The crossing over of the line into the Tierra Adentro, the sense of abandoning the known and the explained, and the tension of the parenthesis of deviation from the known and the explained during the period spent over the line supply the winning interest of a text like *Excursión.* It is for this reason that the moment of transgression (the literal crossing over, the metaphoric abandoning of what is contained by rational explanation) is a breathless, dramatic high point in the text:

> Voy a penetrar, al fin, en el recinto vedado.
>
> Los ecos de la civilización van a resonar pacíficamente por primera vez, donde jamás asentara su planta un hombre del contorno mío.
>
> Grandes y generosos pensamientos me traen; nobles y elevadas ideas me dominan; mi misión es digna de un soldado, de un hombre, de un cristiano, me decía; y veía ya la hora en que reducidos y cristianizados aquellos bárbaros, utilizados sus brazos para el trabajo, rendían pleito homenaje a la civilización por el esfuerzo del más humilde de sus servidores.
>
> Aspiraciones del espíritu despierto, que se realizan con más dificultad que las mismas visiones del ensueño, ¡apartaos! (109)
>
> (I am at last going to penetrate the forbidden territory.
>
> The echoes of civilization will resound peacefully for the first time where no man from my background has ever set foot.
>
> Great and generous thoughts bring me; noble and elevated ideas rule me; my mission is worthy of a soldier, of a man, of a Christian, I told myself; and I could already see the hour in which those barbarians, brought under control and Christianized and their arms put to work, would render homage to civilization through the efforts of the humblest of its servants.
>
> Aspirations of the awakened spirit, which are brought to fruition with greater difficulty than the visions of one's dreams, be gone!)

Significantly, the intensity of the moment of crossing over the line is complemented by the rush of a patriotic thrill in the face of the opportunity to assimilate the Indians of the barbaric unknown into the known world of Christian civilization. The narrator's ironic stance toward his patriotic visions may, from the perspective of mature reflection at the moment of inscribing the emotions of an earlier and uncritical moment, undercut this patriotic thrill. But it does not dismiss what is the compelling motivation for Mansilla's text: the need to take stock of the Tierra Adentro in terms of the cultural priorities that propose to contain it politically.[10]

10. "And *Una excursión* is, as many of its contemporaries saw as the volumes of the work appeared, a veiled assertion against 'civilization,' as incarnate in certain men (Sarmiento in particular). What happens is that today its message appears hidden or diffused in the face of other aspects of the work" (Emilio Carilla, *Literatura argentina, 1800–1950 {esquema generacional}*, 41).

Excursión, of course, is an inaugural and powerful containment of the Tierra Adentro through the medium of descriptive and analytical discourse. No matter how much Mansilla as a narrator may be overwhelmed by the spectacle of the unknown or how repulsed he may be by the strangeness of the material he feels he must convey to his reader, his text is predicated on the assumption that an explanation can, in fact, be provided and on the absolute conviction that it is possible to attain a satisfactory level of knowledge about what must be known. The faith in the ability of the individual to see things with his own eyes and to bring to bear upon what he sees the power of his interpretive intelligence validates *Excursión,* since it can only be of pragmatic value (if not political, then intellectual) if it fulfills its promise to provide both a reliable account and an adequate interpretation of all that is to be seen in the Tierra Adentro:

> el deseo de ver con mis propios ojos ese mundo que llaman Tierra Adentro, para estudiar sus usos y costumbres, sus necesidades, sus ideas, su religión, su lengua, e inspeccionar yo mismo el terreno por donde alguna vez quizá tendrán que marchar las fuerzas que están bajo mis órdenes, he ahí lo que me decidió no ha mucho y contra el torrente de algunos hombres que se decían conocedores de los indios, a penetrar hasta sus tolderías, y a comer primero que tú en Nagüel Mapo una tortilla de huevo de avestruz. (3)

> (the desire to see with my own eyes that world called the Outback, to study its uses and customs, its needs, its ideas, its religion, its language, and to inspect on my own the terrain where perhaps one day the forces under my command might have to march, here is what decided me not so long ago and against the torrent of some men who claimed themselves to be knowledgeable about the Indians, to go as far as the wigwams and to eat before you an omelette made from ostrich eggs in Nagüel Mapo.)

Three elements are mixed in this assertion of purpose: the criterion of military information, individual intellectual curiosity, and a personal competition with his immediate narratee that suggests the quality of their friendship. None of these three goals is in contradiction with the others, and they are unified on the basis of the possibility of attaining the goal of knowledge in the Tierra Adentro. Certainly, Mansilla is writing from the perspective of having already undertaken his adventure, having returned safe and sound, and having been satisfied that he achieved the purpose of his expedition. The historical present with which much of *Excursión* is written, however, suspends the division between the past of that expedition and the present of its recounting (which is reasonable, since Mansilla prepared his text very soon after the expedition it describes). Mansilla defines the categories of his quest for knowledge on the basis of what he set out to learn (a precondition of the exercise of his seeing) and at the same time on the basis of what he had already seen (an inventory of what actually did come to his attention). In either case, the narrator speaks convinced of the possibility of acquiring this knowledge, of assimilating it appropriately in terms of his personal intellectual universe, and of transmitting it adequately to Santiago through his letters:

> "No se aprende el mundo en los libros".
> Aquí era donde quería llegar.
> Siento tener que desagradar a mi ático amigo Carlos Guido, cuyo buen gusto literario los abomina. Sírvame de excusa el carácter confidencial del relato.
> Sí, el mundo no se aprende en los libros, se aprende observando, estudiando los hombres y las costumbres sociales.
> Yo he aprendido más de mi tierra yendo a los indios ranqueles, que en diez años de despestañarme leyendo opúsculos, folletos, gacetillas, revistas y libros especiales.
> Oyendo a los paisanos referir sus aventuras, he sabido cómo se administra la justicia, cómo se gobierna, qué piensan nuestros criollos de nuestros mandatarios y de nuestras leyes.
> Por eso me detengo más de lo necesario quizá en relatar ciertas anécdotas, que parecerán cuentos forjados para alargar estas páginas y entretener al lector. (163–64)

> ("Knowledge about the world does not come from books."
> Here is where I want to get.
> I regret having to displease my Attic friend Carlos Guido, whose good literary taste finds them abominable. May the confidential nature of my story serve as an excuse.
> Yes, knowledge about the world does not come from books, but rather from observing and studying men and social customs.
> I have learned more about my land by going to the territory of the Ranqueles Indians than I did in ten years of burning my eyes out reading opuscules, pamphlets, clippings, specialized reviews, and books.
> By hearing my fellow citizens tell their adventures, I have learned how justice is administered, how one governs, how our people feel about our leaders and our laws.
> That is why I perhaps take longer than necessary to tell certain anecdotes, which must seem like only stories invented to fill these pages and to entertain the reader.)

There is no reason to have to pardon Mansilla for the insouciant confidence of the superiority of his method of knowledge, since for him to feel otherwise would vitiate the whole purpose of his text and the real-life adventure on which it is based. But it is necessary to underscore the unquestioned conviction in the possibility of attaining knowledge. Book knowledge may need to be displaced by the knowledge of actual experience, but it is a question of the efficacy of method, without a doubt as to the power of knowledge attained and explained. Thus, the will to interpret the Tierra Adentro through the medium of his memoir becomes the primary textual principle upon which *Excursión* is based.

As a first-person narrator self-charged with recounting his own exploits (if not heroic, at least worthy), the Mansilla of *Excursión* cannot help but project the validity of his own scrutiny of the phenomena of the Tierra Adentro, at least as a zero degree of narrative practice. While it is true that there are moments when an ironic stance mediates between a desired level of control over the circumstances being narrated and the narrator's minor failures, this neutral transparency of successful reportage is consistently maintained. *Excursión* is therefore not surprisingly punctuated by references to the probing glance of the narrator, which serves as the initial step in the registering of information that will be explicated for the reader: "Yo veía todos estos preparativos, echando miradas furtivas al interior del toldo" (I watched all of these preparations, casting furtive looks inside the tent; 193). Understandably, predicates relating to primary perceptions (the five senses) and to secondary ones (the cognition and ratiocination based on the senses) figure prominently in a text like *Excursión,* where an appeal to the perspective of the narrator, judged to be privileged (because of the opportunity to be present) and superior (because of self-attributed knowledge or the circumstances of rank), confers upon his text a legitimate convocation of our attention.

The primary thrust of Mansilla's memoir is the *explanation* of phenomena as he interpreted them by virtue of his expedition to the Ranqueles and his detailed consideration of what he saw and experienced there. On the basis of this accomplishment, Mansilla's personal narrator allocates to himself the right to engage in a wide-ranging analysis of facts and beliefs, interpreting them as he sees fit and legitimizing his interpretations on the basis of his personal attributes as a witness and the depth of his acquired learning. It is a learning that, as we have noted, circles back on itself when the traditional "book knowledge" still prized by the society of his day is overshadowed by the defense of personal experience in the theater of natural phenomena: a direct contact with "reality" bestows upon the adventurer a privilege to interpret that reality, and Mansilla as raconteur avails himself extensively of that advantage: "¡Cuánto he aprendido en esta correría!" (How much have I learned in this adventure!; 317).

Mansilla's text is a spiraling narrative built around the chronology of events related to the expedition among the Indians but complemented and supplemented by numerous digressions in the marshaling of other information that will assist in the clarification of the main events being explicated. As a consequence, it is a matter of opinion as to how the blocks of description and analysis may be classified, especially since categories clearly overlap. However, a tentative inventory, one sufficient for the purpose of emphasizing the discourse importance of analysis and interpretation in *Excursión* without the need to submit the quality of such disquisitions to independent historiographic and anthropological validation, reveals seven types of explanation. The encyclopedic quality of these explanations and their degree of accuracy is a matter for the evaluation of *Excursión* as a primary social-science source. As a cultural text, the abundance of these explanations and the variety of topics to which they address themselves are important features as such, irrespective of their historical or anthropological accuracy, as indicators of how *Excursión* invests itself with the primary function of revealing the truth about the matters it correlates with the Mansilla expedition.

These seven categories include primarily details about the customs and practices of the Ranqueles Indians, their social organization, their beliefs, and the conduct of their daily lives (I). In the process of reporting on these details, the narrator contrasts Indian sociocultural practices with those of Argentine and European society (II); these contrasts are not always flattering to the latter, although it must be stated that Mansilla usually does not question nineteenth-century racial and ethnic attitudes about the inferiority of indigenous culture. Since *Excursión* has as its major goal the acquisition of information about the Ranqueles to satisfy the needs of military intelligence and personal curiosity, the accuracy of information is of considerable importance. Thus, the narrator takes pains to indicate when his report is correcting prior information that he judges to be erroneous (III).

Mansilla, like many men of his age blessed with a classic academic formation, viewed himself as quite a linguist. In addition to ample quotes from popular Spanish-language sources that demonstrate how Mansilla identified with the still embryonic Argentine cultural tradition, he displays his familiarity with English, Latin, Greek, French, and Italian—and, of course, with Araucanian, a dialect of which is spoken by the Ranqueles. Without becoming a major source of linguistic information about Araucanian, *Excursión* reveals Mansilla's appropriate interest in acquiring information about one of the major languages of the frontier (IV). Concomitantly, Mansilla takes note of the still uncharted wilderness that serves as the setting for his expedition, noting the compelling need for Argentines to take stock of their own country (V). Note how, in the following passages, the implied imperative to render a correct description of the Argentine countryside is underlain by a corrective attitude toward reports that already exist, thereby validating the specific information *Excursión* provides:

> Los que han hecho la pintura de la pampa, suponiéndola en toda su inmensidad una vasta llanura, ¡en qué errores descriptivos han incurrido!
>
> Poetas y hombres de ciencia, todos se han equivocado. El paisaje ideal de la pampa, que yo llamaría, para ser más exacto, pampas, en plural, y el paisaje real, son dos perspectivas completamente distintas. (55)

> La impaciencia patriótica puede hacernos incurrir en grandes errores; el estudio paciente hará que no caigamos en la equivocación.
>
> *No puedo hablar como un sabio: hablo como un hombre observador.* Tengo la carta de la República en la imaginación y me falta el teodolito y el compás. (61; emphasis added)

> (Those who have painted the Pampa, supposing it in all its immensity to be a vast plain, have no idea of the errors they have fallen into!
>
> Poets and men of science have all been mistaken. The ideal landscape of the Pampa, what I, to be more exact, would call the Pampas in the plural, and the real landscape, are two completely different perspectives.

> Patriotic impatience can lead us to make major mistakes; patient study will keep us from falling into error.
>
> *I cannot speak as a learned man: I speak as a man who observes.* I have the chart of the Republic in my imagination, and I am lacking the theodolite and the compass.)

Finally, Mansilla's narrator fills in details of two specialized areas: features of military life (VI) and special terms relating to geography, flora and fauna, and the protocols of intercultural diplomacy (VII). Mansilla takes very seriously the privilege of providing this ample spectrum of information related to the complex details of his incursion into the Tierra Adentro, and it is understandable that *Excursión* has been viewed as one of the most outstanding handbooks of the period regarding the Argentine frontier and relations between the Indians and the representatives of the newly reorganized nation state that needed so badly to contain them.

Excursión must be viewed as a fundamental strategy in this exercise of containment: in providing so much information about Indian society and culture and in detailing the complexities of the contacts between indigenous and European Argentines on the dividing line of the frontier, Mansilla's memoir views itself implicitly as an instrument in that process of containment. It may be unfortunate that the final conflict between Buenos Aires and the Indians of the Tierra Adentro did not come in the form of a manipulation of the latter via the knowledge acquired through expeditions like Mansilla's, but in the form of a successful military campaign of armed overpowering and outright extermination. In this way, the "Indian problem" was resolved in a fashion that rejected categorically the program of cultural assimilation and submission contemplated by Mansilla. If this adds a pathetic note to the patriotic idealism invoked by the narrator of *Excursión,* it does not undermine the sustained appeal to knowledge and explanation, to description and interpretation, as the basis of an approach to cultural otherness. Rather, it lends Mansilla's document a singular poignancy in the context of the clash between cultural writing and political expediency. Ironically, a text that postulates the superiority of direct experience over book learning is countermanded by the harsh realities of the political imperatives of 1879.

But, of course, Mansilla could not have foreseen how his careful efforts at clarification and analysis of the full range of topics associated with life on the frontier would ultimately be of little use to those who saw the best way to deal with the Other to be a policy of elimination. Mansilla must, in making his document legitimate, validate in multiple ways the correctness of his text in order to confirm over and over its usefulness as a form of knowledge. In addition to the appeals to a personal experience that we are asked to accept by virtue of keen curiosity, superior learning, and unique privilege, the narrator asks us to accept what he is explicating because it comes from a reliable source in which he has faith:

> Yo era yo, y a la vez el soldado, el paisano ése, lleno de amor y abnegación, cuya triste aventura acababa de ser relatada por sus propios labios, con el acento inimitable de la verdad. (71)
>
> Me acomodé lo mejor que pude en el suelo para escucharle con atención, convencido de que los dramas reales tienen más mérito que las novelas de la imaginación. (96)
>
> Conozco este episodio de su vida, porque él mismo me lo ha contado. (184)
>
> (I was myself, at the same time the soldier, that countryman, filled with love and abnegation, whose sad adventure had just been told by his own lips, with the inimitable accent of truth.
>
> I made myself as comfortable as I could on the ground to listen to him attentively, convinced that the real dramas have more merit than novels of the imagination.

I am familiar with this episode in his life, because he himself told it to me.)

Such validation by reference to the reasonableness of what is being reported or by the assurance that it comes from a source the narrator considers reliable (including a circumstance that he considers a guarantee of authenticity) is an important component of *Excursión* as a text that pretends to provide a correct and useful characterization of life on the frontier. Whereas the sense of verisimilitude is adequate for fictional narratives, to the extent that Mansilla is primarily concerned with the image of literal truth, as a narrator he is constrained to validate periodically his exposition. Even after he has repeated a particularly unpleasant case of injustice (many of the soldiers in the *ejército de línea* were forced conscripts discharging penal sentences), the narrator guarantees the truth of what has been recounted by the terse lament: "Ese es nuestro país" (This is our country; 190).

Part of the convoluted narrative texture of *Excursión* derives from the anecdotal digressions that Mansilla inserts strategically in his text. In addition to the straightforward chronicle of his experiences among the Ranqueles and the analyses of the information gleaned as a part of these experiences (the details about society, language, customs, and so on to which reference has already been made), the narrator finds it opportune to interrupt his exposition to include an ample range of stories that relate tangentially to life on the frontier. While some of these stories are narrative parentheses whose principal merit is to satisfy curiosity about rural life (in this sense, Mansilla is satisfying the *costumbrista* interest still prevalent in midnineteenth-century Latin American literature), the principal function of the approximately one dozen anecdotes scattered throughout the sixty-eight chapters is to provide an informative counterpoint between the Indians and the non-Indians who inhabit the frontier.

Since there is a necessary interpenetration between the two groups, the experiences of non-Indians who live on the frontier are an integral part of Mansilla's effort to provide an accurate picture of this farthest reach of the national republic. Rather than engage in sociological disquisitions about the problems of these marginal Argentines, Mansilla chooses to allow them to tell their own story in the form of anecdotes that he repeats. In addition to men who serve with him as refugees from society or as society's convicts, the narrator also listens to the stories of frontier settlers and men who have gone to live among the Indians (but not, interestingly enough, *cautivas*, several of whom are mentioned without their story being told). These personal narratives also include the story of the Indian chieftain Mariano Rosas, who lived among the non-

Indians and who was adopted as an *ahijado* by the dictator Rosas, Mansilla's own uncle. The bulk of these stories constitute narrative exempla: autonomous narratives that nevertheless impinge, because of the conflict about human affairs they demonstrate or the moral about life to be drawn from them, on the general context into which they are inserted. Such exempla, of course, enhance the overall narrative quality of *Excursión* and underscore Mansilla's commitment to demonstrating the nature of life on the frontier and authenticating the truth of his exposition by referring to "los dramas reales."

A narrator who ranges over such a vast repertory of information—the facts of his own person and the details of his historically important incursion into the Tierra Adentro, the multiplicity of information about both European and indigenous culture that pepper his text, the many interesting anecdotes about a whole gallery of marginal individuals who cross his path during the expedition—most assuredly sees himself in full control of his text and the events it purports to chronicle. The relationship of power between events and text is bidirectional. The self-confidence held by the narrator with respect to the successful outcome of his expedition allows him to prepare a document that touts the reliability of the information and the analyses derived from his personal experiences. Yet, the unwavering assertiveness with which the narrator of *Excursión* chronicles those experiences and the assurance with which his interpretations are rendered induces the reader to assess retrospectively the success of the expedition.

Through the medium of his text, Mansilla relates the success of his determination to go to the Tierra Adentro, the success of his dealings with his own men and with the Indians, who are never able to get the better of him (hence, the immediately apparent narrative irony of the observation "Mariano Rosas creyó engañarme" [Mariano Rosas thought he was deceiving me; 148]), the success of his deciphering of the language and customs of the Ranqueles, and the success of his return to "civilization" to prepare his memoir. It is not so much a question of how *Excursión* may be marked by a disingenuous masking, through the force of its assertiveness, of any gaps in the success of the Mansilla expedition. Rather, what is of interest is the strong self-confidence about the efficacy of the knowledge to be derived from the project and the inherent value of the memoir based on it. What is to happen less than ten years after the publication of *Excursión* in the matter of bringing the indigenous population within the pale of European civilization and subjugating them to the central authority of the republic belies the textual power of Mansilla's report precisely because it ignores virtually everything on which it is based, beginning with the patriotic ideal of assimilation and including both the possibility of peaceful relations between the Indians and the forces of authority and the value of all of the information about indigenous culture amassed by Mansilla, the man of culture, and others. The story that would be written subsequently is based on the textual power to justify the subjection and extermination modeled by Roca's expeditionary forces; the principles of personally acquired experiential knowledge on which *Excursión* is based would be subverted by the discourse of political legitimation.

Miguel Cané's *Juvenilia:* Autobiography and the Ideologizing of Adolescence

> Más de una vez he procurado rehacer en mi memoria los cuentos estrambóticos que me hacía; me queda algo confuso, y si no he ensayado escribirlos, es en la seguridad de que les daría mi nota personal, lo que no era mi objeto.[11]
>
> (I have on more than one occasion attempted to reconstruct in my mind the outlandish stories that he told me; it remains a little confusing for me, and if I have not attempted to write them, it is out of the certainty that I would give them my personal note, which was not my goal.)

It has been widely acknowledged that one of the characteristic cultural features of the Generation of 1880 in Argentina is the considerable presence of autobiographical and semiautobiographical writing: the former in the nature of the personal recollections of the many singular protagonists in this important period of Argentine social history, the latter in the form of fictional narrators whose first-person accounts bear various degrees of relationship to the known facts of their historical authors (for example, Eugenio Cambaceres's *Pot-pourri: silbidos de un vago,* 1881).[12] At least from the perspective of a global interpretation of the cultural priorities of these writers, such manifestations of autobiographical narration are understandable, in terms of the definitive emergence with this generation of a group of cultural notables whose personal stories are in many ways coterminus with and particularly indicative of a specific sociohistorical consciousness that accorded preeminence to the individual's secure self-image in a society that could be pronounced as finally modern, sophisticated, or developed.[13] The self-confidence cus-

11. Miguel Cané, *Juvenilia,* 32. Hereafter cited parenthetically in the text by page number.

12. "Autobiographical literature in fashion a little after 1880, whose principal example is Cané's *Juvenilia*" (Adolfo Prieto, *La literatura autobiográfica argentina,* 157).

13. "*Juvenilia* crystallizes feelings and concerns that were in the spiritual air of the 80s" (Antonio Pagés Larraya, "'Juvenilia': un título y una actitud en nuestra literatura," 42). David Viñas provides an excellent and probing characterization of the development

tomarily attributed to the writer of the Generation of 1880 is symptomatic both of Argentina's emergence as a society strongly tied to the centers of the dominant social ideology of Western Europe and its satellites and of the Argentine's absolute conviction of his ability to partake fully of that ideology (characteristically, the masculine pronoun will prevail in a discussion of this society, since its culture is virtually without public feminine voices).

Within this group of writings, perhaps no text has enjoyed greater reception than *Juvenilia* (1884) by Miguel Cané (1852–1905). Cané, who enjoyed a varied public life free from the tensions of the more noteworthy achievers among his contemporaries,[14] is best remembered for his role as the founding dean, in 1900, of the Facultad de Filosofía y Letras of the Universidad de Buenos Aires. Yet, Cané did not make much of a contribution to the letters of his day. Besides *Juvenilia,* which runs to barely more than a hundred and a quarter pages in most editions, his travelogue *En viaje* (1884) is his one other most studied work.[15] As has often been said of the writers of the Generation of 1880 as a group, Cané appeared to view writing more as a gentlemanly pastime than as a program either of personal fulfillment, in the Romantic sense of the profound expression of the self, or of rhetorical persuasion, which we associate with the committed writings of social reformers like Zola and the Naturalists during the high period of bourgeois capitalism.

Yet despite whatever commonplaces concerning the fragmentariness of the essentially prose works of the writers of this generation one may wish to echo, in the tradition of Ricardo Rojas's famous characterization,[16] *Juvenilia* stands out both as a minor classic of Argentine literature and as an example of autobiography that may be demonstrated to adhere to a clear set of principles for the explication of a formative period of the narrator's youth.

Cané was a student in one of the early classes of Buenos Aires's prestigious Colegio Nacional, an institution that has trained some of the

---

of Cané's sociocultural values, "Cané: miedo y estilo." See also Hugo Rodríguez Alcalá, "En el 'centenario' de la generación del 80: releyendo *Juvenilia.*"

14. León Rebollo Paz, "Miguel Cané a través de su archivo inédito: el hombre privado, el artista, en argentina cabal."

15. Cané was one of many writers of the Generation of 1880 to author travelogues that bespoke their interest in recording an emerging Argentine elitist concern with becoming "men of the world." These travelogues, to be sure, are another form of the autobiographical writing of the period (Schade, "Los viajeros").

16. Juan Carlos Ghiano echoes the features of this alleged fragmentariness in "Miguel Cané y su tiempo," 71.

most distinguished leaders, intellectuals, and writers in Argentine history.[17] Although its roots go back to the colonial and early republican domination of education by the clergy, during the post-Rosas period in which Cané was a child, the Colegio enjoyed the services of Amédée Jacques, a Frenchman who exercised a decisive influence both on the course of study of the Colegio and on higher learning throughout the country, particularly in science education.[18] Like many of the leading figures of the Generation of 1880, Cané was born during the Rosas period (in his case, within months of Rosas's fall), and his coming of age coincides with the transition of the country, more specifically Buenos Aires, from the reactionary dictatorship of Rosas to the Liberal (but not particularly democratic) republicanism of those men who were exercising power by the time he wrote his memoir of the five years spent in residence at the Colegio.

Juvenilia assumes interpretive dimensions that far outstrip its value as a charming series of anecdotes about the good old schooldays of one's youth. Repeatedly naming explicitly or evoking indirectly by allusion classmates who have gone on to achieve public acclaim, Cané effectively achieves a special resonance in the minds of readers for whom the years spent at the Colegio are, more than a personal experience, the molding of a generation of leaders:

> No todos se han desvanecido y algunos brillan con honor en el cuadro actual de la patria. Si estas páginas caen bajo sus ojos, que el vínculo del Colegio, debilitado por los años, se reanime un momento y encuentren en estos recuerdos una fuente de placer al ver pasar las horas felices de la infancia. (33)

> (Not all of them have vanished, and some glow with honor in the current portrait of the country. If these pages come to their attention, I hope their ties to the Colegio, weakened by the years, are restrengthened

17. A. A. Roig, "A. Jacques, un ecléctico francés en el Río de la Plata: un capítulo de la influencia del pensamiento francés en América Latina."

18. According to Ione S. Wright and Lisa M. Nekham in the *Historical Dictionary of Argentina*, the Colegio Nacional de Buenos Aires was an "important secondary school founded in 1863 as part of President Mitre's educational policy; its first director was Eusebio Agüero; it occupied the historic site of the first Jesuit headquarters (1622), then, in 1767, became the Colegio Máximo de San Ignacio, followed by the Colegio Convictorio y Universidad Máxima de San Carlos (1768), the Real Colegio de San Carlos (1783); in 1810 it served as barracks for the Patricios, in 1813 it was occupied by the Colegio Seminario and in 1817 this was followed by the Colegio de la Unión del Sur; it was used by the new University of Buenos Aires (1821) and by the College of Moral Sciences of Buenos Aires (1823); the Jesuits returned to it for a brief period in 1836" (p. 193).

and that they will find in these memoirs a source of pleasure as they see the happy hours of infancy pass by.)

As a consequence, Cané's book takes on the configurations of a collective memoir, both to the extent that its author is directly recalling a roster of illustrious fellow students who have assumed roles of influence in Argentine national life and to the extent that his personal recollections may be read as synecdochical of the academic formation of many others in a group of which he is a prototype. This prototypic element exists not so much in his personal accomplishments (which were modest), but due to his being the colleague who actually sat down to describe the shared experiences of the Colegio Nacional.[19] In this sense, *Juvenilia* must be seen as an important ideological document of the Generation of 1880. Despite the apparent simplicity of its structure, which is dominated by the urbane first-person narrator, and the anecdotal nature of the material covered, this memoir is underlain by a coherent sociocultural interpretation of the individual's self-identity and his perception of the society in which he moves. By examining the implicit assumptions of a text whose autobiographical nature exemplifies a form of writing during the Generation of 1880, we may understand how Cané's narrative persona, both as an adolescent and as a mature man remembering his adolescence, speaks on behalf of a generation.[20] It is for this reason that *Juvenilia* has enjoyed such a prominent place in the writing of the period. And, if it is true that the programs of the Generation of 1880 continue to hold sway over many sectors of Argentine society and culture, Cané's memoir may still be appreciated as a document enjoying a sustained meaning for its readers.

Take, for example, the various ways in which Cané, a writer who will go on to head the Facultad de Filosofía y Letras, speaks of the literary culture imbibed at the Colegio Nacional. Coming from a family of intellectuals, Cané arrived at the Colegio with considerable prior exposure to

19. Note should be taken of the appendix to *Juvenilia*, "Algunos hombres, cosas y recuerdos de El mundo [*sic*] de *Juvenilia*," 133–42.

20. "*Juvenilia* is a work lacking organic structure. . . . The structure derives from that 'we' that is its protagonist. Even in this it reveals the goal of producing a 'book of origins': the protagonist is a group of men" (Santiago González, *Miguel Cané*, 44). Raúl Castagnino speaks of the "aristocracy of the culture," *Miguel Cané: cronista del ochento porteño*, 21–24. Castagnino sees Cané's insistence on the cultivation of "the spirits without any utilitarian purpose" as a counterweight to "the materialism of [the novel's] setting" (p. 21). Nevertheless, it is clear that the modernized programs of the Colegio Nacional must have been designed in great part to meet the demands of a scientifically and technologically more complex utilitarian society.

literature. However, both the traditional education still prevalent at the institution and the modern, Liberal program of studies developed by Jacques afforded many opportunities to acquire an extensive literary culture in the classics, and in Hispanic, French, and English literature. Moreover, Cané describes how the formal reading of the curriculum was in his case complemented by the clandestine consumption of the historical works of Dumas and the legion of romantic adventure writers whose books had invaded the Argentine market during the period that we now view as one of intense Europeanization.

It is not necessary to have an index of the authors referred to in *Juvenilia* to gain an idea of the range of readings Cané recalls, since the references appear on virtually every page. In addition to the simple citation of books that were part of the program of studies and of his leisure reading, the narrator engages frequently in a form of antonomasia whereby persons and events are characterized as reminiscent of literary models. For example, Cané describes the nocturnal escapades of his group of friends in terms of such an allusion:

> Durante un año y siendo ya mocitos, nos hemos escapado casi todas las noches para hacer una vida de vagabundos por la ciudad, en los cafés, en aquellos puntos donde Shakespeare pone la acción de su Pericles, y sobre todo, en los bailes de los suburbios, de los que algunos condiscípulos, ignoro por arte de quien, tenían siempre conocimiento. (44)

> (During a year while we were still very young, we got out almost every night to lead a life of vagabonds in the city, in the cafés, in those points where Shakespeare sets the action of his Pericles, and above all else, in the dances on the outskirts that some one of us, I have no idea how, always knew about.)

While recounting the time he was summarily expelled from the Colegio for gross misbehavior, Cané likens the sudden finding of himself abandoned to his own devices, baggage and all on the sidewalk beside him, to the plight of a Dickens character:

> Eran las ocho y media de la noche: medité. Mi familia y todos mis parientes en el campo, sin un peso en el bolsillo.
>
> ¿Qué hacer? Me parecía aquélla una aventura enorme y encontraba que David Copperfield era un pigmeo a mi lado; me creía perdido para siempre en el concepto social. (59)

> (It was eight thirty at night: I meditated. My family and all my relatives in the country, without a peso to my name.
>
> What to do? The whole thing seemed to me like an enormous adventure, and I found that David Copperfield was a pygmy alongside me; I thought I was lost forever as far as society was concerned.)

There are many such allusions in *Juvenilia,* the mark of a well-read gentleman who enjoys a learned complicity with his readers in the form of explicit reference to privileged knowledge that they have in common. Moreover, since the knowledge shared by Cané and his ideal readers is the result of the education received at the Colegio Nacional, such a display of allusion becomes a symptom of the incorporation of that education into the public personality represented by the memoir exchanged between author and reader.

But there is an even more singular manner in which literary culture is incorporated into the discourse texture of *Juvenilia.* The educational opportunity of the Colegio Nacional, in the context of the formation of an elite class, becomes a device to distinguish between those who are in and those who are out, between those who remain tied to an inferior culture (Argentina's Hispanic past) and those who can subscribe to and assimilate a modern, superior culture (the dominant European models). Thus, the description of a fracas between Jacques and a student of legendary mental density is expressed in terms of a system of antithetical cultural references:

> Así, cierto día que Jacques nos explicaba que los tres ángulos de un triángulo equivalen a dos rectos, Corrales, oyendo como el ruido del viento la explicación, desde los últimos bancos de la clase, estaba profundamente preocupado en construir, en unión con su vecino el cojo Videla, que le ayudaba eficazmente, un garfio para robar uvas de noche. De pronto Jacques se detiene y con voz tonante exclama: "Corrales, tú eres un imbécil y tu compadre Videla otro: ¿cuánto valen los dos juntos?"
>
> "¡Dos rectos!", contestó Corrales, que tenía en el oído esas dos palabras tan repetidas durante la explicación, y sin darse cuenta, en su sorpresa, de la pregunta de Jacques. Éste se le fue encima y nos fue dado presenciar uno de los combates más reñidos del año. . . .
>
> Pero Corrales era un simple montonero, un Páez, un Güemes, un Artigas; no había leído a César, ni al gran Federico, ni las memorias de Vauban, ni los apuntes de Napoleón, ni los libros de Jomini. Su arte era instintivo y Jacques tenía la ciencia y el genio de la estrategia. (63–64)
>
> (Thus, one day when Jacques was explaining to us that the three angles of a triangle are equivalent to two right angles, Corrales, who listened from the back rows of the desks to the explanation as though hearing the roar of the wind, was deeply occupied in fashioning along with his desk companion, Limpy Videla, who was helping him with efficiency, a hook to steal grapes at night. Suddenly Jacques stopped cold and thundered: "Corrales, you're an imbecile, and your companion Videla is another one: What do the two make up together?"
>
> "Two right angles!" Corrales answered, having heard the words repeated over and over again during the explanation and failing, in his

surprise, to grasp Jacques's question. The latter descended on him, and it was our lot to witness one of the hottest combats of the year. . . .

But Corrales was nothing but a mountaineer, a Páez, a Güemes, an Artigas. He had not read Caesar, nor Frederick the Great, nor the memoirs of Vauban, nor Napoleon's notes, nor Jomini's books. His art was instinctive, and Jacques had at his disposal the science and the genius of strategy.)

The ideological distinctions of this passage are immediately evident. Jacques, the teacher of French origins and the repository of superior intellectual and scientific knowledge, cannot help but be the victor in the battle against Corrales, the rustic who acts by instinct alone. Within the context of the early conflict between *unitarios* and *federales,* those who subscribed to European models versus those who subscribed to Rosas's version of a Hispanic reactionism, the conflict is also between the citified and the provincials. Elsewhere Cané remarks that, during his stay at the Colegio, the conflicts between these two poles of Argentine society continued and that there was a very real animosity between the students from the provinces and those from Buenos Aires. Cané (who was, of course, from Buenos Aires) does not say whether Corrales was from the country. But his characterization of his stupidity, his cunning deviousness, and, in the passage cited, his manner of fighting make him for the purposes of this characterization an emblem of the *barbarie* pitted against Jacques's *civilización.*

Moreover, the Colegio during Cané's time was the scene not only of surviving friction between descendants of *unitarios* and *federales,* but of the conflict between *crudos* and *cocidos* as well. The former, in the tradition of the *unitarios,* defended the autonomy—and political and economic hegemony—of the province of Buenos Aires and its capital city of the same name, while the latter insisted on the federalization of Buenos Aires as the national capital and the relegation of the province of Buenos Aires as coequal among the others. Two years before the writing of *Juvenilia,* the *cocidos* were successful in seeing Buenos Aires federalized, a move that ultimately benefited the *porteños* who had fought such a move.

These differences of opinion, rehearsed and replayed in the conflicts between the students of the Colegio Nacional, make the latter in both reality and within the confines of *Juvenilia*'s narrative universe a microcosm of the ideological conflicts in Argentine culture during the period of the memoir. Thus, the battle between Jacques and Corrales is much more than an incident of violence between a rebellious student and a teacher who resorts to physical violence to discipline him. It is, rather, a contest between the sociocultural legacy represented by Corrales, the rude instinctual behavior of the popular Gaucho heroes Cané likens

Corrales to, and the superior military strategy drawn from his readings in the European tradition at the disposal of Jacques. Moreover, Corrales, who was hardly given to acquiring knowledge from books, conducts himself in conformance with principles drawn from an oral tradition that had become part of Argentine popular culture. By contrast, the foreign teacher's advantage is the result of his familiarity with a long tradition of elitist, non-Hispanic texts.

Cané's characterization of the battle between Corrales and Jacques is an emblem of a particular form of class consciousness exemplified by the author throughout his memoir.[21] Underscoring throughout his text the diverse social elements that were represented by the students of the Colegio Nacional during his stay there, Cané, from the perspective of a public official writing during the 1880s, chooses to emphasize and to praise the cultural legacy installed by Jacques. Cané devotes some of the most memorable and most frequently cited pages of *Juvenilia* to Jacques's sudden death and the reaction to it of the students. This description is an unabashed apotheosis of an influential individual in the narrator's cultural formation:

> Uno por uno, por un movimiento espontáneo, nos fuimos arrodillando y posando en [su mano] los labios, como un adiós supremo a aquél a quien nunca debíamos olvidar. Su espíritu liberal, abierto a todas las verdades de la ciencia, libre de preocupaciones raquíticas, ha ejercido su influencia poderosa sobre el de todos sus discípulos.
>
> Le llevamos a pulso hasta su tumba y levantamos en ella un modesto monumento con nuestros pobres recursos de estudiantes. Duerme el sueño eterno al abrigo de los árboles sombríos, no lejos del sitio donde reposan mis muertos queridos. Jamás voy a la tumba de los míos sin pasar por el sepulcro del maestro y saludarle con el respeto profundo de los grandes cariños. (68)

> (One by one, in a spontaneous movement, we knelt and put our lips [to his hand], as a supreme farewell to he who had never forgotten us. His generous spirit, open to all the truths of science, free of rickety concerns, has exercised its powerful influence on all of his disciples.
>
> We bore him to his tomb, where we constructed a modest monument with our modest resources as students. He sleeps the eternal sleep, pro-

21. "The men of the 80s feel that history has assigned to them an enormous open space that they must put in order, not exactly a physical space, which they take for granted undoubtedly because they own it, but a social space, a society in which there is nothing they cannot correct or order. The country is born and its institutions constitute the realm in which the birth takes place. The men of the 80s watch with awe the first steps taken by those institutions" (Jitrik, *El 80 y su mundo*, 77).

tected by the somber trees, not far from where my beloved dead rest. I never visit their tomb without passing by the sepulcher of the master and greeting him with the profound respect of greatest respect.)

While it is reasonable to assume that someone like Corrales must have belonged to a group of students not completely enthralled by Jacques's intellectual example, Cané's characterization implies that this is the case, in a rhetorical gesture designed to exclude any traces of contradiction to the monumentalization of the foreign culture the teacher exemplified. What is more, Jacques remains a living memory for the narrator, one closely bound up with his own ancestors who are buried near him in the cemetery. Aside from whatever literary intertextuality one might wish to allege inspired this touching evocation of Jacques's death, it is of a whole with the sustained encomium to the exponent of a specific cultural ideology exemplified by *Juvenilia* as a schoolboy's memoir.

Along with the abundance of literary and cultural references in *Juvenilia,* there is one notable absence that should be immediately apparent. With the exception of the oral traditions implied by the mention of Páez, Güemes, and Artigas and a few Romantic novelists devoured along with Dumas and company, Hispanic literature is virtually ignored by Cané in recalling his education. Although Cané had internalized Sarmiento's disjunctive formula of *civilización* versus *barbarie,* expressed at the height of the Rosas tyranny and generally accepted by post-Rosas social thinkers and activists, there is no allusion to Argentina's most important nineteenth-century writer. And, not surprisingly, no other Argentine writer is recalled by the narrator in his constant references to literary culture. Certainly, it is arguable that Argentine literature did not have much to read and cite, but this is exactly the reason M. Jacques and his cultural models were deemed so important. This was a period in which Argentine leaders were concerned with forging a national culture that could transcend the deleterious influence of its Hispanic heritage in favor of the beneficial sophistication of dominant European cultures. The readings of the young autobiographical protagonist of *Juvenilia* confirm this goal, as do the recollections of the mature narrator who chooses to use these preferred cultural models as an organizing point of reference for his text.

Part of the "charm" customarily attributed to *Juvenilia* is a consequence of the fashion in which it is structured as narrative. The author introduces one of his recollections toward the end of the text in the following manner: "Como escribo sin plan y a medida que los recuerdos vienen, me detengo en uno que ha quedado presente en mi memoria con una clara persistencia" (Since I write with no plan, but as things come back to me, I stop before one that has remained present in my memory with a clear persistence; 112). While it is impossible to determine if Cané worked from any sort of outline, the impression that his text gives is that of a rambling and free-form reminiscence held together by the central fact that whatever is recounted belongs to the autobiographical narrator's recollection of personal experiences. There is a rough chronology of events, but the general impression is that transition from one recalled happening to another is more a function of thematic associations than it is the consequence of the adherence to historical time.

Divided into thirty-six segments that rarely run to more than two or three pages, Cané's memoir depends on the discourse authority of concepts like *recuerdo, memoria,* and similar predicates. These key terms serve to frame approximately thirty anecdotes (there is some slippage here due to some arbitrariness in determining what constitutes a discrete anecdote), essentially one anecdote per segment. Understandably, there is considerable structural parallelism from one segment to another: the narrator opens with a prefatory comment about the process of recollection, he refers to a specific individual or circumstance, he proceeds to recount a concrete happening, and he usually closes by drawing some conclusion as to the significance of the event recalled.

From the point of view of narrative as innocent storytelling, the events of five years of his youth spent at the Colegio Nacional by the mature writer Miguel Cané are simply an autobiographical memoir given legitimacy by the subsequent importance of the protagonist and whatever intrinsic interest of events attributed to the substance of his recollections. On the other hand, from the perspective of an inquiry into the sociocultural reasons for presenting to a reading public the memories of Miguel Cané adult concerning Miguel Cané adolescent student, *Juvenilia* becomes ideologized in terms of what events are remembered and how they are recreated narratively. The author indulges in the hoary topos of confessing his inadequacy as a writer ("Creo que me falta una fuerza esencial en el arte literario" [I believe that I lack an essential force in the literary art; 24]) and proceeds to legitimate his text on the basis of its alleged appeal to those who had already read it, presumably in manuscript form:

> Ahora, ¿por qué publico estos recuerdos, destinados a pasar sólo bajo los ojos de mis amigos? En primer lugar, porque aquellos que los han leído me han impulsado a hacerlo, a llamarlos a la vida después de los años de sueño ... Pero con lealtad, en el fondo hay esta razón suprema que los hombres de letras comprenderán: los publico porque los he escrito. (25)

(Now, why do I publish these memoirs, destined to fall only under the gaze of my friends? In the first place, because those who have read them have urged me to do it, to call them to life after the years of sleep ... But out of loyalty—at bottom there is this supreme reason that men of letters will understand: I publish them because I have written them.)

The second half of this explanation attenuates the vested interest implied by the first assertion. However, it simply covers the logical question as to why these pages were written in the first place, which can be answered, in part, because they would appeal to those who were to read them. Such an appeal, which aesthetically based criticism attributes to the "charm" of Cané's unpretentious writing, must necessarily result in large measure from the ways in which Cané is able to echo the ideological premises of those who are already familiar with what he has to say. Thus, the narrator remembers the tedium of the life of a boarding-school student and the many discomforts of institutional living, and, apropos of the confinement of life at the Colegio, he remarks, "He conservado toda mi vida un terror instintivo a la prisión" (I have all my life been instinctively terrified of prison; 83). Recalling that he and his fellow students often viewed their residence at the Colegio as a form of imprisonment, the narrator is able to justify their acts of childish rebellion and the clever stratagems employed to evade their *celadores.* Nevertheless, against the backdrop of these real-life feelings, Cané focuses on key events in his remembrances that lead toward the closing encomium to the Colegio Nacional and the educational ideal it embodies:

> Bendigo mis años de Colegio, y ya que he trazado estos recuerdos, que la última palabra sea de gratitud para mis maestros y de cariño para los compañeros que el azar de la vida ha dispersado a todos los rumbos. (132)
>
> (I bless my years at the Colegio, and since I have drawn these memoirs, I want my last word of gratitude to be for my teachers and an expression of affection for those companions that the whims of life have scattered to the four winds.)

The conjunction of remembered events and encomium is hardly circumstantial, since it is obvious that the autobiographical text must lead toward, must justify retrospectively, this closing encomium. Moreover, since it is a paean not just to the Colegio but to the institutional program of studies it imparts, *Juvenilia* legitimates itself as an autobiographical memoir that echoes an established, official view of the acculturation process to be effected by a specific form of the education of juveniles.

As part of how *Juvenilia* confirms an already ideologized concept of cultural formation, the text, along with its hypogrammatical title, establishes the primacy of adolescence as a period of acculturation: "Yo diría al joven que tal vez lea estas líneas" (I would say to the young man who might read these lines; 132). If the period of composition of *Juvenilia* and its initial readings corresponds to the maturation of a specific sociocultural project for a modern Argentina, the one conveniently designated by the term *Generation of 1880,* the period of juvenile formation recalled by Cané is the "adolescence" of the republic, recently restored from the tyranny of Rosas's Hispanic reactionism. Read in this way, Cané's autobiography possesses an ideological resonance by virtue of the paradigmatic relationship it insinuates between the protagonist, as both child and adult, and the men of his day—his readers.[22]

The appeal to adolescence, a period of psychological and biological growth that achieves recognition as a stage of singular personal growth during the late-nineteenth century in the West, is used by Cané to privilege the formative intellectual and cultural processes that occurred during his years in the Colegio Nacional. Once again, a reading of *Juvenilia* that seeks to understand how it is a document of ideological value within the context of the Generation of 1880 must necessarily go beyond seeing the text as nothing more than the pleasant account of the narrator's youth. By recovering an array of formative experiences that are marked off as of special importance both to himself personally and, by extension, to his readers collectively, the narrator establishes a period of his life as a paradigm deserving of particular recognition.[23] Put differently, the text is an implicit answer to a potential question: Why might an individual like Cané stress the importance of this period in his life rather than others, say either his early childhood during the immediately post-Rosas period in Buenos Aires or his subsequent professional career, many elements of which are equally paradigmatic as regards the life of the gentlemen of his age?

By ideologizing a concept of adolescence as a period of special intellectual, moral, and spiritual formation in conformance with a program that Cané attributes retroflexively with the curriculum that evolved at the Colegio Nacional during his stay there, *Juvenilia* makes use of the autobiographical mode to highlight one set of personal experiences as indicative of the consciousness of what emerges as a dominant segment of Argentine society. The favorable reception of the book when it was

22. One important characterization of the production of ideology by literary writing is Michael J. Shapiro, "Literary Production as a Politicizing Practice."

23. Just as José Enrique Rodó will also privilege adolescence in *Ariel* (1900), one of the major documents in the definition of cultural parameters, through the agency of education and academic intellectualism, in Latin America.

published and by subsequent generations of Argentine readers attests to the ways in which Cané's adolescent narrator speaks collectively both for his actual *compañeros* and for those who would like to consider themselves potentially among them.

Cané wrote at a time when the sociocultural ideology of Argentina was redefining itself in the wake of the turbulent years under Rosas and the following decades of national reorganization that made possible the Liberal hegemony of the 1880s and afterwards. He and his generation of writers were in a particularly enviable position. Virtually all of their major works were singular in one way or another within the context of a paucity of national literary models. As a consequence, these works were established as models by the simple virtue of their presence in an uncrowded textual field. Therefore, their constitutive elements in terms of structure, theme, point of view and so on exercised an unusual influence during this inaugural phase of modern Argentine literature. *Juvenilia* creates a certain range of cultural referents that comes to dominate in the program of studies at the Colegio Nacional beginning with Amédée Jacques (studies that contribute to the Europeanization of the Argentine intelligentsia) by stressing the life-long impact of the years that we have now come to call adolescence. And it accomplishes this in the form of a memoir that installs persuasively the perspective of one important member of the Generation of 1880 as characteristic of that of readers who can recognize themselves as his real as well as his aspiring colleagues.

In 1901, twenty years after the original publication of *Juvenilia,* Cané added the following prefatory note, which only serves to confirm the special resonance his autobiographical document had acquired for his readers:

> Si modificara una sola línea de estas páginas, las más afortunadas de las que he escrito, creería destruir el encanto que envuelve el mejor momento de la existencia, introduciendo, en la armonía de sus acordes juveniles, la nota grave de las impresiones que acompañan el descenso de la colina.
>
> Las reproduzco hoy, porque no se encuentran ya y muchos de los que entraban a la vida cuando se publicaron, desean conocerlas.
>
> De nuevo, pues, abren sus alas esos recuerdos infantiles; que vuelen hoy en atmósfera tan simpática y afectuosa como aquélla que cruzaron por primera vez, evocando a su paso imágenes sonrientes y serenas, son los votos de quien los escribió con placer y acaba de releerlos con cierta suave tristeza. (21)

(If I were to modify a single line of these pages, the best I have ever written, I think I would destroy the charm that cloaks the best moment of life, introducing in the harmony of their juvenile chords the grave note of the impressions that accompany a journey downhill.

I reproduce them today because they are no longer in print and many of those who entered public life when they were published wish to know them.

Thus, may those childhood memories once again unfurl their wings and fly in a sky as kind and affectionate as the one through which they passed the first time, evoking in their wake smiling and serene images—these are the wishes of the one who wrote them with pleasure and who has just reread them with a certain gentle sadness.)

Fray Mocho's *Memorias de un vigilante:* Witnessing Society

Estas impresiones, que son las primeras que tuve en Buenos Aires, puede decirse, las tengo presentes, y las siento como si fueran de ayer; veo aún las escenas y las cosas, tal como se presentaron a mí, así en tropel, medio confusas, informes, barajándose de una manera infernal, figuras, espectáculos, diálogos, ruidos y hasta aire de personas absolutamente desconocidas, que yo encontraba en la calle o veía en las antesalas del Ministerio en las horas de facción.[24]

(These impressions, which one might say are the first I had in Buenos Aires, are still very vivid, and I feel them as though they were yesterday. I can still see the scenes and things just as they appeared to me like a stampede, half-confused, formless, infernally jumbled together, figures, spectacles, dialogues, sounds, and even the air of absolutely unknown persons I met in the street or saw in the antechambers of the Ministry during working hours.)

It is generally asserted that Hispanic *costumbrismo* is an outgrowth of the Romantic discovery of the lower classes, both in their rural setting and in their urban presence, and the emerging bourgeoisie, poised between its humble roots and its aspirations to assume the brilliance of the aristocracy. If in the former interest there is a cross between an encomium of the traditional folkways of the peasant and the portrait of the miseries of the humble, in the case of the latter emphasis we find valuable sociocultural information about the comic tensions associated with the attempts to define a new place in society and to hold on to it.[25]

Latin American *costumbrismo* adds to the foregoing elements the con-

24. José Sixto Alvarez [pseud., Fray Mocho], *Memorias de un vigilante,* 46. Hereafter cited parenthetically in the text by page number.

25. Alberto Oscar Blasi Brambilla, "Fray Mocho y su versíon de la transición finisecular"; and Noemí Vergara de Bietti, *Humoristas del ochenta: Eduardo Wilde, Eugenio Cambaceres, Lucio López, Bartolomé Mitre y Vedia y José S. Alvarez (Fray Mocho),* 97–100.

siderations that attend upon the societies of the New World, conscious of being derivatives of older societies, often obsessed with the need to emulate the new bourgeois culture of Europe and the need to transcend their Hispanic past, and involved in the process of forging independent national identities as a consequence of the independence and republican movements of the nineteenth century. Although often read as little more than charming evocations of bygone days,[26] often in editions that appeal to a nostalgic framing of the past,[27] the large block of *costumbrismo* writings in Latin America have yet to be examined in any detail for their role as literary versions of specific social texts.

Argentina's Fray Mocho (the pseudonym of José Sixto Alvarez, 1858–1903) is an excellent example of both *costumbrismo* and writers whose works have rarely been examined as other than merely charming evocations of the dramatic urbanization of Buenos Aires.[28] A provincial from Argentina's fertile Entre Ríos, Alvarez was typical of the late nineteenth-century journalist-writer in Latin America. Involved in a large number of writing activities that ranged from newspaper columns and sketches to works of fiction, Alvarez was perhaps most important for his involvement with the founding of *Caras y caretas* (1898–1939), the most brilliant and most long-lived of the cultural journals in turn-of-the-century Latin America in the tradition of the English *Punch*.[29] *Caras y caretas* was a natural extension of Alvarez's personal writing. The journal combined editorial writing with *costumbrismo* sketches about life and customs, a wide variety of popular artwork with the inventive graphics of the new art of commercial advertising, and an interest in displaying the models of privileged foreign cultures (typically, French and British) all with the perceptive scrutiny of the details of national society. This publication, which reached well over 1,000 issues during its existence, may be considered the zenith of *costumbrismo* in Argentina.[30]

The idea of a coherent platform for the scrutiny of the rapidly evolving national society of its day is one of the distinguishing features of

26. Carlos Mastronardi, "Fray Mocho, espejo de criollos"; and Ernesto Morales, *Fray Mocho*.

27. For example, José Sixto Alvarez [pseud., Fray Mocho], *Cuentos de Fray Mocho*.

28. Roberto F. Giusti, "Fray Mocho."

29. According to Héctor René Lafleur, Sergio D. Provenzano, and Fernando P. Alonso, *Caras y caretas* was founded by Alvarez, Eustaquio Pellicer, and Emilio Mayol, and 2,139 issues appeared between October 8, 1898, and October 17, 1939 (*Las revistas literario argentinas, 1893–1979*, 28).

30. Howard Fraser, *Magazines and Masks: "Caras y caretas"*; and Jorge Ruffinelli, *La revista "Caras y caretas."*

Caras y caretas, which in a sense became Alvarez's last major work, even if he was only one of many writers associated with it. But the idea of creating a specific focus for local-color sketches, replacing the random and shifting point of reference of those authors who often appeared to write on whatever struck their fancy at the moment, was one of Alvarez's contributions to the extension of *costumbrismo* into late nineteenth-century writing. The increasingly complex culture deriving from the implantation of Liberal, bourgeois capitalism demanded forms of writing that both replicated this complexity and provided textual strategies for probing with sustained detail the types and themes that were of dominant concern.

Memorias de un vigilante (Memoirs of a cop; 1897) was one of Alvarez's mature works that can be said to fulfill to some degree that implicit demand. Although Alvarez was often accused of "only" reporting on the circumstantial anecdotes of life around him rather than creating original fictional works, the interest he continues to hold for the student of Argentine culture lies in his talent for narrating a specific block of national social history.

Memorias is composed of sixteen chapters, all of which, with the exception of 14, "Mundo Lunfardo," run no more than a few hundred words. As a whole, these sketches are purported to be the memoirs of Fabio Carrizo, a peasant who becomes a member of the Buenos Aires police force. Carrizo describes his reactions to the fast-changing metropolis, and he concentrates specifically on the criminal underworld with which his duties as a policeman bring him into contact. Significantly, Carrizo arrives in Buenos Aires in 1880, the year of the separation of the city from the province of Buenos Aires and the creation of the Distrito Federal as part of the centralization of the national government in the service of the new Liberal society.

Alvarez's narrative is structured along two axes that underscore the changes that were taking place during the period covered by Carrizo's memories: the displacement from countryside to city, and the interaction between an expanding gentile society and a concomitantly burgeoning marginal class of criminals. In the same sense that the dominant society is becoming more complex and variegated, this marginal class also comes to assume considerable internal variation and stratification. Having devoted a separate work to the underworld of criminal types,[31] in *Memorias de un vigilante* Alvarez works from a narrative framework with reference to an integrated social panorama.

31. I have been unable to consult Alvarez's *Vida de los ladrones célebres de Buenos Aires y sus maneras de robar,* purportedly published in 1887.

Born in an impoverished rural setting, Carrizo is turned over to a mule-driver by his father; presumably he is sold as a servant, although this detail is never made clear. As a consequence of this arrangement, Carrizo is both freed from the poverty of his origins and introduced into a larger society, which he reveals to his reader. For the personal voice, as well as that of the narrator, the inauguration of the narrative has echoes of its picaresque origins ("Mi nacimiento fué como el de tantos" [My birth was like that of so many; 13]) and underscores the narrator's impoverished origins in a forgotten corner of the republic.[32] As the result of his indenture to the mule-driver, Carrizo comes into contact as a young man with an array of rural culture, which he summarizes in chapter 4, "De oruga a mariposa." In an unusually long chapter for *Memorias,* the narrator describes a rural party, which is introduced in the following nostalgic fashion:

> Recuerdo, como si fuese ayer, las circunstancias en que fuí tomado [para ser soldado] y voy a tratar de pintarlas, no con la intención de hacer un cuadro sino con la intención de presentar una escena de nuestro campo, vulgar y corriente en tiempo no lejano, pero hoy ya casi exótica, debido a las exigencias de la vida. (16)
>
> (I remember, as if it were yesterday, the circumstances in which I was conscripted, and I am going to try to paint them, not out of a desire to make a picture but with the intent of presenting an image of our countryside, common and everyday as it was not so long ago, but now today almost exotic, owing to the exigencies of life.)

Chapter 4 is divided into two parts: the depiction in idyllic terms, with quotations from the folk poetry, of the party, and the arrival of military police, who press the narrator into army service. The practice of the day was to force peasants without papers showing they were gainfully employed to do service in the army, which was still occupied with containing the Indian population. Often little more than human barricades against the marauding Indians, these soldiers were more prisoners than they were professional soldiers, and more often than not Gauchos carted off in this fashion did not return from the front.

But Carrizo does return, and in his recollections service in the military made a man of him. After ten years in the army without a blemish on his record (a virtually incredible accomplishment, given the condi-

32. Of course, one can easily see how the bulk of Alvarez's urban characters are modern pícaros, and it is appropriate that Guillermo Ara title one section of his study "Este mundo de pícaros" (*Fray Mocho: estudio y antología,* 15–28); the picaresque opening of *Memorias* is discussed on pp. 24–25.

tions of service before the professionalization of the Argentine army), Carrizo is released with a letter of recommendation for the police chief of Buenos Aires. In this fashion, Alvarez established one of the underlying axes for his narrative. There are few subsequent references to Carrizo's rural origins and his forced abstraction from a tranquil rural settlement to become a cog in various versions of the enforcement of social order in late nineteenth-century Argentine society. But the reader bears in mind, because of the conditions of this introit, its picaresque elements and the nostalgic terms in which Carrizo describes his young life as a Gaucho, that the narrator as a witness of the theater of Buenos Aires society has made the long journey from a backwater settlement to the metropolis. This trajectory is one of the fundamental conditions for the creation of the Liberal bourgeoisie: the expansion of the capital on the basis of a centripetal demographic growth stimulated, in large measure, by the formation of a proletarian substructure. In the case of Buenos Aires, this substructure was based in equal parts on the wholesale attraction to the metropolis of peasants and the importation of vast numbers of impoverished immigrants.

Carrizo, as a new arrival in Buenos Aires from the extremely marginal rural settings in which the army functioned at this time, is an awe-struck witness to the hurly-burly of a dynamic modern city. Inaugurating the variety of references to the act of *seeing,* the narrator describes how he is overwhelmed by the new world into which he has moved. His narrative assumes the category of an inventory of all of this new reality with which he must become familiar in order to perform his new function as a protector of urban order:

> El principio de mi carrera fué penoso y mortificante. Carecía hasta de las nociones más elementales de lo que formaba la vida de la ciudad, y todo era para mí motivo de asombro y de curiosidad.
>
> Las calles, los tranways, los teatros, las tiendas y almacenes lujosos, las jugueterías, las joyerías, las iglesias, no era extraño que me arrastraran hacia ellas con fuerza invencible y que no tuviera ojos ni oídos sino para observarlas y asombrarme: era que todo me llamaba, todo me atraía.
>
> No conocía ningún detalle de la vida civilizada, y cada cosa que saltaba ante mi vista era un motivo de sorpresa. (38)

> (My career began painfully and mortifyingly. I lacked even the most elementary notions of what constituted city life, and everything was for me a cause for astonishment and curiosity.
>
> The streets, the trolleys, the theaters, the luxurious stores and shops, the toy stores, the jewelry stores, the churches—it was not surprising that I was drawn toward them with an invincible force and that I had only

eyes and ears to observe them and be astounded. Everything beckoned me, everything attracted me.

I was unfamiliar with a single detail of civilized life, and each thing that sprang up under my eyes was a cause for surprise.)

Observar and *asombrarse* become linked as initial action and logical consequence of this taking stock of a new social reality repeated for thousands upon thousands of new arrivals in the city, rural peasants and foreign immigrants (who, of course, were in the main rural peasants in origin, thereby experiencing a compounded overwhelmedness in their doubly new society). This pattern of awakening is linked with the imperative to acquire an awareness of "civilized life" in order to discharge adequately the demands of the narrator's new "career." And, finally, all of these awesome elements constitute an alluring, seductive presence, an "invincible force" that is irresistible for someone of Carrizo's origins. In a few sentences, Alvarez summarizes the powerful points of reference for his protagonist's awareness of the radical transition that has occurred in his life not only as a figure of countless citizens of his day but as, specifically, a unique witness by virtue of the privileged focus of his memoir:

> Mi cabeza era un volcán: todo lo oía, todo lo interpretaba y mi cuerpo se debilitaba en aquellas horas de agitación y de fiebre.
>
> ¡Buenos Aires entero, con sus calles y sus plazas y su movimiento de hormiguero, bullía en mi imaginación calenturienta! (40–41)

> (My head was a volcano: I heard and interpreted everything, and my body grew weak in those hours of agitation and fever.
>
> All of Buenos Aires, with its streets and its plazas and its antlike movements, bubbled in my fevered imagination!)

It is in the privilege of his imagination and the act of his interpretation of this newfound social reality that Alvarez's protagonist establishes the first controlling axis for his narrative.

The second dominant axis in *Memorias* is the more far-reaching circumstance of the policeman of humble origins called upon to defend the property of the wealthy and the small business owners who aspire to economic success. This social disjunction provides a major element of cohesion for the narrative in that it both legitimizes a particular way of characterizing the urban social elite and affords a verisimilar opportunity for reporting on the social subclass that implicitly challenges the rights of that elite:

> El sargento Gómez y Renier—mi maestro inolvidable más tarde, en los días en que ya la fortuna comenzó a sonreirme y que me sirvió de guía para penetrar en el bajo mundo social de Buenos Aires, cuyos misterios

haré desfilar ante la vista de mis lectores en curso de estas Memorias—me fueron enseñando poco a poco a distinguir los caracteres de las cosas que como en un kaleidoscopio pasaban ante mi vista. (119–20)

(Sargent Gómez and Renier—the latter my unforgettable later teacher in the days in which fortune began to smile on me and he served me as a guide for entering into Buenos Aires's social underworld, whose mysteries I will pass before the eyes of my readers in the course of these Memoirs—taught me little by little to distinguish the features of the things that like a kaleidoscope passed before my eyes.)

In this way, Carrizo's contact with Buenos Aires involves a learning process that provides him with a means of becoming a functioning member of his new urban society. He learns his way around the city, he assimilates the wonders of an expanding world in tune with the concepts of progress of the day, and he acquires the ability to discriminate among the multiple human species that inhabit this teaming circus. In the process, Carrizo becomes a servant of the social organization into which he has been thrust. The aggressive professionalization of the modern police apparatus, providing educational opportunities and a financial security that have turned police into members, if still securely at the bottom, of the class they serve, tends to obscure for the modern reader the fact that someone like Carrizo in reality has his origins among the very peasants turned proletarian criminals that he is called upon to police.

In terms of the world of Alvarez's *Memorias,* what this means is that the panorama of 1880 society in Buenos Aires is viewed through the perspective of a narrator who serves to bring together both ends of the social spectrum. Alvarez has created a first-person narrator who, while a member of a marginal class, is in a position to observe the privileged elite at the other end of the scale from his own origins and occupation. This he does by virtue of the fact that he is, in his first assignments, obliged literally to stand in vigil over the possessions and privileges of the powerful:

Mi primer servicio en carácter de vigilante fui a prestarlo a los veinte días de mi ingreso, bajo la dirección del cabo Pérez; el teatro elegido fué el Ministerio del Interior, donde se requería, por no sé qué causa, ayuda de la fuerza pública. (44)

(My first service as a cop came twenty days after I joined the force, under the direction of Corporal Pérez. The chosen arena was the Ministry of the Interior, where, I don't know why, the assistance of the police force was required.)

It is significant that, in the following paragraphs Carrizo mocks the self-importance of Cabo Pérez, a Spanish immigrant as powerless as

Carrizo himself. But Pérez is filled with the sacredness of his mission and the belief that he and his colleagues serve "como ejemplos en la historia de la humanidad civilizada" (like examples in the history of civilized humanity; 44). The narrator's eloquent remark in the face of such faith is "¡Pobre Pérez!" (Poor Pérez!; 44). Yet, aside from such moments of reflection, Carrizo is content to report on the willingness with which he fulfilled the assignments that were given to him and on his slow but sure rise in the force in recognition of his talents and dedication.

Carrizo, therefore, becomes assimilated into the social structure of which his origins had initially maintained him on the margins. The disappearance of the picaresque attitude of the opening chapters of *Memorias* gives way to the interest in the last half of the narrative in a detailed report from the point of view of the police officer about the new urban pícaros, the inhabitants of the Mundo Lunfardo. In the process of achieving this perspective, Alvarez's narrator impresses upon the reader, as he has impressed upon himself, the sociology of the *vigilante.* The *vigilante* possesses a superior vision, the result of specialized training and the simple imperative of survival in his job, that allows him a privileged place in his society. But that "privileged place," a term reminiscent of the perquisites of society's powerful, is not based on either influence or financial gain. Rather, it is the privilege that comes with a heightened horizontal mobility in society and the power of information that accrues to that mobility—moving in and out of all spheres of society, both those that he protects and those that he punishes. The police officer acquires a superior knowledge about society not available to those who remain fixed within the limited horizons of their class, no matter at which end of the social spectrum it might be.

As a consequence, Carrizo is a privileged narrator, and it is no accident that his memoirs are organized in terms of repeated references to the *cuentos* that he is willing to share with his reader. It is important to note that the role of the *vigilante* is neither a neutral nor a natural one, in the sense of something that we can predict from the human condition. Rather, it is the consequence of a social order that "creates" (within whatever parameters of determinacy one wishes to subscribe to) a criminal class, control over which requires the services of a police force. Seen from this perspective, Carrizo's social role is the result of a particular form of social order—let us call it surplus-value capitalism for want of a better term, an economic order that provides some individuals with goods of which they can be deprived by other individuals and a legal order that determines when the practice of depriving the former of those goods is criminal.

Carrizo's role as a narrator is the result of his social role, which affords him the opportunity to witness society in a memorable fashion and to report on what he has witnessed. Alvarez creates a narrative persona homologous with the persona of the *vigilante* created by society, and the interest of the vigilante as narrator is confirmed by this homologous relationship. Put in more pedestrian terms, Carrizo's memoirs are of interest because of the role society assigns to him and because of the reader's interest in, and recognition of the irony of, that role.

By discovering for us a world of capitalistic opulence that requires and demands police protection in order to survive, Alvarez's *vigilante* recognizes implicitly an emerging complex social structure whose newness, both in terms of what needs to be protected and the sectors from which it needs to be protected, legitimates Alvarez's book. Perhaps the reason that we cannot find, before *Memorias de un vigilante,* an example in Argentine literature of a first-person narrative by an agent of the forces of law and order is that the social and legal structures had not evolved to a point at which such a narrative could be of any interest to a reader. By the same token, it is the evolving coherence of a social order in which the *vigilante* had a precise role to play and within which his experiences could enjoy particular sociocultural resonance that makes a book like *Memorias* the sort of literary document one would expect the period to produce. The unique privilege that is bestowed upon Carrizo is evoked in the closing paragraphs of his memoir, the last chapter of which is appropriately entitled "Los misterios de Buenos Aires":

> Yo penetré el movimiento de los hombres en sus calles estrechas, las pasiones que encierran los palacios y los conventillos, los intereses que se juegan diariamente desde la Bolsa a los mercados, y, nacido en las más humildes esferas, ascendí peldaño a peldaño la larga escala social, tendida entre el humilde vigilante, que, parado en una esquina, expuesto a las inclemencias del tiempo, ignora todo lo que no se relacione con el pequeño radio puesto a su cuidado, y apenas sospecha los sucesos de más volumen que ocurren fuera de su parada y la vida turbulenta y accidentada de los hombres del mundo. (145)

> (I penetrated in the movement of the men in their narrow streets, the passions enclosed within the palaces and the tenements, the interests played out daily from the stock market to the marketplaces, and I, born of the humblest realms, ascended step by step the steep social ladder that stretched from the humble cop who, standing on the corner and exposed to the inclemencies of the weather, is ignorant of all that is not related to the small radius under his care, barely suspecting the greater events that

occur beyond his station and the turbulent and fateful life of the men of the world.)

A more ambitious and more properly "novelistic" account than the *costumbrismo* sketches Alvarez provides in these *Memorias* might well have taken the sense of the complex panorama of a new social reality in order to work out in detail the ascendancy of the humble *vigilante* Carrizo as consonant with the maturation of late nineteenth-century Argentine society. This formula is basically what we find in the great Realist novels of the period in England and France and even in the United States. It is not to be regretted that Alvarez does not subscribe to these foreign models or that he does not develop his own unique variation on them. The matter is only worth mentioning to the extent that his narrator's words at this closing point in *Memorias* reinforce the parallelism between social dynamics and a personal career and suggest a perception of the way in which the two might be demonstrated by a narrative as inextricably bound.[33] It is, of course, this suggestion, made implicitly throughout the *Memorias,* that justifies the interest of what Carrizo has to say. That Alvarez's narrative is more descriptive than analytical in the fashion of High Realism does not detract in any way from the importance of his vigilante-narrator from the point of view of a socially significant text.

One of the most salient features of *Memorias* is chapter 14, the longest section—fully one third of the book, which is devoted to reporting on the array of criminal types to be found in the Mundo Lunfardo. The extent of this report is justified, in terms of the sociocultural meaning of *Memorias,* in terms of the sociology of the *vigilante.* If, on the one hand, there is the opulence of urban Argentina to be protected, on the other there is the criminal world from which it needs to be defended. Knowledge of the varieties of types to be found in the Mundo Lunfardo and of their particular argot is not a matter of idle curiosity. It is a logical consequence of the demands placed upon the agent of law and order. The ethnography of the criminal must be examined fully in order to combat it adequately, and, as one of Carrizo's mentors asserts, it is a question of knowledge that can only be acquired in practical terms, out on the street, so to speak: "¡Mis maestros, amigo, son los que deben tener ustedes ... , si quieren servir para algo: los ojos, los oídos y las piernas!" (My teachers, Friend, are the ones you should have ... , if you want to amount to something, eyes, ears, and legs; 70).

One is immediately struck, reading chapter 14, with the complexity of the underworld, the language of which Alvarez was presenting to many

33. Miguel Angel Viola, "Fray Mocho y la incomunicación argentina," 12.

Argentine readers for the first time. It is customary for editions of *Memorias* to be accompanied by a glossary of the Lunfardo terms that the author uses, in the italics that befits their unfamiliarity for readers of his day, despite the fact that many of these words have now become an integral part of colloquial urban Argentine Spanish.[34] It would not be inappropriate for one to hypothesize that the complexity of Argentine criminal society at the end of the nineteenth century duplicates the social diversification of the law-abiding world with which the former enjoys a necessarily symbiotic relationship.[35] Furthermore, the stratification Carrizo describes among the various classes of criminals, their accomplices, and their techniques cannot help but echo the increasing specialization of an evolving capitalistic society:

> Entre los *lunfardos* hay cinco grandes familias: los *punguistas,* o limpiabolsillos; los *escruchantes,* o abridores de puertas; los que dan *la caramayolí, o la biaba,* o sea los asaltantes; los que *cuentan el cuento,* o hacen el *scruscho,* vulgarmente llamados estafadores, y, finalmente, los que reunen en su honorable persona las habilidades de cada especie: estos estuches son conocidos por de *las cuatro armas.* (91)
>
> (Among the crooks there are five large families: the *punguistas* or pickpockets; the *escruchantes* or those who break and enter; those who use *caramayolí* or *biaba,* that is those responsible for assault and battery; those who *cuentan el cuento* or engage in *scruscho,* commonly known as con men; and, finally, those who bring together in their honorable person the skills of each type: these are known as four-armed bandits.)

The subsequent fragments of the chapter are devoted to characterizing in detail each one of these aforementioned types and their derivatives. It quickly becomes obvious that, just as there is a well-defined hierarchy of

34. Morales has a not very useful chapter on "El lenguaje de Fray Mocho" (*Fray Mocho,* 130–35). Alvaro Yunque provides extensive observations, without much in the way of linguistic or lexicographic precision, in *Fray Mocho, precursos del lunfardo: versos rantes,* 17–47.

35. Marta Marín speaks of how Alvarez's characters—and, presumably, his narrators also—in general are unaware of the controlling dynamics of their society: "The feeling that it is unnecessary for what has been acquired to match the deservedness of the one who obtains it reaches such an advanced degree that we could speak in general of a blindness of individuals toward their own conditions, which has much to do with the blindness of the politics of reigning liberalism. Just as the country lived dominated by the blind faith in its potential wealth and believed it was marching forward on an endless path of progress, Fray Mocho's characters not only trust unconditionally in a Providence that will allot public positions and social ascendancy, not only trust that merit will have nothing to do with this allocation, but they moreover seem not to have the least idea of the distances that separate the position in which they find themselves from the one they aspire to" (*Fray Mocho,* 46–47). A general introduction on *Memorias* is provided by Miguel Angel Andreetto, "Temas de las *Memorias de un vigilante* de José S. Alvarez."

social types within the world protected by the law, among the lawless there is also a typology based on a ranking of respect and disdain: "Los que *dan caramayolé* [*sic*] o *la biaba* son los ladrones de la clase más ínfima, es la plebe del mundo lunfardo: ellos no necesitan para realizar sus empresas usar el mínimum de talento" (Those who are responsible for assault and battery are thieves of the lowest class, the plebes of the underworld, requiring for their operations not one shred of talent; 113).

It is fascinating to note in the foregoing that, in addition to the reference to social hierarchy, the relative merit among criminals of such-and-such an act of thievery is based upon *talent,* that precious commodity of a competitive society that weds natural endowment with acquired knowledge and permits the possessor to seek an appropriate level within the complex pecking order based upon its dynamics. A significant counterpart to the typology of talent is the reference to the limitations placed upon the pursuit of police work in what today would be called an "underdeveloped" country. What is delightful about this comment is that it bespeaks once again Carrizo's assimilation of the discourse of his superiors, who, in their commitment to the progressive modernization of Argentine society, are engaged in the acquisition of the specialized knowledge Carrizo's report on the Mundo Lunfardo represents:

> Aquí se vive a ciegas, con respecto a todo aquello que pueda servir para dar luz sobre un hombre: la policía, para desempeñar su misión, tiene que hacer prodigios, y parece imposible que obtenga los resultados que obtiene, dada la clase de gente en que las circunstancias la obligan a reclutar su personal subalterno y el medio en que actúa.
>
> Las policías de Londres, París y Nueva York, dotadas de mil recursos preciosos, no tiene nada de extraño que puedan encontrar un delincuente dos horas después de haber cometido el delito: lo admirable sería que pudiesen hacerlo aquí. (75)

> (One lives blindly here, as regards anything that can be used to throw light on a man: the police, in order to carry out their mission, must perform miracles, and it seems impossible for them to get the results they do, given the class of people from among which circumstances oblige them to recruit their subalterns and the setting in which they operate.
>
> There is nothing surprising in that the police of London, Paris, and New York, endowed with a thousand valuable resources, can find a criminal two hours after he has committed his crime: what would be admirable is that they could do it here.)

Carrizo conveniently overlooks the fact that he is part of the *clase de gente* from which the Buenos Aires police force is obliged to recruit—former peasants who have survived the deprivations of the *ejércitos de línea* without being killed by attacks of the Indians or the abuses of their superiors. Built around the opposition between the chance of conducting business *a ciegas* and the development of knowledge that can shed light on criminal practices, this passage serves as one point of departure for conferring importance on the investigation into and the description of the extensive varieties of types to be found in the Mundo Lunfardo.

This specialization and the diverse manifestations of it in actual criminal cases that he recollects become the basis for the extent of Carrizo's narrative: the greater the diversity of criminal activity, the larger the number of anecdotes available to him to recall for the reader. In this sense, the multiplicity of criminal elements makes possible Carrizo's *Memorias,* and at one point there is even a contamination between *cuento* as a term for the anecdotes Carrizo is recounting and *cuento* as the specific instrument of criminal activity of the con man: "Otro *scrucho* o *cuento* lindo" (127): the *vigilante*'s casebook examples are, in their original pre-text form, just so many *scruchos* worked in endless transformations upon their hapless victims. The difference, of course, is that while the latter are the tools of criminal deception, in the process of Carrizo's retelling they become textbook exempla in the education of his reader as regards the Mundo Lunfardo. The *cuento* as *scrucho* becomes the *cuento* as *lección* in the service of the system of law and order that Carrizo as *vigilante* personifies.

Alvarez's *Memorias de un vigilante* is a minor classic of Argentine literature, to the extent that it is frequently cited for its author's extensive and interesting treatment of the Mundo Lunfardo and for the "charming" feature of having a police officer who moves among that element report on the details of the many types with whom he came to deal in his service. Yet it is not necessary to argue for any degree of sophisticated writing on the part of Alvarez (sophisticated, at least, in the sense of a densely wrought text requiring careful critical interpretation) to recognize that there is something particularly relevant about *Memorias* as a social document. Any way in which Carrizo's narrative goes beyond being simply a series of loosely connected vignettes recounting the activities of an average police officer must lie with Alvarez's choice of a narrator, the details of his origins, the process of his assimilation to the criterion of law and order against a carefully defined criminal class, and the evolution of specialized knowledge as integrally related to the complexities of a dominant society.[36] Within the scope of these features, *Memorias de un vigilante* is a unique literary text.

36. Marín asserts that Alvarez represents, in the realm of literature, a form of professionalization that is a synthesis of the culture that stems from the Generation of 1880 and its social consequences (*Fray Mocho,* 24–25).

Nostalgia and the Literaturization of Nature in Joaquín V. González's *Mis montañas*

todo esto se escucha en medio de esas montañas; es su lenguaje, es la manifestación de su alma, henchida de poesía y de grandeza.[37]

(all this can be heard amidst those mountains; it is their language, it is the manifestation of their soul, swelled with poetry and grandeur.)

Joaquín V. González (1863–1926) must be considered the paradigm of the intellectual in the Generation of 1880.[38] González was born and raised in an obscure corner of the country, the town of Nonogasta, in La Rioja, the province that gave Argentina the legendary figure of Facundo Quiroga; note the reference in *Mis montañas* (My mountains) to this infamous fellow citizen (269). González received the sort of rudimentary education available at that time. However, after his studies at the Universidad de Córdoba, where he obtained his law degree in 1886, González embarked upon a brilliant career in politics that allowed him time to author a wide array of political, legal, and social documents. During his tenure as Ministro de Justicia e Instrucción Pública, the Universidad Nacional de La Plata was created in 1905, twenty-five years after that capital assumed importance, with the federalization of Buenos Aires in 1880, as the new capital of the province of Buenos Aires. González served several terms, beginning in 1906, as president of the university, and his contributions to the evolution of higher education in Argentina during the early twentieth century must be considered one of the most outstanding contributions of a man who was also one of the Argentine promoters of the new social science of sociology.[39]

In a certain sense, the establishment of the Universidad Nacional de La Plata is an intellectual capstone of the Generation of 1880. Argentina's three major universities represent three distinct stages in the pedagogical, and consequently intellectual, development of the country. The Universidad de Córdoba, founded in 1623, was controlled by the Jesuits until their expulsion in 1767 (and then by the Franciscans), a bastion of

37. Joaquín V. González, *Mis montañas,* 185. Hereafter cited parenthetically in the text by page number. The edition cited includes the "Carta de don Rafael Obligado" (167–82), which was written as a review of *La tradición argentina.* Critics have often pointed out Obligado's discreet chiding of González for his overly enthusiastic style: "cierta floración que oculta en demasía el verde de la planta" (a certain floweriness that hides by its excess the green of the plant; 180).

38. Arturo Marasso, "Joaquín V. González, el artista y el hombre"; and Salomón Wapnir, "Joaquín V. González, el soñador."

39. Diego F. Pró, "Joaquín V. González (1863–1923)."

one major variant of Spanish colonial culture in the Southern Cone. The Universidad de Buenos Aires was established in 1821 by Bernardino Rivadavia, Argentina's first president, for whom the university was to represent Enlightenment and Free-Mason ideas. Finally, González's tenure at La Plata corresponded to the consolidation of the positivist ideology in Argentina, and the university was early on a center of advanced scientific research and a leader in the social sciences.[40]

The Generation of 1880 brought together both Porteños and provincials like González in the common cause of forging a new and definitive national identity in the wake of the regressive period of Rosas and his Federalist legacy. González's dedication to the implementation in various spheres of the guiding social and cultural values of the Buenas Aires–based Generation of 1880 was mitigated, however, by his deep commitment to preserving his provincial roots. This sentiment, which can be variously characterized as Romantic reactionary (in the sense of attenuating the primacy of the progressive metropolis) and patronizingly sentimental (in the sense of recovering a traditional culture yet to benefit from civilization), is exemplified in *La tradición nacional* (1888), a meditation on the premodern components of Argentine culture that can be viewed as constants in a unitary national identity. This book, González's first literary (or, at least, nonempirically speculative) work, must be counted undoubtedly as an inaugural work of the nativist tradition of writing about the Argentine consciousness and national identity. As Burns has stated, "To [González], the rugged and quiet countryside with its noble people constituted the 'real,' the 'original' Argentina."[41]

40. Arthur P. Whitaker discusses briefly González's plans for the Universidad de La Plata, including its emphasis on the sciences and his European and American sources, particularly the University of Pennsylvania, in *Argentina,* 60. González published several works on university education, including *La Universidad de la Plata* (1905) and *Universidades y colegios* (1907).

41. Burns, *The Poverty of Progress,* 83. Whitaker refers to González as an "early exponent of nativism" within the context of those intellectuals of the Generation of 1880 who took exception to "so much aping of Europe" (*Argentina,* 61). One of the most ardent defenders of "nativism" in Argentine culture was the literary scholar Ricardo Rojas, who used his influential position as the founding director of the Universidad de Buenos Aires's Instituto de Literatura Argentina to promulgate his autochthonous cultural hypotheses against the predominant Europeanist conviction. It is, therefore, to be expected that he endorsed González's views; compare his *Elogio de Joaquín V. González.* *Julio R. Castiñeiras, Algunos aspectos de la obra de Joaquín V. González,* is a good example of the many uncritical paeans to González's place in Argentine intellectual history. See also the note by González's own son, Julio V. González, in *El juicio del siglo, o cien años de historia argentina* by Joaquín V. González.

Mis montañas (1893) is a much more personal work. Coming during his third term as a national congressman for La Rioja, this long essay on the life and customs of his native province is constructed in terms of an explicit juxtaposition between the turmoils of public life and the solace to be found in the return to the tranquillity of one's native soil:

> Buscando reposo, después de rudas fatigas, de esas que rinden el cuerpo y envenenan el alma, quise visitar las montañas de mi tierra ya para renovar impresiones apenas esbozadas en un libro, ya para refrescar mi espíritu en presencia de los parajes donde transcurrió mi primera edad. (183)

> (In search of repose following heavy tasks of the kind that tire the body and poison the soul, I sought to visit the mountains of my native land, whether to renew impressions barely sketched in a book, or to refresh my spirit in the presence of the places where my first youth took place.)

This play on the venerable *corte/aldea* antimony is the opening paragraph of *Mis montañas*, and it serves to lay the groundwork for the two dominant semantic axes of the text: the relationship between traditional modes of provincial life and the development of a progressive national civilization based in Buenos Aires; the relationship between the landscape and its people of La Rioja and the *yo* of the narrator. *Mis montañas* is organized in terms of a textually constituted first-person narrator who functions as a bridge between the progressive if turbulent metropolis from which he has come and the traditional but tranquil society to which he is returning. It is a journey of both recovery (the substitution of turmoil with revivifying tranquillity) and discovery (the analysis of traditional folkways in terms of the enhanced knowledge of someone who now represents an advanced, civilized, progressive culture).

These two axes constitute the basis of an unresolved tension in *Mis montañas:* the degree to which life in La Rioja is superior to that of Buenos Aires (always present by implication, if never identified explicitly), by virtue of what a contemporary vocabulary might call the authenticity of the former, and the degree to which life in the provinces is marked by an ignorance that has yet to be remedied by the benefits of civilization. González, like many provincials called to defend the ever-increasingly monolithic culture of Buenos Aires, must have been deeply torn between loyalty to native roots and identity with the globalizing mentality of the metropolis. Unlike their contemporaries in Spain's Generation of 1898, most of whom were provincials but virtually all of whom came to defend the primacy of Castile, the provincial members of the Argentine Generation of 1880 cannot have helped but see the culture of Buenos Aires as still raw enough not to win their allegiance completely. Like Sarmiento almost fifty years before, who still retained in *Recuerdos de provincia* (1852) a profound commitment to a personal variety of the rural Hispanic past, González does not write as the social scientist out to explicate the barbarianism of the provinces in need of civilization, but as a poet who sees his most fundamental identity in what continues to survive yet untouched by the spreading waves of metropolitan culture.

The key to González's personal recreation of La Rioja lies with the way in which he "literaturizes" natural and social reality. All writing is, of course, an act of literaturization, in the sense that texts are interpretations of the concrete and the experiential within the conventions of writing.[42] The rhetoric of writing and tropic effects of language transform "reality" into the cultural text. This is an axiom of the semiology of literature and other cultural texts, and critical analysis becomes a matter of demonstrating the various strategies authors employ in the process. But what is different about González's literaturizing process is not just how he represents rhetorically the details of La Rioja as he understands them, but the fact that he sees in the landscape of La Rioja a poetic text that he will interpret for the reader.[43] Thus, *Mis montañas* becomes a confrontation between two texts, La Rioja as it "is" as a primary poetic text and the author's various ways of evoking and describing that primary text.

Needless to say, conceiving of La Rioja as a poetic text is the fundamental metaphoric trope of *Mis montañas,* and in this sense it is the motivating textual strategy: the best literary representation of the provincial landscape is to demonstrate how it is poetry itself, and not merely a circumstantial commingling of nature and people. For an age that elevated academic poetry into the paragon of cultural expression—colloquial expression becomes formal writing, which in turn is presided over

42. David William Foster, *Para una lectura semiótica del ensayo latinoamericano,* focuses on elements of literaturization in the modern Latin American essay. See also Foster, "Elementos de literaturización en un *diálogo* de Bartolomé Hidalgo."

43. González's concern to literaturize physical geography is evident in his earlier *La tradición nacional,* where the second paragraph establishes the correlation of nature as a theater of natural poetry: "All of the features, all of the tendencies, all of the passion have an apparent arena in the varied nature of our country . . . from the smiling banks of the great rivers, the abode of native poetry, where there is no doubting the national muse hides, watched over by the morning mists" (p. 19). The most valuable analysis of the mythification of the land in Güiraldes is provided by Eduardo Romano, *Análisis de "Don Segundo Sombra."* Unfortunately, Romano does not trace the extensive ancestry, reaching back to the Generation of 1880, of this ideological component in Argentine sociocultural history.

by the special artistic province of literature, whose most perfect manifestation is poetry—to consider a natural and social landscape as poetry is to do much more than repeat Romantic commonplaces. Whereas the Romantic saw nature as a form of primitive and, therefore, "natural" and pure poetry, for the Generation of 1880, imbued with the specialized knowledge of an academic age, poetry is the most perfectly crafted expression of language.[44] Therefore, to view the La Rioja countryside and its inhabitants as poetry is a striking hyperbole of dignification that permeates *Mis montañas* from the very beginning of the text:

> Es imposible el silencio; el eco de las montañas es la nota, la armonía que vive latente en su seno como en un arpa gigantesca: el aire que frota la peña enhiesta arranca el sonido musical, la falda vecina lo recoge con caricia, y robustecido lo despide a su vez; diríase que aquellas moles de ruda apariencia, a lo lejos semejantes a tormentas que se levantasen amenazadoras, negras, silenciosas, para estallar sobre nuestra cabezas, tuvieran un alma difundida por las grutas, los intersticios, las cuevas, los nidos y los árboles. El eco es su voz. El modula y expresa todos los tonos: el canto triste del pastor que habla a solas con la inmensidad, el ruido terrorífico de la mole desprendida de su quicio, los gritos destemplados del combate y los alardes estruendosos de la victoria.
>
> Todo es y cuanto en la creación tiene un sonido, se escucha y se sabe más allá, de manera que no hay silencio tan inquieto como aquel solemne silencio de las montañas, donde el vuelo de un ave alarma todos los nidos, las guaridas y las viviendas. (192–93)

> (Silence is impossible; the echo of the mountains is the note, the harmony that lives latent in their depths in a gigantic harp: the air that rubs the jagged peak draws forth the musical sound, the neighboring mountainside picks it up with a caress, and sends it along on its way reinforced. One could say that those rude appearing masses, which from a distance seem to be dark, silent, and threatening gathering storms that will break over our heads, had a soul diffused throughout the grottoes, the spaces in between, the caves, the nests, and the trees. The echo is their voice. It modulates and expresses all tones: the sad song of the shepherd who talks alone with the immenseness, the terrifying sound of the unhinged mass, the off-key shouts of combat, and the thundering cries of victory.

44. Ricardo Levene speaks directly to González's preoccupation, certainly typical of a late nineteenth-century aesthete's view of culture, with art as an organizing principle: "Art was the passion of his life that glowed with a burning flame. Religion, history, sociology had all been seen in terms of his temperament as an artist, intuited with the heart and ennobled by the ideal of beauty" (*Ideas sociales directrices de Joaquín V. González,* 70). César Tiempo makes a similar statement: "Joaquín V. González is first and foremost a poet. 'Poetry is the unconfessed religion of every soul,' he said" ("Joaquín V. González," 48).

> Everything that is the full measure of sound in nature is heard and known beyond, such that there is no silence as restless as that solemn silence of the mountains, where the flight of a bird startles all the nests, the preserves, and habitats.)

There is a concentration of figures referring to the "landscape as a poetic text" in the initial chapters of *Mis montañas.* Subsequently, this inaugural characterization gives way to the array of specific topics and supporting anecdotes that the narrator dwells on in the process of portraying his personal version of provincial life and customs. However, these disquisitions are dependent upon such a characterization, since each specific detail is, to extend the author's metaphor, a constituent in the overall poetic text. Moreover, in conformance with the emphasis during the period of Spanish American Modernism on establishing the homologies between various artistic forms, which were viewed as multiple transformations of each other, La Rioja is not represented as just a poetic text. Poetry may enjoy aesthetic privileges in a literary text since both are elaborations of language. But La Rioja is as much a musical, theatrical, pictorial, and sculptural phenomenon as it is a verbal one:

> Alzando los ojos a las cimas, pueden distinguirse sobre el fondo límpido del cielo los contornos caprichosos de las rocas, que ya figuran torreones o cúpulas ciclópeas, ya grupos de estatuas levantadas sobre tamaños pedestales. (186; see also 213, 221, and 227)
>
> (If you lift your eyes up to the peaks, you can make out against the limpid backdrop of the sky the capricious outlines of the rocks, which look like towers or cyclopean cupolas or like groups of statues placed on as many pedestals.)

The opening chapters of *Mis montañas* are a torrent of metaphors, often one right after the other in an irrepressibly enthusiastic enumeration, based on all of the prized artistic genres. Although the concentration of literaturizing metaphors may become somewhat attenuated in the subsequent chapters (there are twenty-one, each with its distinctive topical title), there is hardly one of them without some reference to the inherent "poetry," "musicality," "theatricality," or "pictorial/sculptural" quality of the landscape and its natural phenomena. Indeed, in some cases, as in chapter 19, "El cóndor," the entire text is built around such conceits, leading up to the summary statement "el cóndor es un ave simbólica, de esas en cuyas formas y hábitos los pueblos sintetizan los más altos ideales" (the condor is a symbolic bird of the kind in whose forms and habits the people find the synthesis of their highest ideals; 361). La Rioja as a poetic text in the broadest sense of the word replaces the objective data that might have formed the basis of a more properly interpretive analysis by one of Argentina's first professional sociologists.

The substitution of poetry for sociology also emerges in the role of the first-person narrator, who substitutes for the impartial and depersonalized analyst of the protocols of the social sciences. It must be noted that on several occasions, however, González refers specifically to his interest, returning twenty years after his original departure to La Rioja, in the examination of its natural and social features from the perspective of a sociologist:

> yo quiero reflejar en estas páginas los caracteres sociológicos de mi pueblo, su fisonomía y su alma, arrancando su secreto a los despojos del tiempo y de la Naturaleza, a las obras mutiladas de los hombres y a las huellas medio ocultas de los que levantaron los primeros cimientos de la ciudad civilizada. (246)

> (I want to reflect in these pages the sociological features of my people, their physiognomy and their soul, wresting their secret from the ravages of time and Nature, from the mutilated works of men and the half-hidden traces of those who built the first foundations of the civilized city.)

Yet the simple fact is that González does *not* undertake a sociological analysis, in any of the senses in which the term had come to be used by the end of the nineteenth century, not even in the sense of a speculative essay concerning the values, customs, and beliefs of a people. Although there is some of the latter, particularly with reference to the relationship between primitive traditions and Christian practices (231, 242, 250–51 inter alia), the dominant discourse throughout is the one that I have described as the literaturization of natural and social reality and the interaction between that reality and the *yo* of the personal narrator.

Within the complex panorama of nineteenth-century Argentine social history, González strikes a delicate balance in the juxtapositions between city and countryside, between Hispanic legacy and European (that is, non-Hispanic) civilization, between the millenary Incan heritage and the Christian overlay. While Rosas trumpeted the return to Christian and Hispanic, pre-Independence values (he called himself the Restaurador de las Leyes), which included the primacy of the rural population over the urban citizenry, González portrays his family as being among those provincials who resisted the rule of the *caudillos,* among whom Rosas was the first among equals. Thus, he is proud of the exodus and suffering of his family during the Tyranny, is pleased to underscore how they represented an adherence to *lo culto* in the face of the barbarism of the 1830s and 1840s and how the culture he presents, which he returns to claim in the odyssey of *Mis montañas,* embodies the quintessence of a nuclear Argentine identity. Certainly, this is the identity González detailed in his earlier *La tradición nacional*,[45] and there can be no mistaking the way in which both documents are part of a paean to a substratum of values that the provincial implies must be recognized for a global national identity. The very fact that La Rioja lies on the fringes of the republic only serves, it would seem, to underscore how this identity must involve the country as a whole, not just the cosmopolitan turbulence from which the narrator emerges to recover the culture of his *montañas.* (One might also add that the geographical juxtaposition is also eloquent: the flatlands of the Buenos Aires center versus, but in tandem with, the monumental geology of far-flung provinces like La Rioja.)

González's narrator—let us call him González himself, since there is every reason to believe that such a confluence is intended between narrator and author—sees himself at the center of a system of relationships. These relationships involve, on the one hand, a homology between the historical past of La Rioja and the narrator's own personal and familial past and, on the other, an assimilation between the La Rioja he seeks to recover and describe and the historical present of a country in need of elements for a unified national identity. If this system has as a consequence the stepping back from a properly speaking sociological analysis, it is, after all, of a whole with the gestures of continuity between narrator and nature (200, 214, 288) and the pathetic fallacy of nature (283) and the anthropomorphization of its organic and inorganic constituents (267, 348).

The return to La Rioja is motivated by a nostalgia for a precise social order that dates back to the Hispanic roots of Argentine provincial culture (not, of course, that evoked by the barbarian *caudillos* and Rosas, but rather an authentic one exemplified by the narrator's progenitors). *Mis montañas* involves the suggestion of a compact series of nostalgic correspondences between land and society, between tradition and personal identity that permits an alternative to the modern-world strife from which the narrator is escaping in the opening sentences of his memoir:

> Mirado desde la altura, donde está la casa de mis abuelos, aquel conjunto de luces dispersas sin orden en el arenal de enfrente, hace el efecto de una bahía silenciosa y en calma, donde arden los farolillos de las embarcaciones.
>
> Pero allí, en el seno de las familias propietarias, la escena es diferente; la alegría repercute en el vasto corredor donde se ha armado la charla con todos los que han venido trayendo criaturas y sirvientes. Ninguno se sentía desgraciado, porque un vínculo amoroso los reunía en una sola ambición noble y pura. (263)

(Seen from on high, where the house of my grandparents is, that collec-

45. William Rex Crawford, "Positivism and Idealism in Argentina," 114–15.

tion of lights dispersed without order across the expanse of sand before it produces the effect of a silence and becalmed bay where the lamps of the vessels burn.

But there, in the bosom of my family's holdings, the scene is different. Happiness resounds in the vast corridor as part of the conversation develops around everyone arriving with children and servants. No one feels out of place because a loving link joins them all together in a single noble and pure ambition.)

It is curious to note how these passages, which constitute a frank and unembarrassed eulogy to a concept of hereditary landed gentry that by implication complements the new bourgeois entrepreneurial class González has left behind in the capital, is fraught with ambivalence as to verbal tense. Writing now in the present, now in the imperfect (that is, nonterminal) past, González moves back and forth between his recollections as to what life was like as a child in the bosom of this beneficent patriarchy and how the elements of it still remain to be rediscovered in his journey of personal recuperation. I suspect that the tirade against the threat to the equilibrium of this microcosm in the pages following the passages quoted above refers more to Facundo Quiroga and company than it does to Liberal capitalism (268), which, at least in terms of Buenos Aires society, is only in part coterminus with the agricultural and cattle baronies that had by the end of the century made Argentina economically prosperous. Since it is true that late nineteenth-century Argentine capitalism monumentalized itself with reference to myths of a rural oligarchy that only used Buenos Aires as a port for the exportation of its products and the importation of the luxuries permitted by its newfound wealth, it is not difficult to understand González as conceiving of his La Rioja aristocratic roots as part of the overall constellation of the gentry that had come to control the country.

From this point of view, the unspoken agenda of *Mis montañas* is to propose, with all of the eloquence involved in the complex process of literaturizing nature, how La Rioja must figure prominently in the forging of a rural aristocracy and the geographic settings of its primacy. Despite all of the effort expended on the development of Buenos Aires as the financial and political capital of a (finally) unified Argentina, the mythification of the *campo* is one of the major ideological criteria of the period. As a provincial who, by the time of the publication of *Mis montañas,* had established a solid reputation in the many spheres of public life in which a gentleman moved in Buenos Aires, González (re)turns to his native La Rioja as part of an ideological effort to cast himself as retrieving a noble heritage that is an inspiration and a solace in the face of the turbulent urban life that he (and his class) had come to lead. As a *locus amoenus,* the monumental landscape of La Rioja provides a fitting setting for the sociologist-poet to construct a renewed identity with the land. *Beatus ille,* he is blessed who can attain the heightened emotion of such an identity:

> Cuando después de veinte años de ausencia he vuelto a visitar aquellos sitios consagrados por la poesía y los ensueños de mi infancia, lo confieso: he llorado a solas sin poderlo resistir. (266)
>
> (When after twenty years of absence I have returned to visit those places consecrated by poetry and the visions of my childhood, I confess that I have cried in private without being able to control myself.)

González's encomium to La Rioja is a profoundly personal statement about renewing contact with one's roots after a long absence, particularly one marked by the sort of success and multiple experiences as González enjoyed during two decades. Moreover, the hyperbolic manner in which he evokes the landscape and recalls the traditional life of the province can be understood in the first instance as a function of the enthusiasm of the narrator's return to the land of his youth.

Yet the ideological dimensions of *Mis montañas* clearly extend beyond the limits of a personal memoir. As a paradigm of the intellectual of the Generation of 1880, González stood in a position to bespeak, in addition to the enormous scientific growth of his age in Argentina, the special properties of the poetization of sociocultural reality. By proposing the landscape, the history, and the traditions of La Rioja as a multiple literary and artistic text, González, after bracketing the urban society from which he undertakes to absent himself, proposes a reinvigorating alternative for the sophisticated but sensitive gentleman. Certainly, it is possible to see in this position one of the origins of a deification of the *campo* in Argentine culture that culminates with Ricardo Güiraldes's *Don Segundo Sombra* (1926), the mythification of traditional, rural life.

In the process, González contributes to the naturalization of the myths of the primacy of the rural aristocracy in Argentine culture at the time when the complex problems of urban growth demand a legitimating point of reference in the vast, unspoiled rural preserve lying beyond the encroaching frontiers of the metropolis. In the penultimate chapter, 20, "Una cacería," González describes in great detail a hunting expedition, a traditional sport, which his father offers to him on the eve of his departure in order to be schooled; it is this departure from which he returns twenty years later. In addition to the sport of the hunt, González's father wishes to show him the far reach of his property which his son will one day inherit. Presiding over this expedition in the memory of the narrator are its grandiose dimensions as an integral part of his provincial identity: "el cuadro que comienza, la escena de corte épico" (376). Thus, again, this recollection is colored by all of the literaturization that forms the basis of González's text, beginning with the "magnitud del teatro" (383) of the setting so dramatically evoked.

First personifying history and then metaphorizing the evolution of human society as a journey through the landscapes of nature, the narrator assimilates to the sweep of human history his detailed re-creation of the geography and the ethnography of La Rioja, synthesized in the symbol of the condor:

> La Historia es una inmensa llanura donde alternan a vastos intervalos los desiertos inconmensurables con los oasis regeneradores, los laberintos sin salida con los valles de verdor eterno y corrientes de cristal, y la raza humana, viajera sin reposo, no tiene otros guías que los astros, las cumbres, los relámpagos y los incendios, pero siempre la luz y las alturas. . . . ¡Oh, si mi patria no olvidase que hacia el Occidente se levantan las cumbres más elevadas de América, y que más arriba de ella tiene su región soberana el cóndor de los Andes . . . ! (363)
>
> (History is an immense place wherein limitless deserts alternate at vast intervals with regenerative oases, labyrinths without exits with the valleys of eternal green and crystal streams, and the human race, wandering without repose, has no other guide than the stars, the crests, the flashes of lightning and the forest fires, but always the light and the heights. . . . Oh, if only my fatherland were not to forget that to the West rise up the highest peaks of America, and that farther to the north the condor of the Andes has its sovereign realm . . . !)

It is in these terms that *Mis montañas* assumes the dimensions of a paean to a nature conceived of as a poetic text that can speak to all Argentines capable of reading productively its signs in the manner exemplified by González's autobiographical narrator. Physical geography as exemplified by the mountains of La Rioja is a source of "natural poetry," and those individuals who accept the primacy of art and poetry as ennobling factors in human experience will see in the return of González's narrator to the wellspring of his personal identity a peaceful reunion with the bountiful Nature of childhood from which he as an adult had become separated (400). This quest for a renewed innocence in the presence of a recovered natural poetry emerges as a strong counterweight to the cosmopolitan imperative of the Generation of 1880.

CHAPTER 2

Rewriting National History

The Rosas tyranny was a traumatic experience for the young Argentine republic. In addition to the terror Rosas wielded in order to solidify and sustain his power over the confederacy, he represented a putative return to Hispanic traditions and a repudiation of the principles on which independence from Spain had been based. Since these principles were based on a criticism of the Hispanic tradition, the differences between Rosas and the founding fathers could not have been more pronounced.

Rosas's fall, the alleged return to the ideals of the founding fathers, and the implantation of a Liberal hegemony corresponded to the rise of professional historiography in Argentina as in the rest of the West. It is therefore possible to refer to important documents executed with the goal of providing the reconstitutionalized republic with a scientific and enlightened national history. This historiography, of course, served the ideological needs of the period of national reformation and the Generation of 1880, giving concrete form to the major economic, social, and political interests of the period.[1]

The enormous output of popular literature by Eduardo Gutiérrez during the final decades of the century constitutes, however, a narrative alternative to academic historiography. Dealing with themes like local *caudillos,* popular folk heroes, and, inevitably, Rosas, Gutiérrez's *folletines* (which were often based on the same sources being rewritten by establishment ideologues) constitute an important vehicle of knowledge for a growing reading public.[2] Although Gutiérrez was not himself identified with the mainstream of the Generation of 1880—his family remained loyal to the primacy of the province of Buenos Aires and opposed the federalization of its port city—*Juan Manuel de Rosas: los dramas del terror* (Juan Manuel de Rosas: The dramas of terror) is a fundamental text in the interpretation of the infamous tyrant.

By the same token, Ramos Mejía's interpretive essay, *Las neurosis de los*

1. Tulio Halperín Donghi, "La historiografía: treinta años en busca de un rumbo."
2. Horacio C. Morando, "Eduardo Gutiérrez: populismo y fama literaria."

hombres celébres en la historia argentina (The neuroses of celebrated men in Argentine history), the first example of psychobiological history in Argentina, weds historical knowledge with hypotheses of the new discipline of psychoanalysis to address the central question of what made possible the Rosas phenomenon. Although Ramos Mejía's study strives for a scientific accuracy irrelevant to Gutiérrez's popular narratives, it too serves as a primordial point of reference for the important task of interpreting national history as part of the project to provide Argentina with a Liberal identity. This essay is only one small fragment of Ramos Mejía's extensive psychobiological or protopsychiatric writings about historical and public figures. As an important intellectual and man of science in the professionalization of knowledge in Argentina during the period of the Generation of 1880, Ramos Mejía's collected writings in this genre constitute an especially useful point of entrance into how his generation was going about the task of interpreting the past and defining, if often only by implication, the principles by which its own participation in the national life was to be judged. By charting in such considerable detail the defects, both in inheritance and in willful action of historical protagonists, Ramos Mejía's psychobiology pruned away from the chaotic garden of variegated human behavior all those elements that were considered anathema to the prevailing concept of the public man.

Theatricalizing History: Eduardo Gutiérrez's *Juan Manuel de Rosas: los dramas del terror*

> El espíritu se conmueve, el corazón se estremece sollozante y la inteligencia se resiste a creer en los horrores de aquellos tiempos inolvidables. . . .
>
> El espíritu, aterrado, cree asistir a una alucinación fantástica, porque parece increíble que el espíritu humano pueda asimilarse de aquella manera con los instintos bestiales de la fiera.[3]

> (The spirit is moved, the heart shudders with sobs and the mind resists believing in the horrors of those unforgettable times. . . .
>
> The spirit, terrified, believes that it is witnessing a fantastic hallucination, because it seems incredible that the human spirit can match in that way the bestial instincts of the wild animal.)

Juan Manuel de Rosas: los dramas del terror, published originally in *La Patria Argentina* between December 1881 and December 1882 and brought out in book form in 1882, is one of the essential sociocultural documents

3. Eduardo Gutiérrez, *Juan Manuel de Rosas: los dramas del terror,* 9. Hereafter cited parenthetically in the text by page number.

written by an adherent to the establishment ideology of the Generation of 1880 that define the Rosas period of Argentine history (1835–1852).[4] Rosas, who had as governor of Buenos Aires exercised dictatorial power on a national level, touted himself as the Restaurador de las Leyes within the context of a program of reactionary political action that sought to overturn the Enlightenment-Romantic attitudes at the heart of the independence movement of the Argentine founding fathers.[5] It has become customary to view the Rosas dictatorship as a parenthesis between the ideals of these founders (ideals that were sustained and developed further by the Argentine intelligentsia in exile in Chile, Uruguay, and elsewhere between 1835 and 1852), and the new founding of the capitalist bourgeoisie that the Generation of 1880 carried to its conclusion throughout the final decades of the century. As a consequence, Argentine literature of the period is filled with images of Rosas.[6]

The interpretation of Rosas as a diabolic dictator who based his power on a well-orchestrated campaign of terror has essentially held firm, despite attempts to write a revisionist history of Rosas and to see in his personalist populism and in the persecution of a Europeanized elite the roots for subsequent varieties of disestablishmentarian opposition—anarchism, the radical movement, Peronism, the revolutionary left, and a Third-World sentiment in general. A variety of this interpretation, of course, might well be to see the successive military dictatorships of modern Argentine history, particularly the so-called *guerra sucia* of the late 1970s, as nurtured by a legacy of official terrorism dating back to Rosas.

Gutiérrez may have, with a work like *Juan Moreira* (1879), seen fit to mythify aspects of the world of the Gauchos on which Rosas based a large part of his political power, as part of an ideology of the return to populist roots, and from which he drew many instruments in his program of organized terror (see below, pp. 153–72). But he had no use

4. This should not be taken to mean that Gutiérrez should be identified with the leading ideologues and literary representatives of the Generation of 1880, only that a work such as this was part of the generalized repudiation of the Rosas period. In fact, Gutiérrez and his family were identified with the policies of Bartolomé Mitre and the defense of the old Creole primacy of the province of Buenos Aires at the expense of a country united under a central administration, not dominated by any one province, which is what the Generation of 1880 proposed. One of the ironies of the Rosas period, of course, is that Rosas's own background was among the founding Creole stock. The best survey of the works of Eduardo Gutiérrez and the controversies surrounding the literary merit (or lack thereof) of his writings, is Jorge B. Rivera, *Eduardo Gutiérrez*.

5. John Lynch, *Argentine Dictator: Juan Manuel de Rosas, 1829–1852*.

6. Harry Lee King, Jr., "Juan Manuel de Rosas and His Epoch as Portrayed in Argentine Fiction."

for the political program that turned around the figure of Rosas, and *Juan Manuel de Rosas* is only one of his many *folletines* dealing with the period broken by the battle of Caseros in 1852. Works like *El Chacho* (1884) and *Los montoneros* (1886) are narrative versions of the resistance to the ultimately successful attempts at national hegemony by the central, Buenos Aires–based government during the post-Rosas period. Indeed, they are eloquent in the denunciation of the excesses of the federal armies in the struggle by Buenos Aires for centralized political control. *Juan Manuel de Rosas,* on the other hand, focuses both on the establishment of the reign of terror as part of Rosas's consolidation of power and on one singular case of the use of terror and injustice in the pursuit of that power.

The first part of *Rosas* concerns the establishment of the Mazorca, the avatar of all subsequent death squads and parapolice operations in Argentine history. Made up of the dregs of society and empowered to maim and kill at random while expropriating for their own use the property of their victims, the members of the Mazorca were the undisputed owners of the night during Rosas's reign. Either entertaining themselves with the random choice of victims or following up on the most casual hint of the Restaurador that so-and-so constituted an inconvenience to the spirit of federalism, the *mazorqueros* are essential points of reference for Gutiérrez in the definition of the horrors of life under Rosas. The narrator spares few details in the portrayal of their activities. In addition to stock, melodramatic "Gothic" evocations of the impact on decent citizens of these thugs run wild, undoubtedly confirming for Gutiérrez's audience the worst fears of law-and-order readers as regards the dangers of unfettering the lower classes, there are graphic descriptions of the standard practices of the Mazorca of beating women senseless and slitting men's throats, often with the dullest blade possible.

Moreover, Gutiérrez surely must have made even his least refined readers catch their breath with his forthright description of how the Mazorca got its name: Rosas's denizens early on adopted the practice of using corn cobs to impale their victims, either before or after slitting their throats and beheading them. These details are provided by the section entitled "La Mazorca":

> El Carpincho puso en el suelo su carga de maíz, y tomando una mazorca y armado de una astilla de leña, se dirigió al cuerpo de Baigorri, caliente aún. Ninguno se sospechaba cuál era la intención de aquel bandido.
>
> El Carpincho dió vuelta al cadáver y valiéndose de la astilla de leña como de un mazo, introdujo la mazorca en aquel cuerpo. Aquella opera-

ción impía e infame hasta lo fantástico, aquella afrenta, digna de Satanás, fué acompañada de un eco de alegres carcajadas, e imprecaciones de todo género. (43–44)

(El Carpincho placed his load of corn on the ground and taking a cob in his hand and armed with a piece of kindling, he turned to Baigorri's still warm body. No one had any idea what that bandit's intentions were.

El Carpincho turned the body over and wielding the kindling like a club, he introduced the cob in that body. That ungodly and infamous, even fantastic, operation, that insult worthy of Satan, was accompanied by an echo of happy laughter and imprecations of all kinds.)

The second part of *Rosas* deals with the frame-up of the Reynafé family for the death of Juan Facundo Quiroga. Quiroga, the *caudillo* or popular leader of the province of La Rioja, is, of course, the subject of Sarmiento's *Facundo* (1845), the most famous interpretation of Argentina under Rosas.[7] Quiroga, despite his brutal career as a champion of the federalist cause, came to be seen by Rosas as a major challenge to the latter's authority. Thus, Rosas had Quiroga assassinated at Barranca Yaco in 1835. Since it was necessary to find a scapegoat for this murder, Rosas had the Reynafé family framed for Quiroga's murder. Gutiérrez describes in great detail the mechanics of this aberration of justice: how the Reynafés are set up, how they become victims of false witness, how they are subject to every possible form of physical abuse, how their trial and sentencing is a travesty of the legal system manipulated by the Restaurador de las Leyes, and how they serve to symbolize the final consolidation of power of the tyrant Rosas. Gutiérrez makes full use of the documents from the period available to him, many of which he quotes in his text, and he enthusiastically pursues every possible narrative strategy available to him in the literature of the day to enhance his descriptions of the Reynafés as sacrificial victims to Rosas's implacable reign of terror.

Rosas fed upon a morbid interest in a period that had already by the 1880s become invested with all of the negativity European culture had associated with the Dark Ages. Gutiérrez's writing merely served to confirm the prevailing interpretation of that period and to confirm the legacy of *unitario* values that the Generation of 1880 was in the process of implanting and, after its own fashion, consolidating.

There must be, from the point of view of Argentine literary history, considerable interest associated with *Rosas* as a key interpretive reading of a founding historical period. In this sense, it is a point of departure,

7. Armando Zárate, *Facundo Quiroga, Barranca Yaco: juicios y testimonios*.

like José Mármol's *Amalia* (1851) before it, for the Gothic interpretation of Rosas,[8] as well as a point of reference for all those works of Argentine literature concerned with the horrors of the *chusma,* the rabble, turned loose on the decent defenders of a civilized society.

As a consequence of this importance as a founding reading of the social text, *Rosas* invites an investigation into its specific narrative strategies. The opening of the narrative is based on a reiteration of a topos of incredulity that is reinforced for the reader by the receding image of what by the early 1880s was already a historical period, one to which considerable legendary material had already accrued. Gutiérrez's ploy for framing his text from the outset is to announce to his reader that, no matter what they have already heard about the debaucheries, the persecutions, and the assorted horrors of the Rosas period, his narrative will make clear that the facts are far more horrible than can be imagined. In this variant of the venerable topos of "you have no idea of what really went on"—and, therefore, "I will be the one to inform you adequately"—the narrator subscribes wholeheartedly to the discourse maxim of the originality of the information about to be imparted to the reader. That is, the reader's attention is engaged on the basis of the privileged information of the narrative that goes beyond whatever the reader may have already known. It is for this reason that there is a concentration of transformations of the tropes from the opening words of the text that have already been cited as epigraphs to this study.

The assertion that what is to be revealed strains credulity is complemented by the narrator's assurances that what he will recount will leave little—if any—doubt about the terror of the period: "Pero son verdades pálidas y débiles [las conocidas hasta el momento] al lado de otros horrores más ignorados, que exhibiremos de manera a no dejar la más remota duda" (But these are pale and weak truths alongside lesser-known horrors which we will place in exhibit in order that there cannot be the remotest doubt about them; 9). Although these tropes do not constitute a recurring echo in *Rosas,* their strategic placement at the outset of the narrative serves to establish the basic foundations of Gutiérrez's narrative and the special criterion of his appeal to the reader. To enter into the world of his narrative is to accept the responsibility to face, if we are to believe the narrator, the most direct representation possible of the facts surrounding Rosas's abuse of power.

Yet Gutiérrez's narrative is not unmediated. No discourse can constitute an unmediated representation of Truth or Reality for the simple

8. David William Foster, "*Amalia* como novela gótica."

reason that language is a metaphor of whatever it purports to speak of. It is not necessary to subscribe unconditionally to a deconstructionist hypothesis about the inadequacies and the distortions of language to understand how narrative representation is far from a transparent window on an autonomous but fully recoverable meaning. If language is in most neutral form a metaphoric discourse that displaces the experiences or meanings it sets out to represent, the sort of rhetorical language associated with narration in a specifically configured narrative, can hardly be viewed as unmediated in any reasonable sense of the notion of "direct representation."[9]

It is no surprise to find Gutiérrez's narrative colored by a host of features associated as a matter of course with the narrative modes of the time. The two most obvious are direct speech attributed to historically verifiable individuals, beginning with Rosas and including the lowliest members of the Mazorca and their hapless victims, and the indirect reporting on the thoughts of these individuals. That is to say, Gutiérrez does not exemplify the interior monologue of high Realism, but rather he makes extensive use of the free indirect style whereby the narrator speaks with the voice of specifically identifiable characters. Concomitantly, the narrator feels free to report confidently the feelings and motivations of the cast of characters he assembles. But these are all stock features of the sort of narrative customary in the period, and it would be rash to seek any originality on Gutiérrez's part in this regard.

What does emerge as the most salient feature of *Rosas* is the decision to report on the period in terms of a complex network of dramatic allusions. Aside from the repeated use of words like *escena, espectáculo, farsa,* and other casual or circumstantial commonplaces referring to the dramatic quality of the events being narrated, Gutiérrez postulates his evocation of the Rosas period as a constellation of *dramas del terror.* This interpretation is announced by the subtitle of the book, and it is carried out on a sustained basis in both parts of *Rosas* as the principal configuring strategy of the narrative.

This configuring strategy assumes the form of a flow of narrative—a succession of evocations, dialogue, and commentary— that gives the im-

9. Contemporary historiography has come to share with literary criticism an interest in the mediating nature of narrative and to view historical writing as a form of mediating narrative, which, to be sure, does not mean to imply that what historians write should be viewed as a variety of fiction; see F. R. Ankersmit, *Narrative Logic: A Semantic Analysis of the Historian's Language,* and Hayden White, *The Content of the Form: Narrative Discourse and Historical Representation.* It is important to note that Gutiérrez's narrative is frequently treated as a historical primary source and that it is classified as history by American libraries.

pression, in the best parajournalistic fashion adhered to by Gutiérrez, of a straightforward representation of an array of interlocking events. The image of a continuous fabric of reality is abetted by the historical character of the material being narrated and his readers' presumed familiarity with many of the names and happenings. However, this apparently uncomplicated flow of narration is punctuated at regular intervals both by the aforementioned words and their derivatives and by judicious parenthetical elaborations on the theatricality of the panorama being portrayed. These asides serve to confirm the subtitle of Gutiérrez's narrative, as well as to remind the reader that the narrator is interpreting events as much as he is simply representing them. That is to say, the recurring references to the theatricality of the Rosas period sustain *Rosas* as a specifically weighted analysis of the federal period rather than as merely an unmediated re-creation of certain infamous events associated with it.

This characterization of his narrative material reaches a high point in the description of the execution of the Reynafé family and their alleged accomplices at the end of the second part of the novel. Much more than simply the unjust execution of a group of hapless scapegoats, this event is presented against the backdrop of a broad canvas of a citizenry that assembles to witness the well-orchestrated spectacle that Rosas has carefully planned:

> La ciudad ofrecía un raro aspecto de vida y de muerte. Las casas de familia en su gran mayoría estaban cerradas, como una débil protesta a aquellos asesinatos bárbaros, que debían celebrarse con toda la pompa federal.
>
> La sociedad de Buenos Aires estaba conmovida y aterrada con las escenas de vandalaje que empezaban de aquella manera. Las mismas casas de negocio que no eran las pulperías de los grandes mazorqueros, estaban cerradas en señal de duelo. El pueblo de Buenos Aires no sabía la época funesta que le esperaba, y aún se atrevió a protestar, aunque de aquella manera muda y temerosa.
>
> Entretanto, los grupos de la chusma cruzaban las calles dando desaforados gritos de vivas y mueras. Para mostrar la preponderancia que tenían sobre la gente decente, iban golpeando las puertas de las casas que estaban cerradas, insultando a las familias y amenazándolas de muerte con sus enormes dagas.
>
> Algunos grupos cuya estación en las pulperías había sido más larga, marchaban alegremente al son de sus guitarras, en festejo de la gran fiesta que la Federación les preparaba. Ver fusilar a un gobernador, acompañado de sus hermanos y cinco personas más, no era espectáculo que se ofrecía a cada momento. (183)

(The city offered a rare appearance of life and death. Family houses in

> the main were closed, like a weak protest against those barbarous assassins, who must have celebrated themselves with all federalist pomp.
>
> Buenos Aires society was shaken and terrified by the scenes of vandalism that began in that fashion. The very houses of commerce other than the dives of the principal *mazorqueros* were closed as a sign of mourning. The people of Buenos Aires had no idea of the terrible times that awaited them, and they even dared to protest, although in that mute and fearful way.
>
> Meanwhile, rabble groups traversed the streets yelling wildly. In order to show the sway they held over decent folk, they would pound on the doors of the houses that were closed, insulting the families and threatening them with death from their enormous daggers.
>
> Some groups whose stay in the bars had been longer marched happily to the sound of their guitars, celebrating the great feast that the Federation was preparing for them. To see a governor shot, accompanied by his brothers and five others, was not a frequent spectacle.)

This sort of mediating characterization is a natural consequence of the description of an essential anecdote that has been presented as part of "nuestra dramática historia" (our dramatic history; 181) and as a chain of events that constitutes "aquella tragedia que debía concluir [con la muerte de los acusados] en la plaza de la Victoria" (that tragedy that was to conclude [with the death of the accused] in Victoria Square; 114). One might argue that the recurring references to *drama* and *espectáculo* and their synonyms are nothing more than the use of standard commonplaces in Spanish to refer hyperbolically to events that the narrator wishes to impress upon his readers. But the subtitle announces a dramatic conception for the narrative and the major aspects of the story being unfolded are characterized in terms of a theatrical spectacle that the narrator allows the reader to witness. These strategic aspects of Gutiérrez's discourse thereby underscore how his narrative description moves in the direction of a firmly grounded ideological analysis: the entire Rosas project was nothing more than a tragic farce organized and executed by the tyrant in his brutal manipulation of political power. The narrator asserts with respect to Rosas's plans for the execution of the accused that

> Esta era la sentencia feroz con que Rosas iba a aterrar a la población. El espectáculo de los cadáveres suspendidos en horcas durante seis horas, era para él la parte maestra de la sentencia. Sería el golpe de muerte asestado a la cabeza y al ánimo de los salvajes unitarios. ¿Quién se atrevería en adelante a conspirar contra Rosas? (153)
>
> (This was the ferocious sentence with which Rosas was going to terrify

the populace. The spectacle of the bodies hanging from the gallows for six hours was for him the masterful part of the sentence. It would be the death blow to the head and soul of the savage unitarians. Would they dare conspire against Rosas in the future?)

The theatricalization of society by Rosas as a tragic farce and Gutiérrez's representation of the events of that farce as a spectacle to be witnessed by his reader are enhanced by the references to the carnivalization of social life during the period of Rosas's terror. The concept of carnivalization in culture, as proposed by the Russian critic Mikhail Bakhtin, is intimately linked to the idea of a form of text production (whether written or social texts). The conventional structures of society and the ideologies they represent are called into question through a series of processes that invert or subvert them, that reverse the poles of meaning, that explore the possibilities of other—scandalous, taboo, or perverse—conjugations of the signs to which the fossilized structures give rigid and exclusive meanings at the expense of those that just might represent a liberation of a repressed human spirit.

If Bakhtin's guiding metaphor is the carnival, with all its complex parodies and burlesques of the seriousness of our closed-off existence, his principal literary reference is Rabelais, whose writings have served as an enormously influential model of the disarticulation of the nascent stage of an orderly and predetermined social discourse. Certainly, this conception of a culture that defies established values by opening them up in the process of carnivalization is continuous with a concept of revolutionary, or at least diametrically different, cultural practices. It has been a particularly productive mode in contemporary Latin American writing,[10] and criticism has been anxious to find roots for it in even the earliest and most monumentalized forms of Latin American literature. By the same token, I know of no work of literature in which carnivalization is juxtaposed to an alternate model of established society in defense of the latter, unless it is Gutiérrez's *Juan Manuel de Rosas.*

Gutiérrez, like the constellation of even more establishment writers of the 1880s, writes in defense of the Liberal establishment that felt it was constructing an orderly Argentine society in the wake of the political, social, and economic chaos that had reigned since independence.[11] As a consequence, throughout this writing we find posited as a thoroughly naturalized point of reference, one that cannot be questioned since it is

10. Emil Volek, "La carnavalización y la alegoría en *El mundo alucinante,* de Reinaldo Arenas."

11. Tulio Halperín Donghi, "Una nación para el desierto argentino."

accepted as so undeniably and self-evidently correct, the image of a bourgeois society that is defined in terms of an idealized social order.[12] Any deviations from this ideal are simply examples of moral perversion and social maladjustment. One result is the use of the conventions of European Naturalism, not to criticize a destructive social dynamic, but to confirm a specific social order and to condemn any deviations from it by misfits and outcasts who are unable to abide by its conditions and profit from its benefits (see below, pp. 122–27, 139–50).

Although Gutiérrez does not describe this ideal in any detail in *Rosas* (see, however, the comments below on the *nosotros* versus *ellos* disjunction in the novel), his narrative is committed basically to the repudiation of the Rosas model of Argentine life as a corrupt and depraved deviation from the seigneurial lifestyle exemplified by the victims of the Mazorca as described in the first part of this book. While this lifestyle is only sketchily maintained by the subsequent adherence to a model of economic expansion and modernization that is the basis of the Liberal establishment, Rosas's Argentina serves as a firmly anchored negative pole to whatever else can be imagined by implication and inference as the basis of social life in the country.

It is therefore not too surprising, to find that Gutiérrez views Argentine society under Rosas not only as a meaningless farce, but more importantly as an orgy in which the accepted values of an orderly and decent society are degraded by Rosas's exploitation of the worst impulses in the *chusma* at his command. The details concerning the practices of the Mazorca, the ways in which the free-floating, murderous pandemonium scandalizes the decent Buenos Aires citizenry, and comments concerning the protracted kangaroo-court trial of the Reynafé family include frequent references to the generalized carnival atmosphere of public life at the time. In addition, the narration of the execution of the accused is firmly grounded on an image of Rosas's society as alien in its manipulation by the corrupt tyrant to any "normal" sense of propriety and justice. That is, it is a society that has been totally carnivalized:

> —¡Mueran los inmundos salvajes unitarios!—resonó en azoteas y balcones. El grito fué recogido por la multitud, para repetirlo entre un vocerío imponente y estruendoso.
>
> Las cajas tocaron atención, toque que repitieron las cornetas, y aquellos veinte mil ojos se clavaron en el arco principal del Cabildo. Acababan

12. Jitrik, *El 80 y su mundo.*

de aparecer en él los tres hermanos Reynafé y Santos Pérez, entre una compañía de infantería. Poco más atrás venían los otros cinco infelices que debían servir de alimento a la ferocidad de aquellas turbas ebrias y mercenarias.

¡Mueran los asesinos del general Quiroga! ¡Mueran los ladrones y cobardes!—aulló aquella multitud enfurecida a la proximidad del terrible espectáculo.

Los Reynafé miraron serenos a aquella canalla, y siguieron avanzando penosamente, entre una doble fila de soldados. Tenían los pies tan hinchados y tan destrozadas las piernas por los grillos, que aquella corta marcha era para ellos un verdadero vía crucis. Los tres venían igualmente tranquilos y serenos. No parecían hombres que marchaban a una muerte terrible e inevitable. Miraron tranquilamente a la multitud, que los devoraba con su injuriante curiosidad, y en seguida descansaron la mirada sobre la horca y el banquillo.

Indudablemente, la vista de todo aquel aparato, y sobre todo el de la horca, debió hacer en aquellos hombres una impresión terrible, pero la dominaron instantáneamente hasta la sonrisa. Ni el mismo sacerdote pudo apercibirse del menor temblor. Llegaron a los banquillos, y desde allí miraron a la plaza y sus alrededores con una mirada noble y tranquila. La multitud, que había callado un momento, volvió a atronar los aires con sus grandes alaridos.

¡Viva el gran Rosas! ¡Mueran los asesinos del general Quiroga! ¡Mueran los Reynafé!—aulló aquella canalla. (185)

("Death to the dirty unitarian savages!" resounded on the rooftops and balconies. The cry was taken up by the multitude and repeated with an imposing and roaring clamor.

The drums called for attention, a roll that the bugles repeated, and those twenty thousand eyes were nailed on the principal arch of the town hall. The three Reynafé brothers and Santo Pérez had just appeared, with an infantry company. A little behind came the other five unfortunates who were to serve to feed the ferocity of those drunken and mercenary hordes.

"Death to the assassins of General Quiroga! Death to the thieves and cowards!" roared that multitude enraged by the proximity of the terrible spectacle.

The Reynafés looked serenely upon that mob, and they advanced painfully between a double row of soldiers. Their feet were so swollen and their legs so destroyed by the irons that that short march was a true via crucis for them. All three were equally tranquil and serene. They did not look like men marching to a terrible and inevitable death. They looked tranquilly at the multitude, which devoured them with an insulting curiosity, and their gaze quickly fell on the gallows and the bench.

Without a doubt, the sight of that whole apparatus, especially the gallows, must have made a terrible impression on those men, but they overcame it instantly and smiled. Not even the priest himself could perceive the slightest trembling. They reached the benches, and from there they looked at the square and its surroundings with a noble and tranquil gaze. The multitude, which had fallen silent for a moment, once again made the air thunder with their great cries.

"Long live the great Rosas! Death to the assassins of General Quiroga! Death to the Reynafés!" cried that mob.)

It is this *canalla* that Rosas has completely carnivalized by promoting in it the affirmation of values of social disorder and unchecked violence, a social dissolution that is the antithesis of the respectful observance of the bounds of law and order to which Gutiérrez assumes his readers to subscribe and which the Reynafés exemplify in their disdainful indifference to the braying of the rabble. Rather than an attitude that promotes the liberation of the individuals in their escape, the Mazorca-Rosas carnival is a form of social repression that victimizes the standard-bearers of a decent Argentine polity: "Aquello era una fiesta federal, pero una fiesta federal ruidosa" (That was a federal festivity, but a noisy one; 34); "Con este motivo se renovaba la algazara y chacota" (That provided for renewed clamor and merriment; 51); "la chusma acudía a la cárcel a gozar del espectáculo miserable. Y los Reynafé eran exhibidos como cualquier galeote, ante aquella chusma desenfrenada que los llenaba de improperios y de groseros insultos" (the rabble went to the jail in order to enjoy the piteous spectacle. And the Reynafé were put on exhibit like any prisoner before that uncontrolled rabble which hurled curses and gross insults at them; 173).

Surely this image of an orgiastic collective behavior has come to constitute a standard image in Argentine culture; compare the many images of the Peronista masses, marching here and there, shouting their prepackaged slogans and beating their *bombos,* and washing feet swollen by this enthusiastic display of mobilization in the pseudoclassic fountains of Buenos Aires. Although Esteban Echeverría's short story "El matadero" (1841), which represents Argentina under Rosas as a bloody slaughterhouse, was written during the author's Uruguayan exile, its discovery by Gutiérrez's brother Juan María and publication in 1871 quickly led it to be considered a paradigm for life under Rosas.

The depiction of the antithetical opposition between the Reynafés and the *chusma* is built around the motif of the orgy of uncontained and deliberately inflamed savagery. It is also viewed by the narrator as a pitiful spectacle in which men of decency and honor are the actors, and their tormentors are an unruly audience for whom they must play out the tragic script of their victimization. Throughout, Rosas contemplates the scene both as the carnivalized spectacle's best audience and as its adroit ringmaster:

> Como si esto hubiera sido calculado, apareció en aquel momento en los balcones del Cabildo la satánica fisonomía de Juan Manuel de Rosas. Todo, sin duda, preparado de antemano. . . .
>
> Rosas estaba pálido y desencajado. Sus ojos azules y hermosos brillaban como los de un tigre. (189)

> (As if this had been calculated, the satanic physiognomy of Juan Manuel de Rosas appeared at that moment on the balconies of the town hall. All undoubtedly prepared in advance. . . .
>
> Rosas was pale and his eyes were wild. His beautiful blue eyes glowed like those of a tiger.)

One of the salient characteristics of Gutiérrez's reporting of the speech of Rosas's supporters, one that is readily evident in the fragments that have been quoted so far, is the use of formulas like "¡Viva el ilustre Restaurador de las Leyes!" and "¡Mueran los salvajes unitarios!" These phrases have entered the stock of Argentine cultural tropes, much as "Give me liberty or give me death" forms an integral historical part of American social discourse. Concomitant with the juxtaposition between the debauched carnival of Rosas's society and the noble but trammeled values incarnate in the victims of the Mazorca and the Reynafé brothers, *Rosas* examines the corruption of language, whereby seemingly fixed meanings are inverted and subverted to suit the ends of Rosas's terrible farce.

In addition to exclamatory phrases like "¡Mueran los [inmundos] salvajes unitarios!" that serve as epiphonemena in the public discourse of Rosas's supporters and as the standard introit for all public documents, Gutiérrez identifies an inventory of other commonplaces that exemplify the cynical inversion of language during the period. Surely, the very epithet applied to Rosas, Restaurador de las Leyes, must be understood to abstract the entire process of semantic degradation associated with his regime. If it remained unclear that the "restoration" Rosas was committed to was to something Hispanic and traditional that antedated the continental, Masonic, Enlightenment-Romantic inspiration of the Rivadavia-Moreno-Belgrano founders of the Argentine Republic, then Gutiérrez's depiction of the Restaurador made that "restoration" clear by building it around the demonstration of the lawlessness and the abuse of justice characterized by Rosas's use of *las leyes*. Certainly, this is the whole point of the second section of the narrative and the protracted chronicle of the frame-up of the Reynafé brothers.

The Reynafé brothers are the protagonists of this *drama del terror.* However, their portrayal is complemented by the introduction of the lone, brave individual who accepts the challenge to defend them, the nominal federalist lawyer, Dr. Gamboa. Gutiérrez portrays Gamboa as a man of law of unimpeachable honor and credentials who, during these early years of Rosas's rise to power, had chosen to identify himself with the federalist cause. However, and here Gutiérrez underscores Rosas's cynicism, when the Reynafé brothers are obliged to name someone to defend them, Rosas and his public prosecutor, Maza, are outraged that Gamboa would accept the commission.

Gutiérrez spares no detail in describing the efforts made by Gamboa to counter the suit against his clients and to expose the network of falsehoods on which the charges against them are based. As is to be expected, Gamboa is unsuccessful in his application and only damages irreparably his own and his family's security. Through the chronicle of the trial, the narrator refers repeatedly to Gamboa's attempts to counter the corruption of the law that characterizes the case. The following passage synthesizes Gutiérrez's narrative strategy based on a characterization of the corruption of language and the truth it purports to represent; significantly, the point of departure is the transcript of the legal proceedings that serve as the pretext of his own work:

> Aquel cúmulo de iniquidades reunidas en la forma de sumario, constaba de mil ochocientas cuarenta y cuatro fojas. ¡Mil ochocientas cuarenta y cuatro fojas donde no había una sola palabra de verdad, fuera de la defensa del doctor Gamboa! ¡Mil ochocientas fojas donde la calumnia y la impostura desempeñaban el principal papel! Y todavía el doctor Maza tenía la insolencia de elevar la causa con una nota donde se leía este párrafo monstruoso: "La gravedad de la causa, lo complicado de ésta, la extensión del proceso y la cantidad de personas sumariadas, exigían una contracción más detenida, una atención exclusiva que no ha podido tener el juez especial comisionado; procediendo, *para su mayor desconsuelo,* a verificar la entrega de la causa *sin la satisfacción de haber dado una segunda mano a la obra.* Mas en esto, los que la revisen, suplirán y corregirán los defectos que en ella encontraren."
>
> ¡Aquél era el colmo del cinismo y de la infamia! ¡Al juez Maza le parecía poco haber llevado al patíbulo cuatro inocentes, y lamentaba no haber dado a su obra inicua una segunda mano! (151)

(That accumulation of iniquities brought together in the form of a summary judgment consisted of 1,844 pages. In 1,844 pages where there was not a single word of truth, outside of the defense of Dr. Gamboa! Eighteen hundred pages where calumny and fraud played the key role! And still Dr. Maza had the insolence to carry forward the case with a note containing this monstrous paragraph: "The gravity of the case, its complexity, the length of the trial and the quantity of persons examined require a more detailed examination, an exclusive attention that the special judge has not been able to give it; proceeding, *for his greatest disappointment,* to verify the delivery of the case *without the satisfaction of having been able to go over the work.* But those who review it will supplement and correct the defects they might encounter in it."

That was the height of cynicism and infamy! It appeared to Dr. Maza that it was a small matter to have sent to the gallows four innocent men, and he complained about not having given his iniquitous work a second going over!)

The foregoing passage juxtaposes Gamboa's and Maza's respective legal discourses, and Gutiérrez's own narrative discourse. In addition to assuming the function of undertaking such a juxtaposition, it supplements the discourses by pointing out the cynicism of the latter and the privileged representation of the truth of the former. This juxtaposition is the culmination of Gutiérrez's representation of the corruption of meaning at the hands of Rosas's administration of the law (compare, in the description of the activities of the Mazorca, the terrible irony of the gap between their purported cries of defense of the government and its interests and their acts of indiscriminate pillage and murder that were the antithesis of the language of public weal).

The result of Gutiérrez's extensive chronicle of the emergence of a society besieged by official terror, certainly the forerunner of the description by one writer of Argentina under recent military governments as the *estado terrorista,*[13] is a governing disjunction that is the ideological basis of his narrative discourse. This disjunction is between the *nosotros* made up of the narrator, his readers, and the hapless victims of Rosas's terror and the *ellos* of Rosas and his henchmen. The former are bound by a narrative contract that assumes that the readers of *Rosas* can experience nothing but revulsion toward the drama being presented for them, and Gutiérrez's panorama is structured less as a demonstration of the horrors of the period than it is as a confirmation of what had, by the 1880s, become an accepted interpretation of Argentina during the 1830s and 1840s. One of the Reynafé brothers addresses himself, in words of encouragement to one of his brothers, to the opposition between the values they represent and those of their tormentors. Embedded in the discourse of the narrator, they assume an added eloquence deriving from the fact that Gutiérrez's own narrative is the vindication prophesied by the unjustly condemned:

13. Eduardo Luis Duhalde, *El estado terrorista argentino.*

—¡Firmeza, hermano mío!—le decía entonces Guillermo—. ¡Firmeza, que harto la necesitamos todos! Es preciso estrujarse el corazón y morir como debe hacerlo todo hombre honrado que no puede temer el juicio de Dios ni de los que lo sucedan. Algún día esto ha de concluir, y nuestra causa será entonces revisada por hombres de honor, que salvarán nuestro nombre del ludibrio y la infamia a que se lo ha querido condenar. (174)[14]

("Steady on, my brother!" Guillermo said to him then. "Steady on, for we all need to be! We've got to clench our hearts and die like any honorable man would who is not afraid of the judgment of God or those who come after him. Some day this will all be over, and our case will then be reviewed by men of honor who will salvage our name from the mockery and infamy to which they have wanted to condemn it.")

Rosas is such an effort, and it can only function as a form of meaningful sociohistoric interpretation by underscoring emphatically the distance separating two versions of social life, that of Rosas and that of the order that followed in his wake. Such an opposition can only be enhanced by the identification and vindication of the victims of Rosas, and this is the thrust of sketches concerning the activities of the Mazorca and the detailed chronicle of the Reynafé case. It is significant that Gutiérrez's novel focuses on the early years of Rosas's administration, the period of his greatest use of the Mazorca and various forms of organized violence as part of the consolidation of his power over the province of Buenos Aires and, subsequently, the rest of the nation. In this sense, Gutiérrez is less concerned with a comprehensive examination of Rosas's government than he is with detailing the founding acts of the regime.

This investigation into the founding acts of the terror has as an essential point of departure the acceptance of an irresolvable conflict between that regime and the forms of public life to which Gutiérrez's "civilized" readers "naturally" subscribe. In addition, it is constructed around three textual principles: the mediating images of varieties of dramatic spectacles, the destructive carnivalization of social behavior, and the corruption of public language in the interests of consolidating a narrative of unmistakable ideological configurations in the defense of the ordered society Gutiérrez posits by implication as the controlling point of reference for his depiction of the Rosas period.[15]

14. Another occasion when the narrator has his characters speaking with prophetic eloquence is an exchange with reference to the celebration by the masses of the imminent execution of the Reynafés; it concludes with the double lament that the people do not know the terrible future in store for them and that they deserve it for not understanding their fate (p. 187).

15. One of the representative historical interpretations of the period is José Manuel

Psychoanalyzing National History: Ramos Mejía's Interpretation of Rosas

¡Cuántas hogueras se han levantado, cuántas cabezas han caído sin causa, sólo por las exigencias de un cerebro agitado por el aura terrible de incurable neurosis![16]

No era posible tampoco que sucediera de otra manera, dadas nuestras condiciones sociales y políticas. (133)

(How many bonfires have been built, how many heads have fallen without cause, simply because of the demands of a mind addled by the terrible aura of an incurable neurosis!

It was impossible for it to be otherwise, given our social and political conditions.)

Among the welter of material published in the decades following the fall of Rosas, the psychoanalytic interpretation of his personality that is the centerpiece of José M. Ramos Mejía's *Las neurosis de los hombres célebres en la historia argentina* is of special interest.

The first volume was published originally in 1878, with a second volume following in 1882; the first volume was devoted to setting forth the scientific and medical principles in use at the time for the analysis of neuroses and their application to the interpretation of Juan Manuel de Rosas, who had died in exile in England in 1877. The second volume is devoted to similar analyses of other figures prominent in the history of the area, like Paraguay's enlightened despot, Dr. Francia, or Argentina's early naval hero, Guillermo Brown. Ramos Mejía revised his interpretation of Rosas thirty years later, with a significant toning down of the examples used to demonstrate the alleged cruelty of the Restaurador.[17] Nevertheless, *Rosas y su tiempo* (1907), despite a less lurid rhetoric, was a

Estrada's *La política liberal bajo la tiranía de Rosas* (first published in 1873). A comment from Gandía in the introduction to this book underscores how the Rosas period was viewed as a parenthesis that only interrupted a larger continuity as interpreted by the subsequent Liberal ideology: "*La política liberal bajo la tiranía de Rosas* is designed to explain a credo, not a book; to analyze—in the words of Estrada—'the political doctrines of the youthful liberal element which during Rosas's tyranny was preparing itself to govern the country and which has in fact run the country from 1852 to the present day' " (p. xxxiii). In turn, Estrada's opening words are interesting from a rhetorical point of view, since they are based on an unquestionable presupposition: "That Rosas was a tyrant who persecuted rights in every guise, methodically cruel and popular by design until out of fear and ignorance he surrounded himself with mystery—all of this is neither unknown nor denied by anyone" (p. 1).

16. José M. Ramos Mejía, *Las neurosis de los hombres célebres en la historia argentina,* 110. Hereafter cited parenthetically in the text by page number.

17. Lynch lists Ramos Mejía's *Rosas y su tiempo* in his bibliography, but he does not cite him in his definitive study on Rosas.

bestseller. Clearly, Ramos Mejía's psychohistories had a place to fill in Argentines' reading about their national history.[18]

Ramos Mejía (1849–1914) is presented by José Ingenieros as the founder of psychoanalysis in Argentina. As a former student of Ramos Mejía's, Ingenieros describes him as a paradigmatic representative of the Generation of 1880 (12–13) and as a key figure in the introduction into the practice of medicine in Argentina and medical research of the vanguard of European thought on mental illness.[19]

Nevertheless, Ingenieros is quick to point out what might be considered the scientific limitations of *Las neurosis:*

> Verdad es que el autor no se detuvo a criticar el valor histórico de las fuentes a que acudió en busca de datos; tomó por verdades probadas las más burdas patrañas de los panfletisras [*sic*] unitarios, repitiendo disparatadas anécdotas inventadas por la imaginación febricente de algunos proscritos. Sus citas de Rivera Indarte, de Lamas y de otros, parecen hoy rectores de "crónicas de policía" intercaladas por error en un libro de medicina, escapadas de su destino legítimo: los folletos terroríficos de Eduardo Gutiérrez. Pocos años más tarde lo comprendió así mismo Ramos Mejía; en "Rosas y su tiempo" hallaremos otro Rosas que el de las "Neurosis de los hombres célebres." (17)

> (It is true that the author did not stop to critique the historical value of the sources used in seeking data; he took as proven truths the clumsiest hoaxes of the unitarian pamphleteers, repeating absurd anecdotes invented by the fevered imagination of some of those who had been persecuted. His quotations from Rivera Indarte, Lamas, and others seem today like "police reports" mistakenly included in a medical book, in flight from their legitimate place: Eduardo Gutiérrez's terror-ridden pamphlets. Just a few years later Ramos Mejía understood this himself, and in "Rosas y su tiempo" we will find a different Rosas from that of the "Neurosis de los hombres célebres.")

How useful Ramos Mejía's interpretations may be today to medical researchers or to historians seems to have been in question to Ingenieros fifty years ago. However, as one version of the constellation of works by writers associated with the Generation of 1880 devoted to discrediting Rosas's government, *Las neurosis* is of considerable importance. Actually published before Gutiérrez's *Juan Manuel de Rosas: los dramas del terror* (1882), Ramos Mejía's exposition unquestionably enjoys a considerable amount of intertextuality with the former and, although Gutiérrez does

18. Burns, *The Poverty of Progress,* 68–69.

19. Hebe Clementi, "José María Ramos Mejía (1849–1914)"; and Aníbal Villaverde, "Ideas sociales de José María Ramos Mejía."

not cite sources (Ramos Mejía does include a bibliography), it is probable that many of them were the same for both authors, who, in any case, were born early enough to have had extensive personal contacts with individuals who lived during Rosas's government.

Despite the intertextualities with Gutiérrez—and, indeed, with the many other writers of the period who had essentially the same thing to say about Rosas in the same *febricente* vein—the dominant characteristic of Ramos Mejía's treatise is the desire to place his comments under the aegis of scientific inquiry. This means two things: (1) Rosas is described in terms that eschew moral judgment in favor of a rigorous attribution of physical and mental factors that exercised an absolute controlling influence in his erratic and bloodthirsty behavior, and (2) the analysis of Rosas and his regime is accounted for in terms of a novel intellectual or scientific schema that is meant to supersede the anecdotal and nonscientific bases of prior explanations.

It is significant that Ramos Mejía relies heavily on these latter commentaries, violating the criterion of objective and impartial clinical observation that Ingenieros attributes to Ramos Mejía's professional career as a researcher and professor in Argentina and that characterizes the many European (primarily French) sources Ramos Mejía cites in both his introductory comments and his analysis of Rosas's maladies. Thus, there is a productive, if curious, tension between the controlling framework of clinical analysis and the recourse to hearsay, whether in the form of written reports identified by name or vague sources like "se refiere que" (it is said that; 152), "de los cuales hablan algunos historiadores" (of which some historians speak; 157), "dice un historiador contemporáneo" (a contemporary historian says; 159), "la imaginación de todo un pueblo" (the imagination of an entire people; 167), or "otro episodio . . . tomado de las tradiciones orales de la época" (another episode . . . taken from the oral traditions of the period; 177).

The importance of Ramos Mejía's strategy is to assimilate a mass of what in modern parlance would be called prescientific evidence and to analyze it in conformance with a set of scientific principles with the goal of reducing it to a coherent meaning in conformance with an epistemology of greater hierarchy or prestige than that of the oral, popular tradition:

> La aplicación de estos principios [de la ciencia moderna referente a las neurosis] a nuestra historia parecerá impropia porque hemos conocido la vida de casi todos nuestros hombres célebres trasmitida por la tradición fabulosa y desfigurada, o por la biografía meliflua de sus biógrafos amigos, y porque muchos historiadores "han creado" al personaje a su

capricho y nos lo han impuesto difundiendo errores que hoy es difícil combatir. (115)

(The application of these principles [from the modern science on neuroses] to our history might seem inappropriate because we are familiar with the life of almost all our celebrated men as transmitted by legendary and deforming tradition or from the mellifluous biographies prepared by friends, or because many historians "have created" their character at will and have imposed him on us, spreading errors that are today difficult to correct.)

Whether or not Ramos Mejía has, with his approach, "'creado' al personaje" may seem to some contemporary readers an open question. The extent to which such an approach satisfies the criteria of a scientific methodology by present standards or the standards of a century ago is of little importance for the purposes of this discussion. The point is that it represents a significant alternative way of viewing Rosas for Ramos Mejía and his readers. Echoing the principles of biological determinism that will subsequently affirm themselves in more specific literary terms in late nineteenth-century Naturalism, *Las neurosis* depends heavily on a belief in the inevitability of a behavior that derives from the unappealable laws of nature. The author derives the following conclusion from his exposition of the biological, physical, and mental, reasons for Rosas's conduct as a human being:

Se vé, pues, el número y la magnitud de las causas que han influido para producir su neurosis. Todas ellas se han combinado, reforzándose las unas a las otras y aumentando considerablemente su potencia mórbida. . . .

Tenemos, pues, en conclusión, que cuatro de las causas más formidables para la producción de esas perturbaciones cerebrales, han obrado en Rosas de una manera completa y duradera.

Lo que vemos no es sino la consecuencia forzosa de su influencia, el cumplimiento estricto de una ley a la cual no puede sustraerse ningún organismo humano. (188)

(One can thus see the number and magnitude of the causes that have produced his neurosis. They all combine together and reinforce each other to increase considerably their morbid potential. . . .

Thus, in conclusion, we see that four of the most formidable causes for the production of those cerebral disorders have worked on Rosas in a complete and lasting way.

What we see is but the necessary consequence of their influence, the strict fulfillment of a law that no human organism can evade.)

What is even more unique about Ramos Mejía's contribution to the analysis of Rosas's personality—and to the variety of the causes that may be adduced to explain what the post-Rosas period considered to be the urgent need to mark off a period in national history as particularly violent and reprehensible—is the translation of the terms of psychoanalysis from Rosas to the Argentine citizenry during his reign of terror. That is, after analyzing the nature of Rosas's neurosis, the author turns to an analysis of the neuroses inspired among the populace as a consequence of their leader's mental illness. Ramos Mejía approaches this collective reaction on two fronts. First, there is the bloodthirsty behavior of Rosas's henchmen, the Mazorca and other followers. This behavior is the direct consequence of the model provided by their leader and of his manipulation of the aspects of their own origins that made them susceptible to a collective homicidal neurosis. Secondly, the author is especially interested in describing the neurotic behavior provoked among innocent citizens as a consequence of the generalized violent social disorder:

> Al lado de las turbas desenfrenadas que seguían a la Mazorca, estaba esa otra parte de la población hundida en este estupor extremo. Subyugada por el régimen enervante de Rosas, y dominada por el miedo y la desconfianza, había perdido sus hábitos varoniles y debilitado todas sus fuerzas: una decadencia intelectual extremada vino a gravar este estado de embotamiento en que se encontró en presencia de los homicidas de la Mazorca. (192)

> (Alongside the unchecked hordes that rallied behind the Mazorca there was that other part of the populace sunk in this deep stupor. Subjugated by Rosas's enervating regime and dominated by fear and distrust, it had lost its manly habits and weakened all its powers: an extreme intellectual decadence came to encumber this dulled state in which it found itself in the face of the Mazorca's homicides.)

In the case of the evidence Ramos Mejía presents in support of this analysis, he is on the secure ground of clinical analysis, since he is able to refer to many individuals whom he has examined personally, men and women who continued to suffer mental illnesses attributable to a period of recent national experience. Thus, the author sets up a series of scientifically based equivalences expressed in terms of metaphoric equivalences. The illnesses of the human mind may be viewed as etiologically and functionally equivalent to physical infirmities, which is the thrust of the program of psychiatric research on which Ramos Mejía confidently anchors his analyses: the mind is one more organ of the body, albeit a particularly complex one, and it may be examined and treated clinically with scientific principles that are continuous with the medical arts developed for somatic manifestations.

Moreover, if it is true that a society is a collective of human beings composed of body and mind, it may be treated as an organism susceptible to the same forms of neuroses that beleaguer the individual: "Parece que los pueblos, como los individuos, pueden, bajo la acción de ciertas causas, sufrir estas perturbaciones del espíritu, que aunque temporarias, ofuscan la razón y adormecen el sentimiento hasta la oclusión completa" (It seems that towns, like individuals, given certain conditions, can suffer those perturbances of the spirit that, although temporary, disturb the mind and lull the senses until the occlusion passes; 189). Ramos Mejía does not really go so far as to view society as a sort of unitary suprabody. Rather, at this point he seems to wish to stress that, whereas Rosas's mental illness is the result of a vertical transmission of biological inheritance, complemented by specific personal experiences, in the case of the Argentine citizenry under Rosas, there is a horizontal crossbreeding of neuroses. This crossbreeding is the result of particularly horrifying collective experiences that individuals share in common, whether as participants in the drunken brawls and bloodlettings of the Mazorca or as victims of the latter. Thus, the author speaks of both an "epidemia" and of a "contagio nervioso" (211) in his characterization of the collective experiences.

Ramos Mejía unquestionably propounded his analysis of Rosas and the latter's government as an important scientific breakthrough, and this is the sense of many of the contemporary reviews of his work cited by Ingenieros. It would not be surprising to find that current practitioners of psychohistoriography (in Argentina, León Rozitchner might be mentioned as a foremost exponent of this methodology) might find much lacking in Ramos Mejía's putatively scientific approach, even when measured against the limited sources from which he was able to draw. That is, this sort of social science ages fast. However, in the early years of the Generation of 1880, there is no doubt that *Las neurosis* represented a notable addition to the extensive list of treatments of the Rosas phenomenon.

CHAPTER 3

Writing the Tensions of Transition

One may be reluctant to attribute the modern ills of Argentina to the deleterious effect of the aggressive policies of a Liberal economy as imposed by the Generation of 1880, an economy that lasts well into the 1920s, only to collapse with the international crisis of 1929. Nevertheless, it is undoubtedly true that within the fifty-year period that extends from the signal year of 1880, the pursuit of the social and political ideology of the Liberal hegemony created, in addition to the Golden Age of Argentine history, some monumental problems.

The program of external immigration flooded the country with foreign born, each bringing with him or her a legacy of Old World ills and cultural traditions that would be inserted into the old Creole society and the new structures based on concepts of progress and modernization. Internal demographic shifts affected the relationship between Buenos Aires and the rest of the country, and the subjugation of the indigenous population in the center of the country altered radically various subcultures, including that of the Gaucho, in favor of massive exploitation of the land, which brought with it new rural myths. Financial crises in Buenos Aires, particularly as symbolized by the vicissitudes of the stock market in the cycle of novels associated with the 1891 debacle, prompt a questioning from both ends of the political spectrum concerning Liberal programs: anarchism militates for drastic social change, while the traditional elite decries the fluidity and instability stimulated by Liberalism's free marketplace. General phenomena of social dislocation are highlighted by a sort of inverse form of European Naturalism: Is moral corruption rather than progress the result of the profound changes that have occurred in Argentine society as the result of the Liberal program?

If one of the functions of culture is to record and explore the irresolvable tensions in society, the narratives examined in this chapter may be seen as reasonable exponents of the strains produced in the social fabric by the enormous changes that took place in Argentina between Caseros and the end of the century.

Patriarchal Absence in *La gran aldea*

> ¿Qué hombre, qué mujer, por variada y llena de contrastes que haya sido su vida, no tiene allá, en el fondo del recuerdo, la fotografía vaga pero indeleble de las primeras impresiones del mundo?[1]
>
> (What man, what woman, no matter how varied and full of contrasts their life may have been, does not possess there in the depths of their memory, the vague but indelible photograph of the first impressions of the world?)

Characteristic of the development of a critical Realism and Naturalism in Spanish and Spanish American literature is an early phase of *costumbrismo,* a writing that focuses on the features of local customs, manners, and lifestyles. Since the development of Realism and Naturalism is unquestionably a conscious and perhaps even a slavish imitation of French and English models, it might be argued that *costumbrismo* should be viewed as the more original literary activity in nineteenth-century Hispanic letters. Indeed, this ought to be particularly true for Latin America. Although Spain produced an exceptional body of *costumbrista* writing, elaborating enthusiastically on the Romantic principle of the importance of the regional—which would turn Spain itself into one of the cultural motifs of the period—*costumbrismo* in Latin America meant not just the realization of the importance of local quotidian lifestyles, but the opportunity to discover and to describe what was characteristic of the newly formed republics.

Unfortunately, Latin American literary criticism has been divided into those who view nineteenth-century writers in terms of the degree to which they realized an adequate assimilation of European models (which was admittedly the goal of these writers) and those who, while perhaps acknowledging implicitly the greater importance of Realism and Naturalism, prefer to underscore the "primitive charm" of *costumbrista* verism. Freedom from the need to judge nineteenth-century Latin American literature in terms of its success in the imitation of European models does not automatically mean revindication of *costumbrismo* writing, particularly if the critic's concern continues to be why Latin American writers should have felt compelled in the first place to pay such close heed to English and French narrative models. Admittedly, models for Realism and Naturalism had their own roots in the late-Romantic period with works that demonstrate aspects of local color, a style that Dickens

1. Lucio V. López, *La gran aldea: costumbres bonaerenses,* 39. Hereafter cited parenthetically in the text by page number.

had mastered, especially to the extent to which he is able to go beyond the sketch and short narrative in the creation of broad social canvasses.

Latin American *costumbrismo* presents a considerable array of writers, and a certain strain of cultural nationalism among literary critics of the various countries has resulted in a good record of this writing, which ranges from simple descriptions of regional phenomena to the chronicling of events characteristic of local values to full-scale narratives that attempt a degree of social analysis. In Peru, Ricardo Palma's *Tradiciones peruanas* have often been considered the fullest expression of this sort of writing, and it is significant that Palma may be discussed in detail without recourse to an inventory of European writers whose models lend validity to his work.[2] Palma's *tradiciones* exemplify the *costumbrismo* characterization of local lifestyles through the use of a narrative sketch without the degree of character development demanded by the accepted norm of European Realism. Palma drew on a vast repertory of sources for his texts in both written and archival documents and the oral tradition of folklore and legend, and the result is an admirable example of a type of Latin American writing in which the texture of an entire society is conveyed through a mosaic of narrative sketches.

The problem for Latin American criticism has always been to see the importance of *costumbrista* writing without having to redeem it only by an appeal to its "primitive charm." The practice among most critics seems to have been simply to value *costumbrismo* for its anticipation of a more sophisticated Realism and subsequent Naturalism. Palma has, it must be noted, always come off a bit better than the bulk of *costumbrista* writers because of the rich, unifying irony of his narrative voice, which creates a complex mediating level of social analysis usually lacking or only fragmentary in the bulk of Latin American *costumbrista* writers (in Spain, of course, Mariano de Larra stands out for something close to the same sort of unified narrative perspective).[3]

Criticism has spoken with one voice about the distinguishing characteristic of *La gran aldea: costumbres bonaerenses* (The grand village: Buenos Aires customs) by Lucio Vicente López (1848–1894). The novel is the portrait of life in Buenos Aires during approximately a twenty-year period from the 1860s to the 1880s, as seen by a boy who grows to

2. Roy L. Tanner, *The Humor of Irony and Satire in the "Tradiciones peruanas."*

3. There has been virtually no scholarship on *costumbrismo* as a category of Argentine prose writing. See, however, H. Ernest Lewald: "A novelistic technique [is used] to present aspects of the growth and modernization of the capital" ("Aim and Function of Costumbrismo Porteño," 526), a comment that seems to deny López's novel any literary intent whatsoever in favor of a historico-sociological goal.

manhood during the course of the novel; it is primarily of interest for its evocation of life in Buenos Aires at the moment of its transition from a *gran aldea* into a center of bourgeois capitalism; it is a rich repository of descriptions of various elements of Buenos Aires lifestyles during that period of transition as seen from the perspective of the nascent bourgeoisie; it is a veritable *roman à clef* in the details it provides about the personalities of Argentine social history of the period; and it is marked by both a tone of nostalgia toward a lifestyle that has passed into history and a tone of scathing, at times even sarcastic, denunciation toward the social values that have emerged as dominant.[4]

The first thing that needs to be said about *La gran aldea* is that, despite its title and the way in which it is generally pigeonholed by literary historians, López's narrative is much more than a sketch of *costumbres bonaerenses.*[5] Written as a memoir by Julio, an orphan who grows to maturity in the course of the novel, *La gran aldea* takes on a clear structure provided by a unifying point of view invested in a dominant character. As a consequence, it is not just the series of descriptive sketches it is often claimed to be.[6] *La gran aldea,* like many narratives of the period,

4. Several key commentaries are provided by *El 80,* 2:41–50; Myron I. Lichtblau, *The Argentine Novel in the Nineteenth Century,* 143–46; William W. Megenney, "*La gran aldea* de Lucio V. López: novela integral"; Hebe Noemí Campanella, *La generación del 80: su influencia en la vida cultural argentina,* 174–81; Roberto F. Giusti, "La prosa de 1852 a 1900," 2:386–90; Antonio Solari, "Lucio V. López: el escritor, el catedrático, el hombre público"; Ricardo Piccirilli, *Los López, una dinastía intelectual: ensayo historico literarario, 1810–1852,* 157–77; and Bernardo González Arrili, "Lucio Vicente López."

5. The following comment is typical of the emphasis on *La gran aldea* as a series of loosely structured *cuadros de costumbres:* "López conceived *La gran aldea* as a series of sketches of customs or, as its subtitle accurately states, *Buenos Aires customs.* In chapters I-IX the author presents a complex of types and situations that correspond to the Buenos Aires of 1860. These chapters consist of isolated units joined only by a connecting thread, the figure of the protagonist, and, therefore, they lack a novelistic structure. The use of the first person allows for the presentation of a vision of the Buenos Aires of bygone years from a *personal* perspective. Everything is seen through the eyes of the protagonist, who participates in what he narrates. That is to say, the character is present, although as a spectator, in every event the author considers of fundamental importance for the Buenos Aires of 1870. Julio-child *is present and participates* in the events and customs that serve to characterize a period" (*El 80,* 2:42).

6. As the following analysis will make clear, I do not agree with the long-standing opinion that López's novel is poorly structured, an opinion repeated by Campanella: "What is important, beyond the weakness of its conception, is the documentary value of the work, a portrait of the sociopolitical and economic change that took place in the country. . . . There are two well-defined parts to *La gran aldea,* and all critics are in agreement on this; these parts are separated, in plot and structural terms, by Medea's death. The first is the chronicle of a recent past and the second of the present; the first is

appeared in a serialized form in 1884 in *Sud-América,* a publication founded by López, future-president Carlos Pellegrini, Paul Groussac, and others.[7] The novel has often been viewed as a series of newspaper clippings and described as loose and fragmentary. But it may be demonstrated that it is, in fact, underlain by a very clear unifying structure.

Julio is a poor orphan who is taken in by his father's brother, don Ramón, who has married the wealthy daughter, Medea, of a military figure of minor distinction. Medea is a raging and apoplectic woman totally consumed by her own importance as a political influence. She dominates her husband and barely accepts the presence of his orphaned nephew. Life is miserable for Julio as an unwelcome guest in his uncle's home, and his loneliness is relieved only by the idyll of his years away at a provincial school and, when he begins to make his way in the world as a clerk, by the company of don Benito, a generous roué who is a friend of don Ramón. Don Benito takes Julio in and shows him a bit of the world. When Medea dies in a fit of apoplexy at having been crossed, Julio returns to his uncle's home, where he is witness to don Ramón's misfortunes at the hands of another woman, this time a ruthless fortune hunter, Blanca, whom he marries. The novel concludes when the baby girl of the aging don Ramón and his young wife dies in a fire caused indirectly by Blanca's irresponsibility. Don Ramón ends up in an insane asylum, Blanca disappears with her lover, and Julio is left to reflect on the amoral world he has witnessed.

La gran aldea derives its first unifying principle from the role of Julio as a spectator of a segment of a Buenos Aires social reality in transition.[8] Indeed, Jitrik underscores the autobiographical nature of *La gran aldea* by identifying it with "el recuerdo," one of the major motifs of the writing of the period.[9] As is customary in the case of memoirs, there is a blending between the perspective of the individual at the time of the writing of the text and the perspective of the individual who views an

---

loose and fast-paced and the second is novelistic, with its horrifying denouement and the monstrous deformation of the female character" (*La generación del 80,* 178).

It is curious that, in 1983, Campanella appears to be reproaching López for his portrayal of monstrous feminine types, as though women like Medea and Blanca could not exist. Historically, many critics, presumably upholding the standard of the defense of the fairer sex, had excoriated López in this regard. See Aníbal Ponce: "it is difficult to conceive that from the lips of a moderately refined young woman [Blanca] could come the rude cynicism that he attributes to his heroine" ("Lucio V. López," 209).

7. Tim Duncan, "La prensa política: 'Sud-América', 1884–1892."

8. Iber H. Verdugo, "Estudio preliminar."

9. Jitrik, *El 80 y su mundo,* 93.

event at a particular time being recovered by the memoir. Although it is impossible for the narrator to recover unmediated his feelings at a particular time in the past he wishes to report on, his text may strive for such an illusion. Thus, *La gran aldea* may be divided into those segments where the narrator, speaking with the voice of the man who writes the text, looks back and assays what he has seen and those segments where the narrator strives to speak with the voice of the younger Julio—first a boy, then an innocent youth—who participated in those events, if only as an impressionable bystander. López did not exploit this disjunction to any great degree. At least there is no apparent narrative irony arising from the potential conflicts between what Julio thought he was seeing as a boy and how Julio the narrator may interpret what he saw to have been in a deeper or more complicated sense.

The narrator conceives of himself as little more than a clear lens. As such, save occasional asides of a critical and sarcastic nature that may be attributed to Julio the narrator, the young Julio limits himself to taking at face value the individuals and circumstances presented as being of sufficient interest as such for the purposes of the narrative. Narrative irony is a mode that will predominate in the high Realism that is reputed to be the most sophisticated form of fiction in the nineteenth century. Verbal irony—that is, the attribution of the same word or phrase to different individuals, often the narrator versus a character, but with different and usually contradictory meanings—may be found in *costumbrista* writing (this was one of Larra's hallmarks). But *costumbrismo,* as a writing concerned with detailing the surface of presumably heretofore unchronicled lifestyles, has little use for narrative irony. It is the act of discovering a world and collating its constituent parts that is of concern to a narrator like Julio. In the case of a format like the memoir, the differences between the past of the events viewed in autobiographical terms and the present of their setting down do not play a significant role in the characterization beyond the straightforward implication that the accumulation of those events conditions the particular stance taken by the narrator.

In Julio's case, this stance is one of condemnation of a world of vain ambition and false pretense. Although López may have been identified with the intellectual establishment of his day (the periodical in which his novel appeared, *Sud-América,* was one of the organs of that establishment), the transition of events portrayed is not from a period of one outmoded lifestyle (that following the overthrow of the dictator Rosas by a petite bourgeoisie imbued with romantic ideals) to a more modern one (that of the capitalistic, international bourgeoisie epitomized by the Generation of 1880). Rather, Julio recovers for his reader the transition from the corrupt Buenos Aires of the *gran aldea* to the corrupt Buenos Aires of the *gran urbe.*

Julio's narrative is organized in terms of two sets of intersecting relationships, those of the male figures and those of the female figures. The latter set is surely the more interesting, and the two female characters who dominate in the novel represent different phases of life in Buenos Aires in the social stratum that López chooses to portray, and they constitute the two stages in the period of transition that is the time frame of the novel. Criticism has paid insufficient attention to these characters. However, I shall argue that the most outstanding feature of *La gran aldea* is their presence in the novel and the meaning, in ideological terms, of the relationship between them and the male figures.

When Julio is orphaned at the death of his destitute father, he is taken in by his uncle don Ramón. The latter's wife is a veritable tyrant. Medea, possessed of her own self-importance, which she derives from her father's minor military role in the early days of the republic, considers herself a central figure in the political debates of the day, and she has made her house into a meeting place for politicians and their supporters. Medea is a supporter of Bartolomé Mitre and his faction, which led the early battle to separate the city of Buenos Aires from the province of the same name and to convert it into an independent national capital, thereby confirming a strong central government at the expense of provincial autonomy. López was associated with the opposing position, that is, that Buenos Aires should continue to be the capital of a strong provincial government.

In the early chapters of the novel, the grotesque caricature of Medea as an intransigent mother of the republic may appear to be an easy mark for an author of defined political convictions hiding behind a putatively wide-eyed and innocent child spectator. Undoubtedly, many readers have read the descriptions of Medea's character, her diatribes, and the ludicrous proclamations of the politicians who assemble in her salon only in terms of the debate between the nationalists (those who favored nationalizing Buenos Aires as a federal district; that is, Medea's associates) and the autonomists (those who wished to retain it as the provincial capital).

Medea, however, must be seen as the point of reference for the entire society López is representing at this point in his novel—the old Creole aristocracy. These are the individuals who have assumed the glories of the overthrow of Rosas (which promoted the independence of the provinces in order to impose a feudal dictatorship) and who have assigned to themselves the task of forging the republic Rosas's reign of terror suspended. Julio reports these individuals as arrogant, intolerant, self-satisfied, and aggressively anti-intellectual. Julio witnesses the posturings of these individuals and overhears their unconscious parodies of political wisdom. Medea, in one of her few demonstrations of concern for the education of her husband's nephew, counsels him to learn from his betters:

> —Mira, niño—me decía mi tía Medea sin dejarme respirar—; aquél es don Buenaventura; aprende, mira qué traje tan sencillo lleva. Ese que habla con el ministro español, es el doctor Trevexo; aquel que sale, es el coronel Valdelirio.
>
> Y yo miraba extasiado aquel grupo y me decía a mí mismo: "¡Ah, si algún día llegase yo a saber lo que sabe el doctor Trevexo! ¡Si llegase a ser un guerrero como Valdelirio!" Y después, aterrado de mi petulancia íntima, transaba con una fórmula más modesta: "¡Si llegase a ser ministro español!" (87–88)

> ("Look, child," my aunt Medea would say to me without letting me catch my breath, "that's Don Buenaventura. Learn from him. Just look at what a simple suit he is wearing. That one talking to the Spanish minister is Dr. Trevexo. The one just leaving is Colonel Valdeliro."
>
> And I looked with fascination at that group and said to myself: "Ah, if only one day I could get to know what Dr. Trevexo knows!" And then, terrified by my intimate petulance, I fell back on a more modest formula: "If I could get to be Spanish minister!")

It should be noted that don Trevexo has magnanimously shared his wisdom with the young Julio; he advises him not to bother with books, but to read only newspapers:

> —Vean ustedes, señores: llevar hombres jóvenes a la cámara sería nuestra perdición. La juventud del día no tiene talentos prácticos: ¿cómo quieren ustedes que los tenga? Le da por la historia y por estudiar el derecho constitucional y la economía política en libros! Forman bibliotecas enormes y se indigestan la inteligencia con una erudición inútil, que mata en ellos toda la espontaneidad del talento y de la inventiva. ¡Sí, señores, los libros no sirven para nada! Ustedes me ven a mí ... Yo no he necesitado jamás libros para saber lo que sé. (50)

> —Todo eso no sirve para nada, señora [Medea]. Enséñele usted [a Julio] a leer y a escribir y deje usted al talento que se revele solo. Repito a usted que en este país los hombres no necesitan estudiar nada para llegar a los altos puestos.
>
> "¿No me ve usted a mí?" (52)

> ("Look here, gentlemen: it would be our ruin if young men got into the chamber. Today's youth have no practical talents, how could they?

They're interested in history and studying constitutional law and political economy in books! They assemble enormous libraries and upset their minds with useless erudition, which kills in them all spontaneous talent and inventiveness. Yes, sir, books are useless! Just look at me ... I have never needed books to know what I know.

"That's all useless, madam. Teach [Julio] to read and write and let his talent emerge of its own accord. I repeat to you that in this country men do not need to study a thing in order to attain high positions.

"Aren't I proof?")

There is certainly no subtlety in this representation of the range of values to which Julio is exposed in Medea's household, and the foregoing quotations are examples of López's preference for a sarcasm that leaves little doubt as to the corruption of ideals in the hands of the leaders of Buenos Aires in the 1860s.[10] Medea dominates this world, intimidating with her monumental rages those who would raise a voice against her while toadying to the men she believes to be masters of the political arena. This is not a society controlled by Medea or by a set of values invested in her character. Rather, Medea assimilates the values of those whom she lionizes in order to translate them into the guiding principles of the household, a microcosm of the Buenos Aires of the *gran aldea,* over which she reigns tyrannically. Medea may be a raging tyrant, but she is only an instrument of social values she willingly accepts in order to advance the influence of her salon. Medea's death from apoplexy is masterfully grotesque. Significantly, her demise is the consequence of a loss of political influence. The narrative has reached the 1880s, and the elements Medea supports no longer occupy center stage. The sham of republican simplicity has yielded to the decadent opulence of bourgeois capitalism, and for the microcosm of the novel, Medea's grotesque death marks the replacement of the former by the latter.

Julio is no longer the young boy who was a spectator in his aunt's household. He is now a young man who works as a commercial clerk, and his gaze now falls on the occupants of the clubs, theaters, and restaurants of the nouveaux riches who are in the process of transforming the *gran aldea* into the Paris of the Southern Hemisphere. Medea is replaced as the focal point of Julio's witness by Blanca, a brilliant and strikingly beautiful young woman whose carefree and scheming immor-

10. As a consequence of my view of the novel as a trenchant denunciation of ideological structures, I find Lichtblau's characterization too cheerful: "With lively grace and a frequent touch of veiled humor, Lucio López brings to light salient traits of the capital during the 1880's" (*The Argentine Novel,* 145).

ality is the distillation of the new corrupt social values of Buenos Aires. Julio encounters Blanca on several occasions, but one of the longest chapters of the novel (11) concerns Julio's inaugural function at the Club del Progreso, one of the most important centers of social activity for the new masters of Buenos Aires. It is at this grand ball that Julio is able to observe Blanca in all of her splendor. Whereas years before he had observed Medea raging and toadying in her modest Creole household, here he observes Blanca coolly disdaining and outrageously flattering in the club that epitomizes what Buenos Aires has now become:

> La fatiga me rindió aquella noche, pero no pude descansar. La imagen de Blanca me atraía involuntariamente: veíala andar y detenerse burlonamente en mi camino como dándome tiempo para alcanzarla, y cuando creía tenerla cerca, la visión desaparecía, dejando en mi sueño el surco luminoso de su vestido rojo que parecía disolverse en el aire en deslumbrantes e impalpables copos de fuego. (133)

> (I was done in with exhaustion that night, but I could not sleep. The image of Blanca pulled at me involuntarily: I saw her walk and stop mockingly along the same road as though giving me time to catch up, and when I thought she was near, the vision would disappear, leaving in my dream the luminous trace of her red dress which seemed to dissolve in the air in flashing and impalpable bursts of fire.)

Blanca has made it quite clear to Julio, however, that although she may be attracted to him he can entertain no hopes toward her because of his extreme poverty. She outlines her plans to marry a wealthy man, and his age is of no consequence as long as he is able to satisfy her expensive material desires. Blanca does, in due course, fulfill her ambition, and Julio contemplates her determined pursuit of an extravagant lifestyle that pays no heed to the expense of money or human feelings. Although Blanca, now financially secure, is willing to have a dalliance with the still impoverished Julio, he rejects her, and she turns to another young man. At the close of the novel, her baby burned alive as the result of her irresponsibility as a mother (this is the second grotesque highpoint of the novel) and her elder husband driven mad at his loss, Blanca disappears with her lover.

With the schematicism permitted to literature, López has Blanca find her fortunes in Julio's now widowed don Ramón, who has inherited Medea's family wealth. Thus, this Creole inheritance passes to a Europeanizing fortune hunter who uses it skillfully in support of the opulent lifestyle that now reigns triumphant in Buenos Aires (see *La gran aldea,* 163).

The Medea-Blanca axis of *La gran aldea* represents in unmistakable terms the social evolution of Buenos Aires in the twenty-year period of his life that Julio the narrator describes to the reader. There can be little doubt that he finds both women equally repugnant and degrading; I discuss below what Julio may consider a suitable alternative to these feminine points of reference. In terms of the male figures of the novel, Medea and Blanca interact with an axis represented by Julio and don Ramón. Julio's role here is obvious. He is the observer, first innocent and then critical, of the social world around him: "yo, ardiendo de curiosidad, hice todo lo posible por ser espectador lejano" (I, consumed by curiosity, did everything possible to be a distant spectator; 49–50). As a character in the novel, Julio is a boy who comes of age in a world undergoing profound ideological transformations, and as a mature narrator he finds little in either the before or after of this transformation that he can identify with. As a biased observer, Julio is the locus for a profound disgust toward both the old Creole aristocracy and the new capitalistic bourgeoisie. His inability either to come to terms with what Buenos Aires has become or to recall with fond nostalgia an ancien régime marks the controlling narrative perspective of *La gran aldea* as a confrontation with a social panorama of irresolvable corruption. As a cultural text, López's novel transcribes a posture of despair for an individual growing up in a society where the lifestyles that succeed each other are all equally vile.

But the most curious aspect of the novel is the role of don Ramón, the uncle who takes Julio in when he is left an orphan. The Spanish word for an orphan's guardian is *tutor,* but don Ramón serves his nephew as an "antitutor," both in the legal sense and as a guide for his education. Since don Ramón is completely dominated by Medea, Julio is barely tolerated in the household, and he receives no formal education until as a teenager he is sent away to a provincial boarding school. As a figure of the nineteenth-century Latin American patriarch, don Ramón is a pathetic man, and herein lies the curious nature of his role in the structure of meaning of the novel. In conformance with a society of male dominance and privilege, one would expect don Ramón to exercise an important influence in his microcosmic world. However, quite to the contrary, don Ramón is browbeaten by Medea and manipulated by Blanca (their respective styles signal the different rhetoric of their corresponding societies). As a consequence, he can be only an object of pity for Julio, who finds in his *tutor* hardly the sort of male role model prized by the patriarchal society of his day, no matter what its ideological variety may have been. That is to say, if patriarchal dominance was accepted by all of the lifestyles of Argentine society, Julio's *tutor,* in his interaction with the two dominant patterns portrayed in the novel, is nothing more than a puppet in the hands of others.

That don Ramón cannot be a role model in the eyes of his nephew is complemented by the fact that don Ramón is dominated by women who embody lifestyles that Julio rejects in equal measure. Thus, in terms of the values portrayed in the novel, Julio in effect has nowhere to turn. Medea and Blanca are nothing more than embodiments of values defined and pursued by dominant male figures in Julio's society: don Buenaventura and don Trevexo in the case of Medea; her corrupt father in the case of Blanca. However, the degradation of Julio's primary role model by women who are in turn the instruments of remote male figures serves as a conclusive confirmation of Julio's eventual alienation from the society he chronicles. A noteworthy feature of López's novel, therefore, is the decision to structure the microcosmic world of Julio's coming of age in a Buenos Aires undergoing radical transformations in terms of Medea and Blanca. While that world is not dominated by the Medeas and the Blancas, for Julio it is mediated and interpreted by them at the expense of the male figure whom he believes to be his legitimate point of reference.[11] As a consequence, Julio meditates on the profound pathos of his uncle's situation:

> Entonces el martirio debía duplicarse [para mi tío]: aquella aparición deslumbrante de todas las noches [Blanca], que pasaba indiferente por su lado y el de su hija, sin detenerse, que no rendía culto ni a la ley del esposo ni al cariño de la madre, que volvía llena y tibia aún con lo[s] vapores del mundo en que vivía, después de librar la batalla del lujo en la feria de las vanidades; aquella aparición enloquecedora desaparecía, y ante los ojos fatigados del anciano se alzaba el espectro aterrador de doña Medea, riendo con una carcajada satánica, estridente y vengativa, y lan-

11. Paternalism in Argentine literature has yet to be examined in any detail. When it is, one model might be Roberto Schwarz's monograph on the Brazilian Machado de Assis's early novels, *Ao vencedor as batatas: forma literária e proceso social nos inícios do romance brasileiro.* It is interesting to note that one of the major Brazilian novels of the period concerns a protagonist whose principal points of reference are dominant female figures in an environment dominated by the absence of the male center: *Lucíola* by José de Alencar (1829–1877); see Roberto Reis, "O recato da escritura." See also Pérez Amuchástegui on the "oligarquía paternalista" (*Mentalidades argentinas,* 93–99). Elizabeth Garrels examines patriarchalism indirectly in her study of the concept of family in the novel *La novia del hereje* (1854) by Vicente Fidel López, the father of the author of *La gran aldea,* "El 'espíritu de la familia' en *La novia del hereje* de Vicente Fidel López." Mark D. Szuchman provides a superb sociological study of the Argentine family during the period of *La gran aldea* in *Order, Family, and Community in Buenos Aires, 1810–1860.*

zando una blasfemia terrible contra aquel desgraciado del destino, víctima inocente de la suerte, que temblaba de espanto y de impotencia ante el recuerdo del pasado y el cuadro del presente. (171)

(Then his martyrdom must have doubled [for my uncle]: that overpowering apparition every night [Blanca], who passed by him and his daughter indifferently without stopping, who had no use for the rights of her husband or a mother's affection, who came home satisfied and still warm with the vapors of the world in which she lived after doing battle over luxury in the vanity fair; that maddening apparition would disappear and before the tired eyes of the old man the terrifying specter of Doña Medea would rise up with her satanic laugh, strident and vengeful, hurling a terrible curse at that man so ill-favored by fortune, an innocent victim of luck, who trembled with fear and impotence in the face of the memory of the past and the portrait of the present.)

If the decent and honorable don Ramón's miserable situation embodies for Julio the decay and corruption of a world of pretensions and exploitation, a friend of his uncle offers one alternative for coming to terms with that world. Don Benito is a jolly old cynic who takes Julio in when he returns to Buenos Aires from boarding school. It is don Benito who introduces Julio to the demimonde of the Club del Progreso, serving as an effective cicerone in Julio's discovery of the new Buenos Aires. Yet don Benito can only offer his young charge a witty commentary on the vanities and secret lives of the inhabitants of that world and not the refuge from it Julio requires. After the destruction of his uncle's home at the end of the novel, Julio attempts to renew his relationship with Valentina, the sister of one of his classmates. But he finds that she has made a marriage of convenience, and this avenue of consolation is closed to him. Although Valentina is never fully developed as a third feminine figure in the novel, she does represent the sort of simple womanly decency that Julio seeks. In his first encounter with Valentina, she is an alternative to Medea (chapter 9); at the end of the novel, he sees in her a refuge from the specter of Blanca. In both cases, however, Valentina is an elusive figure for Julio, first because she is engaged to marry someone else and subsequently because she has married.

Julio's affection for Valentina is much more than simply a "realistic" note of human sentiment in the novel. Rather, it completes a triangle of possible lifestyles presented to him in the form of a feminine protagonist: Valentina as the romantic feminine ideal, Medea as the aggressive republican matron, and Blanca as the fortune-hunting courtesan. It is significant for *La gran aldea*'s interpretation of the panorama of Buenos Aires society that the only woman with whom Julio identifies is happy in her marriage to a man from the world dominated by the values represented by the other two. As a character representing a fictional but personalized experience, Julio's despair is that of a man who can find no refuge for his personal aspirations. In terms of the novel's use of these narrative schemata for purposes of making a point about *costumbres bonaerenses,* the panorama laid before us by the narrator is one wherein the dominant ideological structures possess no point of identity for individuals like Julio.

In the best tradition of *costumbrista* writing, the bulk of *La gran aldea* is a series of vignettes. The narrator's descriptions of his experiences are framing devices for the presentation of detailed descriptions of the lifestyles of the period covered by the novel. These descriptions abound with detailed references to the material items and the language of the period in an emphasis on the verism that is characteristic of *costumbrismo.* The descriptions of Medea's salon, the grand ball at the Club del Progreso, and functions at the theater that Blanca attends are some of the examples of these vignettes that the narrator frames with references to his discovery of the world in which he lives. In turn, these vignettes confirm for him his evolving interpretations of that world: "El cuadro era digno del satírico pincel de Hogarth" (The picture was worthy of Hogarth's satiric brush; 165).

However, López's novel is much more than the parade of these vignettes. My comments have attempted to show that López fictionalized and concentrated his interest in the ways of life in Buenos Aires between 1860 and 1880 in the figure of a personalized narrator whose human interactions exemplify a series of possible parameters for the identification in ideological terms of those lifestyles. Moreover, the personal dilemma of that narrator testifies implicitly to the spiritual bankruptcy of his world. López may have had deep commitments to the progressive, European values of the leaders of his day, but Julio's status as an orphan reveals an abandonment of the individual in society that is much more than his lack of family and fortune.

La Bolsa: The Narrativization of Social Tract

> —¡Quiera Dios que no sea ficticia esta abundancia que nos rodea! ¡Quiera Dios que mañana no se levante el patriotismo de su tumba, evocado por el espectro del hambre![12]
>
> ("I hope to God that this abundance surrounding us is not fictitious!

12. José María Miró (pseud., Julián Martel), *La Bolsa: la diputación de Alberto,* 143. Hereafter cited parenthetically in the text by page number.

May God keep patriotism from rising up out if its tomb tomorrow, evoked by the specter of hunger!")

There can be little question that *La Bolsa* (The stock market) by Julián Martel (pseudonym of José María Miró, 1867–1896) is the most famous narrative of the Generation of 1880. There have been over a dozen editions of this text since its original posthumous publication in book form in 1898, certainly a record for the titles of the period. Correspondingly, *La Bolsa* has been read and studied as one of the most accurate representations of the personal and social effects of the unchecked economic expansionism of its day, and it is considered the best example of a "cycle" of novels dealing with the famous stock market crisis of 1889–1890.[13] Indeed, Martel completed his novel on the eve of 1891, and there is every reason to believe that he composed it hastily in order to take advantage of the public's interest in accounts surrounding the individuals affected by and, of course, responsible for this crisis.[14]

It is significant to note that *La Bolsa* was originally published in serial form in 1891 in the prestigious newspaper *La Nación,* which eventually sponsored its first edition as a book. A newspaper born of the ideological struggle of the post-Caseros period—it was founded by future-president Bartolomé Mitre in 1870—*La Nación* has customarily been associated with landowning, agrarian interests, in contrast to the capitalistic entrepreneurship represented by the equally venerable *La Prensa.* Indeed, *La Bolsa* adopts an attitude drawn from a rather simplistic, "inverse" variant of Naturalism whereby decent society is besieged by the excesses, whether inherent or willful, of unscrupulous and amoral indi-

13. Campanella, *La generación del 80,* 187–89; Blasi, "Las crisis del noventa"; Lichtblau, *The Argentine Novel,* 149–55; *El 80,* 2:26–36.

14. Segundo I. Villafañe's novel on the stock market, *Horas de fiebre,* was also published in 1891, and, like Ocanto's *Quilito* and Martel's *La Bolsa,* it deals with an unfortunate speculator who is ruined by the "fevered" cycle of buying and selling that led to the 1891 crisis. And like Ocanto's protagonist, Villafañe's commits suicide, complementing the apoplectic death of Martel's Glow. Even more transparent than Martel's novel, Villafañe's is built around a series of stark contrasts, between the protagonist's nouveau riche way of life and the simple Creole practices of his mother and brothers and between his new world of glitter and pretense and the humble poverty of the girl he once courted and who wastes away out of love for him. Of particular note is how the novel is also structured around the homology between *fever* as a metaphor of the intense activity of the stock market and as a literal designation for the malady that undermines the protagonist's health in proportion as his business dealings fail and his life crumbles around him. Regarding the contrasts upon which the novel is built, see Antonio Pagés Larraya, "Estudio preliminar" in *Horas de fiebre.* Pagés Larraya does not, however, comment on the double meaning of *fiebre* in the novel.

viduals.[15] As an unequivocal denunciation of the fever of speculation that both provided for the enormous expansion of the Argentine economy at the end of the century and occasioned numerous financial crises of which the panic of 1889–1890 was but the most alarming one, Martel's narrative implicitly laments the opportunism that had come to prevail among social and commercial leaders.

By extension it also decries the abandonment of the solid principle of wealth based on land holdings, precisely the arrangement of affairs championed by the so-called oligarchic *La Nación.* Therefore, as an initial generalization about *La Bolsa* and the other titles of the stock market cycle, one might say that the novelistic goal is to present a portrait of a society destroyed by the gallery of types whose locus of operations gives the novel its title.[16] The stock market is viewed as the epicenter and a microcosm of a specific segment of Argentine society of the end of the penultimate decade of the century. As a microcosm, it exhibits an inventory of freewheeling financial dealers (the speculators, their attendants, and assorted hangers on) that manipulate the economy of the country for the latter's own personal gain. As an epicenter of this intense activity, the stock market is the controlling point of reference for a series of operations and their successive repercussions that impinge on the economic well-being of the entire nation. In these aspects, *La Bolsa* is not unlike similar American and European novels dealing with the same sort of operations in a type of dominant economy that would become increasingly international, resulting, of course, in the worldwide crash of 1929.[17]

But there is another aspect to *La Bolsa* that also makes it, in addition to the most often evoked novel of the period, the most notorious one. As part of Martel's strenuous efforts to portray in the starkest terms possible the unscrupulousness that flowed (naturally, he would say) from a

15. "Biologism slides over into the attack on the immigrant (*En la sangre,* by Cambaceres, *La Bolsa,* by Julián Martel) and the defense of the values held by the high bourgeoisie in Argentina, whose project was to link themselves up with the bourgeoisie of industrialism" (Jitrik, *El 80 y su mundo,* 96).

16. David Viñas, "Martel y los culpables del 90."

17. The only adequate contemporary analysis of *La Bolsa* is the pamphlet by Nobile, *Análisis de "La Bolsa,"* which provides a very general characterization of the sociopolitical background of the novel, the typology of the gallery of speculators associated with the stock market, and a detailed paraphrase of a plot, which is quite skeletal to begin with. A general commentary from the period is provided by Ernesto Quesada, *Dos noveleas sociológicas—"La Bolsa" y "Quilito,"* which stresses the information the novel provides about social life and public values.

feverish market speculation, his characters emerge unavoidably as caricatures, as fully transparent signs of a cluster of ethical traits. Rather than place all of the blame for the disruption of society brought about by economic adventurism on the shoulders of local investors, who are often as much ignorant victims as they are unscrupulous manipulators, Martel invests a radically disjunctive sign with the role of constituting the synthesis of the evil that corrupts the stock market and occasions the failure of so many unwitting investors. This sign is abbreviated in the person of the Jew, a foreign mountebank who represents an international financial conspiracy (conveniently tied to the Rothschilds) whose goal is to take over the Argentine economy through the calculating exploitation of the economic system, concentrated in the stock market, at the expense of witless local investors.[18]

In *La Bolsa,* Glow is the epitome of the naive speculator, and it is his pitiful downfall that provides the main sequence of narrative events:

> —*¿Et comment allez vous, mon cher docteur?*
>
> Glow le dijo secamente que bien. Claramente se notaban sus deseos de separarse del judío, que no lo dejaba, hablándole en el único idioma común a los dos, en francés, porque el descendiente de Judas no conocía el español, y Glow no entendía el alemán. No ignoraba el doctor que aquel semita era un enviado de Rothschild, el banquero inglés, que lo había mandado a Buenos Aires para que operase en el oro y ejerciese presión sobre la plaza. Lo que el doctor no sabía era que Mackser tenía la consigna de acaparar, de monopolizar, con ayuda de un fuerte sindicato judío, a cuyo frente estaba él, las principales fuentes productoras del país. (73)

> ("Et comment allez vouz, mon cher docteur?"
>
> Glow said fine to him. His desire to rid himself of the Jew was clearly apparent, but the latter did not leave him, speaking to him in the only language the two had in common, French, because the descendent of Judas did not know Spanish, and Glow did not understand German. Glow was not unaware of the fact that the Semite was an envoy of the English banker, Rothschild, who had sent him to Buenos Aires to deal in

18. Leonardo Senkman, in *La identidad judía en la literatura argentina,* mentions Martel only in passing, as though his anti-Semitism were so blatant as not to require commentary. Gladys Onega, *La inmigración en la literatura argentina, 1880–1910,* on the other hand, writes at length on Martel (pp. 109–23). The extent to which the anti-Semitism of *La Bolsa* continues to be a touchy issue in Argentina is shown by how reference to its publication by *La Nación* was censored in a 1986 television documentary on anti-Semitism in that country (Andrés Avellaneda, "El proceso de la censura y la censura del 'Proceso': Argentina, 1976–1983," 26).

gold and to bring pressure to bear on the marketplace. What Glow did not know was that Mackser had orders to corner, to monopolize, with the help of a powerful Jewish syndicate led by him, the principal sources of wealth in the country.)

"Lo que el doctor no sabía" (what Glow did not know) becomes the operating principle of *La Bolsa:* Glow's innocence or naiveté or misplaced trust in the system or whatever conjugation of qualities was responsible for his failure to discover "Baron" Mackser's financial schemes emerges as the tragic flaw in his nature and in the microcosm he represents in the world of the stock market. Certainly it is a flaw inherent to the system, an unchecked dynamic of barely or flagrantly unethical business dealings that, it is clear from both the outset of the novel and the larger historical context in which we must read it, necessarily leads to grief and destruction.

There is no way to argue away Martel's semantic shorthand in concentrating the agency of the exploitation of the built-in flaws of the system in this Jewish archetype. It is ridiculous to attempt, as Lescano wishes to do (31), to argue that the Jewish agent is only one of a cast of manipulators whom Martel denounces. Mackser's characterization is so forthrightly anti-Semitic, involving as it does an ample display of all of the common derogatory epithets (as may be seen in the passage quoted above), that it would be an incompetent reader indeed who would mistake his role as a categorical sign in the novel. To be sure, Martel is not really interested in exploring the person of Mackser in any sort of arrestingly original characterization of his corruption, and his introduction does not deviate in any way whatsoever from the stock image of the rapacious Jew.

Martel's anti-Semitism cannot be labeled as anything but the convenient utilization of a standard figure borrowed from the cultural inventory of the period, which is why I have alluded to Mackser as representing a sort of semiotic shorthand. However, to assimilate Mackser's role in the novel to a particular theory of narrative configuration does not lessen the blatant anti-Semitism of the narrator's handling of him, and this aspect of *La Bolsa* is understandably one of the greatest embarrassments of Argentine literature when viewed in terms of the contemporary standards relating to the treatment of ethnicity. Of particular interest is the long exchange of opinions concerning the historical role of the Jews that takes up most of the seventh chapter of the first part (144–55).

Where this aspect of the novel assumes importance is as an excellent index of Martel's casting of the poles of conflict in his novel. The shrillness of this characterization leaves no room for error as to the point of reference for the inherent defects of a financial system that would admit the likes of Mackser, as though benevolently welcoming the agent of its own destruction. Glow, who personifies the other principal pole of the novel, may treat Mackser with the coldness appropriate to his many personal liabilities: foreigner, non-Spanish speaker, poorly dressed and lacking in social graces, a Jew, and the representative for a powerful and antagonistic financial empire. But his ignorance as to the true extent of Mackser's machinations is one of the consequences of his unquestioning faith in the institution of the stock market.

The stock market achieves virtual anthropomorphization in *La Bolsa.* In addition to the hypostasis of the novel's title, providing the financial institution with a recognition usually considered appropriate to the protagonists who give their name to many of the novels of the period (compare the paradigmatic works of both Thomas Hardy and Émile Zola), the stock market is portrayed as the embodiment of an entire human ethnology:

> Promiscuidad de tipos y promiscuidad de idiomas. Aquí los sonidos ásperos como escupitajos del alemán, mezclándose impíamente a las dulces notas de la lengua italiana; allí los acentos viriles del inglés haciendo dúo con los chisporroteos maliciosos de la terminología criolla; del otro lado las monerías y suavidades del francés, respondiendo al ceceo susurrante de la rancia pronunciación española. . . .
>
> Agolpábase a aquella reja una multitud ansiosa estremecida por corrientes eléctricas. Se veían pescuezos estirados en angustiosas expectativas, con la rigidez propia del jugador que espera la salida de la carta que ha de decidir la partida; ojos desmesuradamente abiertos, siguiendo con fijeza hipnótica los movimientos de la mano del apuntador, al cual, subido sobre su tarima, anotaba las operaciones en las pizarras que, negras, cuadradas, siniestras, se dibujaban como sombras en la pared del fondo. (58–59)

> (A promiscuousness of types and a promiscuousness of languages. Here the harsh sounds of German like someone spitting, impiously mixed with the sweet notes of the Italian language; there the virile accents of English in concert with the malicious flashes of Creole terminology; over there the coquettishness and softness of French, answering the rustling lisp of ancient Spanish pronunciation. . . .
>
> An anxious multitude shaken by electric currents bunched together in front of that grill. Necks craning expectantly were to be seen, with the rigidity proper to the gambler who awaits the outcome of a card that will decide the game; eyes gaping wide open, flowing with a hypnotic gaze the movements of the hand of the marker, who, mounted on a platform, noted the operations on the boards which, black, square, and sinister, stood out like shadows on the back wall.)

One is immediately struck by the intensity of Martel's expression in these descriptions, and only a sort of willful misunderstanding could account for mistaking the complex of social values that underlie such a characterization. For example, the cluster of images is controlled by the repeated term *promiscuidad,* a word belonging to a discourse of social order and moral reserve. Evidently, the stock market is the antithesis of a societal ideal in which identities are maintained and in which there is an ordered separation between what are considered inherently and categorically different phenomena. As opposed to a norm of discreet structures whose differentiation is possible because they are not jumbled together, as much as the fact that their differentiation recommends and impedes their being scrambled, an institution like the stock market is by insinuation "unnatural" because of the cacophony that results from the confusion of different orders. Quite an array of orders are implied by the narrator's statement, both general types and particular nationalities. The overall effect is one of a circus.

This image is extended by subsequent paragraphs in which the narrator focuses on the specific details of the heated activity within the confines of the stock market. Again, the controlling terms are those of disorder, in the sense of a collective action of pandemonium ("agolpábase . . . una multitud ansiosa" [an anxious multitude crowded around]), in the description of grotesque distortions of the human body and senses under the effects of the trading fever: the stretched necks, the hypnotic stares, the anguish and rigidity of the expectant player, and the characterization of the sinister shadow cast by the board that records the figures of the vertiginous operations.

Martel's style rests securely on a principle of accumulatio, the piling up of descriptors that reinforce each other and, as a consequence of their semantic redundancy, exclude any possibility of ambiguity. As a special form of hyperbole, accumulatio promotes relentlessly categorical meanings. In the case of narrative structure, this means the sort of reiterative patterns that emerge from the assemblage of chapters and smaller units that essentially rephrase the same controlling terms with other, circumstantial signs. The narrative blocks, although framed in terms of a progression beginning with Glow's decision to participate in a business scheme and ending with his losing his fortune and going insane, are basically organized as repetitions of the multifaceted ingredients of the destructive financial network that emerged in Buenos Aires around the institution of the stock market. Or, put differently, the chapters detail, like a mosaic, small-scale components of the global, dominant institution of the stock market.

Appropriately, the novel posits Glow against a gallery of unsavory exponents of this institution. Glow is not wholly blameless, to be sure, not at least in the terms of the legendary Creole aristocracy from which his wife derives (111ff.). A member of the system that gave him wealth which he is only too enthusiastically willing to help to sustain, Glow shows only a minimal level of ethical consciousness about the business schemes he is willing to endorse (for example, the blatantly symbolic Sociedad Embaucadora and its too-good-to-be-true land investments; compare the second chapter of part one, "Los entretelones"). Yet, Glow is basically a decent family man (which, of course, counts for much in terms of the social code of the period), and his principal defect is defined as the blind trust in the system he believes will enhance his lot and that of his dependents.

Against the tragically innocent Glow there is ranged a host of monstrous types like Granulillo, the bank president who uses his French mistress to extort large sums of money from the men she seduces; Peñas, the grave robber who is a pawn in Granulillo's scheme to defraud Glow; Fouchez, a fellow investor who will also collaborate in deceiving Glow; and, casting his shadow over them all, Mackser, the vile Jewish agent of foreign monetary interests. In terms of the dynamic of *La Bolsa,* these and other secondary individuals reinforce each other reciprocally by contributing to the scheme of financial skullduggery and, therefore, ethical corruption that will overwhelm the naive Glow.

If the dominant semantic axis of the novel is the polarized relationship between Glow and his fellow financiers, a disjunction that Glow cannot perceive until it is too late but of which the reader is abundantly informed from the outset, Glow's private world is juxtaposed to the public arena of the stock market. In support of the image of Glow as a decent family man for whom financial speculation represents primarily the opportunity to provide a better life for his family rather than an extension of the maniacal greed of his antagonists, the narrator takes pains to portray Glow at home in the bosom of noble domesticity. At the time of the narrative, Glow has just moved his family into a mansion along the Avenida Alvear, at that time the Buenos Aires equivalent of Fifth Avenue. To Glow, this new home is confirmation of the successful life that the son of a poor English immigrant has built for himself; an offering to his adoring wife and precious children of the comfort and secure position he is now able to offer to them; and testimony to his society of the riches available to any man willing to avail himself of the promises of economic expansionism. Glow returns to his home from the stock market as to a refuge from the turmoil of the latter, but also as to a retreat made possible by that institution:

> Contento, satisfecho, el doctor arrojó una mirada a su alrededor, y sus labios volvieron a dibujar la misma sonrisa que se bosquejó en ellos a la entrada de la Bolsa. Pensaba que aquel palacio, situado en el centro de la Avenida Alvear, en pleno barrio aristocrático, era suyo, completamente suyo. Sólo quince días hacía que lo habilitaba, y aún conservaba fresca la impresión que produce en el hombre acostumbrado a llevar una vida cómoda pero sin lujo, el repentino encumbramiento a las más altas cimas de una opulencia improvisada. (106)

> (Content, satisfied, Glow cast a look about him, and his lips once again showed the same smile they had shown when he walked into the stock market. He thought that that palace, situated midway along the Avenida Alvear, in the very middle of the aristocratic neighborhood, belonged to him, was his and his alone. He had moved into it only fifteen days ago, and he still had the impression produced in the man used to living a comfortable but unluxurious life, one of suddenly being thrust to the highest reaches of unexpected opulence.)

The narrator dwells carefully on the inventory of Glow's newly acquired opulence, and again the rhetorical principle of accumulatio holds sway as a way of confirming the importance of the station Glow has recently attained. In the portrait of domestic well-being, of an ordered life, of personal circumspection and interpersonal fidelity, the author constructs a hyperbolic antonym to the pandemoniac circus of the stock market from which Glow has just retired. As in the case of the sustained representations of the corruption of the latter, *La Bolsa* relies equally on a reiterative depiction of Glow's enviable domestic situation. Therefore, when Glow's enemies succeed in bringing about his ruin, it will quite naturally involve the unremitting destruction of this haven of decency. In accord with the notable lack of subtlety in Martel's novelistic practice, the emphatic concordance of all of these elements in terms of two antithetical poles of social, moral, ethical values confirms the ideological posture of *La Bolsa* that no reader has likely been able to misinterpret.

Although there can be no doubting that Glow's home and the stock market constitute diametrically opposed realms of ethical and moral behavior, the formal ball that Glow holds as part of the inauguration of his mansion represents a significant link between those two universes. Glow moves daily between them, and the ambiguousness of his own conduct, not in terms of his presentation to the reader but from the point of view of the compromises he must make, is objectified by the way in which he opens the private domain of his home to the denizens of the stock market. This is amply apparent in the hostility that Glow's wife, Margarita, feels toward Mackser, who has been invited to the ball at the instigation of one of her husband's associates:

> Y ella, que detestaba al judío, invitado por compromiso gracias a la oficiosidad de Granulillo, lo encontraba muy simpático ahora, reprochándose interiormente la animadversión que antes le tuviera. (163)

> (And she, who detested the Jew, who had been invited out of obligation thanks to the intercession of Granulillo, now found him very charming, and she inwardly reproached herself for my former aversion toward him.)

Margarita's feelings toward the Jew, rather than damn her for the prejudices of her class, signal the higher criterion of social politics, just as her subsequently finding him rather charming is a correlative of her elation at the triumph on her part: "ella era el centro de todo aquel aparato decorativo" (she was the center of everything in that whole decorative scene; 162).

Glow's splendid ball, which even the president deigns to attend, is an emphatic element of foreshadowing (from the dating of the novel and the climate of financial speculation described, it would have been Miguel Juárez Celman, who served from 1886 to 1890, before resigning his scandal-ridden office). The scoundrels who will eventually seize Glow's fortune have the opportunity to appraise first-hand the richly appointed mansion that will soon be theirs. Appropriately, the narrator turns once again to the inventorying of the material signs of Glow's financial status, and the chapter closes significantly with his offering to an obviously covetous president one of the prize baubles of his recently assembled collection (170–71).

The narrator's pursuit of a portrait of greed, corruption, exploitation, and fraud is both inexorable in its amassing of details and unswerving in the single-mindedness of its denunciation of the stain of social evil that spreads outward from the personified stock market. It would be pointless to enumerate the continual allusions to the latter as a telling explanation for this or that feature of improper social or moral behavior. For the narrator, it is sufficient to evoke the stock market in order to avoid having to say more about the state of public affairs and the private lives affected by them. Significantly, *Bolsa* must always be capitalized, as much because of its personification of social evils as because it is the name of a recognized institution: "—¡Oh!, ¡La Bolsa!" (103). The expanding image of the stock market as something like a live and organic being with an independent dynamic, like a machine that has taken control of itself against its creator, is enhanced as the novel moves toward its dénouement. When Glow is taken violently ill as the result of his financial collapse, his wife is aided in the nursing by her mother. This gentle and innocent lady is exposed to the horrors of the stock market in the person of the creditors who assault the Glow household (263). And when Glow slips into his final madness as the consequence of a ruin he cannot remedy, he is visited by a phantom of the stock market incarnate, a monster who installs herself as the companion of his delirium:

> Y él entonces, debatiéndose en el horror de una agonía espantosa, ¡loco, loco para siempre!, oyó estas tres palabras que salían roncamente por la boca del monstruo:
>
> —Soy la Bolsa. (271)

> (And then he, struggling with the horror of a fearsome agony, crazy, crazy forever!, heard these four words that came hoarsely from the mouth of the monster:
>
> "I am the Stock Market.")

The hypostatization of both the stock market and Glow's house, the prolix inventory of the gallery of rogues that frequent the latter and the material effects of the former establish the master semantic axis of *La Bolsa.* Glow moves back and forth between these two worlds, striving to exploit the former in order to support the latter, ultimately being ruined by the stock market, to which he must yield up the symbolic preserve of his home.

The emphasis on the materiality of the domains within which Glow moves, however, is double-edged. On the one hand, it is a materiality deriving from the radical expurgation of the "spiritual" from his world, by which the narrator insinuates that we should understand the traditional moral and ethical values that have been corrupted by the financial institutions and economic structure centered in the stock market. This is, of course, the society being forged by the Liberal and Progressive society that holds sway in Argentina around the epochal date of 1880 and whose apogee is the presidency of Julio A. Roca (1880–1886); but the beginnings of decay come soon afterward, during the rule of Roca's son-in-law, Juárez Celman. One of the shadows cast over the details of Martel's narrative is the recurring adynaton, stated either explicitly or evoked by suggestion, to the effect that Argentine society would be less precarious and more honorable were it not for the pace set by a corrupt, ineffectual government (142).

If the principal role of Glow's home life is to signal the sort of sweet tranquillity that can provide refuge from the turmoil of the market, that home's mistress, the virtuous Margarita, presides over it with an unbending dedication to the traditional Creole values of her ancestors. Although Glow is privileged to enter into this universe by virtue of his sanctified union with Margarita, he is, after all, the driven son of a poor immigrant, and the success he attains in life is based on the material riches afforded by the stock market. But there is another way in which materiality dominates in Martel's novel, and that is as a feature of the vague sort of Naturalism prevalent in the Argentine novel of the period. As in the case of novels like Eugenio Cambaceres's *En la sangre,* Manuel T. Podestá's *Irresponsable,* and Antonio Argerich's *¿Inocentes o culpables?, La Bolsa* underscores material details of human society as indices of far-reaching social ills that must be addressed. Rather than stating a concern for the way in which the defects of the social dynamic, whether seen as an inherited biological determinism or singled out as a destructive physical environment, create human victims, these novels identify human types who are a threat to an otherwise honorable social establishment.

Thus, what Martel really accomplishes in his novel via the hypostatization of the stock market is the creation of an institutional point of reference for a gallery of unsavory types, both national entrepreneurs and foreign adventurers, who have created an economic machinery that is destroying the fabric of Argentine society (compare the litany of social ostentation of these types, a litany constructed around the anaphoric predicate "Allá va," which allows the narrator to indulge in yet another inventory; 173–78).

Glow, somehow a member of both domains as a consequence of his affiliations with these types and by virtue of his marriage to Margarita, is ultimately an agent of his own doom, while at the same time being responsible for the destruction of one more constituent of the Creole society exposed to the cancer of the stock market, the home saintly Margarita made for him. The energetic, repetitive description of the whole world of the stock market and its extensions into all corners of polite society, and the argument that the stock market imposes forms of public and private existence that are coming to replace the noble patriotic heritage of the country are all narrative moves on the part of the narrator to underscore the material elements that threaten a weakening social body.

The foregoing description of the narrative processes underlying *La Bolsa* has made insistent reference to rhetorical figures: hypostasis, anaphora, accumulatio, and the like. These figures are not simply metaphoric extensions of more specifically narrative, rather than properly rhetorical, features of the novel. Rather, they are concrete verbal figurations that can be identified at certain points in the text of the novel as stylistic principles around which narrative exposition at those points is built. While undoubtedly these and similar figures may be identified in other novelistic works of the period (indeed, in any literary text), their special concentration in *La Bolsa* points to a fairly singular aspect of Martel's narrative practice.

Surely, none of the so-called Naturalist novels of the Generation of 1880, with the possible exception of Cambaceres's (see below, Chapter 4), can be called a particularly dense representation of character and existential circumstance, despite all of the emphasis purportedly placed by Naturalism on the interactions between individuals and environments. There is something about all of these novels that makes them read much more like sociopolitical tracts than narrative figurations, understanding that these two terms are intersecting axes for prose fiction. But *La Bolsa* is especially prominent (blatant, one might say) in its sustained adherence to a clear thesis of sociopolitical commentary: the horrendously corrupting, destructive effects of a speculative financial system based in a self-propelling yet cynically manipulated stock market. Moreover, the disjunction between the ostentatious society that has evolved from the rapid economic expansionism made possible by the stock market and a vaguely evoked traditional society of stable wealth underlies the alternating exhortations and excoriations of a narrator who makes full use of the omniscience awarded to him by the novelistic practices of the period.

As a consequence, *La Bolsa* is only a very lightly novelized text, to the extent that it is possible to suggest such a relative metric. What is meant by this assertion is that Martel marshals characters and circumstances when necessary to substantiate by example the points being made about the social impact of the stock market. Little attempt is made to propose Glow or the details of his fortune in such a way that the stock market assumes a growing and ultimately definitive destructive role in his existence. Rather, the stock market exists, and Glow and his circumstance are brought in to illustrate the ramifications for decent families of that hypostatized institution. The result is, in bald descriptive terms, a sociopolitical tract that makes use of the exemplum (yet another rhetorical device) of Glow's fate by way of illustration.

None of the foregoing is meant to repudiate *La Bolsa* as an honorable constituent of the novelistic canon of the Generation of 1880. Rather, it is intended to highlight the specific narrative texture of Martel's novel and to emphasize the way in which it is constructed around a starkly defined sociopolitical thesis that subordinates to it the aspects that we customarily associate with the novel, like characterization and the inner logic of narrative events. What narrative logic is operant here is the inevitability of failure for the respectable Argentine investor, rather than more specifically the character-centered plot of Glow as a dense human presence. By comparison to Cambaceres's Andrés in *Sin rumbo,* Martel's Glow is little more than a flat generalization of the whole class of victims of the stock market system.

What *La Bolsa* achieves in the process of this generalization is a compact ideological statement that does not allow the reservations that might come with more complexly developed, and therefore ambiguous, characters and circumstances. Martel makes a clear statement about the stock market system, but, by eschewing a fuller exploration into the character of Glow as a prototypic victim of the financial monster, he turns away (presumably by design) from an inquiry into why the system became installed in the first place and what complicity Glow and company have for its controlling presence. Concomitantly, Martel does not find it necessary to explore the intervention in the system of foreign agents like the detested Mackser and how their machinations are possible in spite of or as an inversion of an honorable Creole society. True, Martel's narrator speaks on several occasions of the naiveté of men like Glow, but why they are incapable of perceiving the concerted assault on their personal fortune and the corruption of their integrity by the deceivers, both foreign and domestic, is never explored. An incorporation of these issues into the narrative of a novel like *La Bolsa* might make for a richer fictional world, one marked by all of the ambiguities and complex motivations prized by high Realism and the psychological novel that develops out of Realism and Naturalism. But it also might well have detracted from the particularly emphatic sociopolitical tract that Martel's novel wound up being.

Debauched Patriarchy: Argerich's *¿Inocentes o culpables?*

> Estas anomalías eternas en las corrientes del pensamiento y que forman en sus remansos lo que llamamos conciencia, se observan en cada "documento humano" y confunden al analista que no acierta en tanto cáos á determinar un "punto matemático" para la moral, aunque encuentre como causas, estados morbosos, impulsiones fatales del organismo, dolorosos efectos de la educación recibida ó productos de las preocupaciones reinantes, —que en todo caso, y ante cualquier juez serían por lo ménos causas poderosas para atenuar el peso abrumador de esa mole de la conciencia que designamos bajo la palabra "responsabilidad."[19]

19. Antonio Argerich, *¿Inocentes o culpables?,* 32. Hereafter cited parenthetically in the text by page number.

(These eternal anomalies in the currents of thought, which for what we call conscience in their backwaters, can be observed in each "human document" and confound the analyst who, because of the chaos, is unable to determine a "mathematical point" for morals, although he might find as causes morbid states, fatal impulses of the organism, painful effects of the education received or products of dominant worries, which in any case for any judge would be at least powerful reasons to ease the heavy weight of that burden of conscience that we designate with the word *responsibility*.)

One can almost perceive a note of grim satisfaction in the description of the trajectory of destruction in *¿Inocentes o culpables?* (Innocent or guilty?, 1884) by Antonio Argerich (1855–1940). Recognized as one of the most explicit novels of its day in Argentina, *¿Inocentes o culpables?* abounds in details concerning the strains of matrimonial sex, the flotsam and jetsam of Buenos Aires's legalized brothels, the clinical details of venereal disease, and even a fragment on the virtues of contraceptives in preventing unwanted pregnancies.[20] The first Argentine novel to focus on an Italian immigrant,[21] it relates José Dagiore's modest success as the owner of a humble inn, his marriage to a social-climbing middle-class woman, and the suicide of their son when the latter falls victim to a serious case of syphilis contracted from a prostitute.

José, the son, is shown fluctuating between being an honest and sincere young man and the sort of dastard spawned by the disorderliness, blind ambition, and irresponsibility of his society. Thus, he alternates visits to the brothels with a tender engagement to a saintly young lady, and it is the thought of not being able to marry her as a consequence of his disease that drives him to take his life. The novelist is particularly taken up with this contradictory behavior:

> José, tanto en el trayecto como en lo de Amalia [the madam of a brothel], hablaba pronto de Carlota y de sentimientos dignos y elevados, y casi sin transicion, al mismo tiempo, descendia á temas licenciosos. ¿Cómo esplicar estas aberraciones? ¿Seria que la educacion y el medio, lo arrastraban, como las olas de un mar embravecido á una débil nave que hubiera perdido el timon? (216–17)

> (José, both in their walk and at Amalia's [brothel], spoke often about Carlota and about noble and elevated sentiments and, almost at the same time and without transition, while at the same time descending to licentious themes. How to explain these aberrations? Might it have been his education or the setting drawing him, like the waves of a high sea pulling at a small boat that'd lost its rudder?)

20. Lichtblau, *The Argentine Novel,* 173–74; and Guillermo Ara, *La novela naturalista hispanoamericana*, 25–26.

21. Luciano G. Russich, *El inmigrante italiano en la novela argentina del 80,* 43.

The novel is marked by rhetorical pondering of this sort and by asides that range the physical and mental constitution of individuals against the temptations of their society. Whether in the form of a hypocrisy on the part of the powerful, the quite understandable ambitions of immigrants and other occupants of the humble strata to make their way in the world, or the pressures of a disorderly society in transition, these temptations, in the narrator's far from subtly expressed opinion, exercise an inescapable fascination on the individual. Moreover, in the best tradition of the biological determinism of the day, the younger José is explained to be at the inevitable mercy of his parental legacy, particularly that of his father, who goes raving mad during the course of the novel. In this fashion, the novel unequivocably answers the disjunctive question of its title in favor of the first possibility, despite all of the conventional beliefs that sustain individuals' complete free will and, therefore, their full responsibility for their actions.

It is apparent from the text that the author had some interest in experimenting with a reform of the orthography of Spanish. Most notable are his representation of the prefix *ex-* by *es-*, his suppression of the accent on the *i* of second- and third-conjugation imperfects and on acute syllables, and his rather inexplicable use of the accent to mark penultimate stresses, but only in some cases. It should also be noted that Argerich adamantly eschews any colloquial representation of his characters' speech (except for an undoubtedly unconscious stray Argentinism here and there). Indeed, he explains in a lengthy footnote (186) that he desires the moral nature of his characters to emerge without recourse to the trappings of their actual speech. This is remarkable, since one usually associates the aggressive anticolloquialism of the Argentine novel of the period with a desire not to offend educated and cultivated readers, thereby increasing the distance between them and the world being narrated on the one hand and enhancing the privileged pact between them and the narrator on the other.

In one sense *¿Inocentes o culpables?* manifests all of the trappings of the Naturalist writing of the period, although the grimness of the narrator's tone may remind one more of Hardy than Zola, who is the principal source of the Argentine understanding of this mode of interpreting human destiny. Certainly, unlike Cambaceres and Podestá, who use Naturalism in an eccentrically innovative fashion to defend society against undesirable elements, Argerich is closer to his European models in the representation of the individual as the innocent and unknowing victim of a corrupt world. Curiously enough, Argerich's preface seems to echo the denunciations of the immigrant, whose bad blood will irremediably pollute the noble Creole stock:

> En mi obra, me opongo franca y decididamente á la inmigracion inferior europea, que reputo desastrosa para los destinos á que legítimamente puede y debe aspirar la República Argentina. . . .
>
> [P]ara mejorar los ganados, nuestros hacendados gastan sumas fabulosas trayendo tipos escogidos,—y para aumentar la poblacion argentina atraemos una inmigracion inferior. (10–11)
>
> (In my work, I am opposed frankly and decisively to inferior European immigration, which I hold to be disastrous for the destiny to which the Argentine Republic can and ought to aspire legitimately. . . .
>
> In order to improve the livestock, our ranchers spend fabulous sums to bring select breeds—and to improve the Argentine populace we attract an inferior immigration.)

Despite these resounding statements, however, *¿Inocentes o culpables?* is hardly the portrait of a society—or of representative figures of it—spoiled by an inferior immigration. The senior Dagiore certainly does exemplify these noxious elements, and his eventual madness, along with an inventory of ugly traits throughout his life, is the confirmation of his constitutional weaknesses. And it is true that the narrator attributes to the erratic and contradictory behavior of Dagiore's son the deleterious influences of his inherited blood and the inauspicious circumstances of his conception. Yet the bulk of the novel is devoted to an unremittingly Zolaesque critique of the world of moral bankruptcy in which the young José comes to unstable manhood. This moral bankruptcy is an amalgam of the blind ambition of those who seek to enhance their political power and, hence, their economic wealth (represented in the novel, significantly, by the cynical Creole governmental minister Ferreol) and the licentiousness of a social class for whom the indulging of the flesh is a part of the quest for worldly sophistication. That the "houses of tolerance" are legal institutions encouraged, patronized, and protected by the power structure only made them an integral part of the social dynamic Argerich denounces.

One of the recurring contrasts in the novel is between ideals and illusions on the one hand and harsh social realities on the other. The plight of the young generation to which Dagiore junior belongs is characterized in terms of this disjunction:

> Ellos que tenian un concepto elevado de la patria y del amor y cuyos corazones eran bien inclinados, latiendo en sus pechos, con noble espontaneidad, al primer llamado de los grandes sentimientos, ¿cómo era posible que descendiesen tanto hasta ir á revolcarse en la inmundicia?
>
> ¿Qué aberración era esta?
>
> ¡Quien les hubiese dicho que estaban al borde de un horroroso abismo—y que cada una de esas noches de equívoco placer, repercutirian tal

> vez,—formando eslabones el dolor,—hasta inocentes vástagos del futuro, degenerando al fin una familia entera! (182)

> (Those who had an elevated concept of the fatherland and of love and whose hearts were favorably inclined, beating in their breasts, with noble spontaneity, at the first call of high sentiments. How was it possible that they stoop as low as to roll in the dirt?
>
> What kind of aberration was that?
>
> Would that I could have told them that they were on the brink of a horrifying abyss, and that each one of those nights of equivocal pleasure would perhaps have repercussions, the pain forming links, unto innocent future offspring, finally bringing degeneracy to an entire family!)

Accompanied in his escapades of erotic abandonment by several scions of decent families (one of whom is the son of Ferreol, and one night they run into the latter in the distinguished gentleman's pursuit of his own pleasure), José is swept along by the circus of a provincial world striving to be sophisticated. The foregoing quotation is prelude to the opening of the latter third of the novel, which is devoted to Ferreol's rise to eminence and José's decline and death. In the best of Naturalist tradition, the narrator pursues relentlessly the traces of the former's corruption and the latter's tragic circumstance. As a consequence of the focus on Ferreol's cynicism as an index of the forces that are reputed to hold sway in Argentine society, there is little opportunity to note the circumstances of the country's unfortunate immigration policy as the cause of either society's corruption or of José's death. Both would be clearly contradictory, especially José's death, since he commits suicide out of despair over his syphilis, which he contracted having a good time as modeled by Ferreol and company, not as a consequence of his bad blood.

That is to say, José lives an irregular life that results in his death imitating, regrettably, the models provided by the patriarchs of his society; he does not die as the consequence of his father's biological legacy. Although this fact may mean that Argerich couldn't keep the thread of his own novel straight or that his preface was a bit of circumstantial opportunism (he refers to impending presidential policies that will exacerbate the negative impact of immigration in the country), it does mean that, in the final balance, *¿Inocentes o culpables?* is more meaningful as a portrait of corrupt social models than it is as an inaugural anti-immigration narrative. And, as a consequence, it is more original and, by extension, more interesting within the context of the writing of the period.

One of the dominant narrative ploys that Argerich uses to underscore the disorderliness and corruption of his society is the casting of the contrast between illusion and reality in terms of a conflict between the culture of Romanticism and the harsh social truths that he is propounding. On at least a dozen instances in the novel, characters of a wide range of social classes are shown to construct their understanding of experience along the lines of the emotional subjectivism of their Romantic reading. In the narrator's opinion, this reading blinds them to the true dimensions of human suffering, which, we understand by implication, he not uncoincidentally is propounding in the pages of his narrative. It is significant to note that the Romantic literature the narrator decries as inculcating a "false notion of love" (242) is part of the trove of reputed foreign sophistication avidly consumed by the aspiring social arbiters of Buenos Aires (see *¿Inocentes o culpables?,* 168, for some of the novels the narrator has in mind).

Since the novel deals with individuals who are hardly able to develop any line of reflective analysis of their irregular and destructive behavior (phrases like "no comprendia" echo throughout the narrative), it is no surprise to find the customary pact of the period between a superior narrator and a presumedly enlightened reader, able and willing to accept the scientifically based interpretation offered by the former. Argerich's narrator gives free reign to his grim satisfaction in contradicting the "false" self-images of his characters, images that he has a tendency to attribute to their poor reading habits; this is certainly a novel addition to the inventory of inexorable traits that lead to the demise of characters in Naturalist novels. And the fact that what they are most unconscious of is really not their biological determinism but the corrupt social dynamic propagated by some and adhered to by all is indeed a notable feature of this famously scandalous novel.

Irresponsable: Naturalism Ideologically Revised

> Nuestro prurito era hacerle hablar, hacernos contar en detalle todos los antecedentes de la muerta; preveíamos algo de romancesco en la vida de ese personaje que se nos presentaba con la faz simpática de una pobreza heroica: la comparación y el tipo están buenos para entonces, para nuestro cerebro, impregnado en aquella época de las lamentaciones elegíacas que nos inspiraban los libros de literatura sentimental que estaban en boga.[22]
>
> Su canto, sus alegrías, sus movimientos, su indiferencia, su edad, todo esto, muy propio para disimular la realidad, nos aleja, al contemplarlas, de reflexiones amargas sobre su situación y sobre su porvenir. (62)
>
> (Our concern was to make him speak, make him tell us in detail all of

22. Manuel T. Podestá, *Irresponsable: recuerdos de la Universidad; novela argentina,* 46. Hereafter cited parenthetically in the text by page number.

the antecedents of the dead woman; we foresaw something novel-like in the life of that character who appeared to us with the charming face of a heroic poverty: the comparison and the type are good then for our minds impregnated during that period with the elegiacial lamentations inspired in us by books of sentimental literature in vogue.

His song, his happiness, his movements, his indifference, his age, everything very appropriate for masking reality, kept us, as we contemplated these features, from any bitter reflection about his situation or his future.)

Irresponsable (Irresponsible, 1889), by the medical man Manuel T. Podestá (1853–1918) is undoubtedly the most eloquent example of how European Naturalism did not fare very well in the trans-Atlantic voyage to South America.[23] Ostensibly the story of the inevitable and unchecked decline and madness of the unnamed *el hombre de los imanes,* Podestá's novel raises a number of difficult questions for the fate of a Naturalistic description of Argentine culture.

To be sure, *Irresponsable* is not a very persuasive novel, and one might well be tempted to dismiss it as an example of incompetent novelizing, not in the sense of being a lamentable imitation of European novels, but for the fact that it is not very successful in awakening in the reader any enthusiasm for what it has to say. Yet perhaps in the ways in which it is unsatisfactory lies the interest of *Irresponsable* for an understanding of the novelistic construal of Argentine society among the writers of Podestá's generation.[24]

There are a number of problems that derive from the attempt to grasp the structural integrity of *Irresponsable.* Some are of considerable interest as novelistic strategies that may be attributed to Podestá's designs as a novelist, while others, although they may not be part of conscious design,

23. Juan Epple, "Eugenio Cambaceres y el naturalismo en Argentina."

24. Podestá's writing has not attracted extensive critical attention. Giusti's description of the novel is typical of the way in which it has been classified by the standard treatments on Argentine literature: "disjointed sketches of society that make up the basis of *Irresponsable,* the pathological biography of a rather phantasmagoric figure which we only know as 'the man of the magnets,' a victim more of hereditary fatality as made popular by Zola: an unbalanced and abulic romantic who dies in an insane asylum" ("La prosa de 1852 a 1900," 3:398). Ara does not question the conventional forms of Naturalism in the novel (*La novela naturalista,* 24–25). The novel is also discussed in passing by Lichtblau (*The Argentine Novel,* 178–79). Alberto Blasi Brambilla's approach, rather than to analyze either the structure or the ideology of the novel, is to examine in considerable detail all of the thematic ramifications it may provide (*Un novelista argentino del 80: Manuel T. Podestá;* see also his "El médico novelista Manuel T. Podestá" and "Manuel T. Podestá," written under the name Alberto Blasi).

are obliquely interesting as regards the ideology of Podestá's writing. First, the narrative point of view of *Irresponsable* shifts inexplicably, about a quarter of the way into the narrative, from that of a participant observer to that of an omniscient and intrusive narrator. Second, nowhere is there an attempt to explain in any convincing detail the specific psychophysical defects of the protagonist that may account for his irrational and destructive behavior—his "stain of original sin" in terms of the Naturalist's view of the influence of heredity and environment. Third, the social setting of the novel, while it may be criticized as regards the lack of taste of the nouveaux riches, is enthusiastically portrayed as the fulfillment of the promise of progress and personal ambition. Fourth, the conflict between philosophy and medicine, between idealism and materialism, although developed in considerable detail, is incapable of articulating a Naturalist vision that might engage the appropriate horror of the reader for the vortex of destruction in which the protagonist sees himself irretrievably trapped. Finally, the most productive disjunction of the novel, that between the narrator and *el hombre de los imanes,* leads away from a Naturalist vision of human society and toward a highly ideologized paean to the Argentina of material progress that the Generation of 1880 vigorously endorsed, with the consequence that the ironically Ibsenian trope "an enemy of the people" is hereby resemanticized in literal terms.

Irresponsable is marked distinctively by the superior tone of the narrator, who, in the tradition of the novel of the day and in particular of the novel that had a specific thesis to promote, intrudes in an unambiguous and irreflexive manner on the inner thoughts and motivations of the characters. Throughout, Podestá's narrator speaks with firm conviction about the traits that impel *el hombre de los imanes* on his path of destruction, and he examines ironically and often patronizingly the pitiful nature of the man:

> Era un contraste ver aquel hombre joven, educado, con la preparación suficiente para labrarse con el trabajo una posición social, con el aspecto mal disimulado de un pobre vergonzante, en medio de aquel bullicio, de aquella feria continua del lujo, de la riqueza, de la distinción, empujado, desairado, mirado con desdén y menosprecio por los que pasaban a su lado, esquivado tal vez por los que fueron sus amigos y condiscípulos, y él, impasible, mal vestido, raído, con manchas en las ropas, mezcla de ridículo y de desprecio por las conveniencias sociales, indiferente, enfermo, caído en el marasmo del abandono, suicidándose poco a poco tal vez por la anemia de un cerebro que funciona con un solo objetivo, con una sola aspiración: no hacer nada, ser inútil, caer en el fango poco a

poco como un palo roto que el mar tira a la playa en una arcada de espuma y de resaca. (64)

(It was quite a contrast to see that young man, educated and with sufficient training to achieve a social position through his efforts, with the poorly concealed appearance of a man of shameful poverty, in the middle of that crowd, that continual parade of luxury, wealth, distinction, shoved about, scorned, looked upon with disdain and belittled by those who passed his side, shunned perhaps by those who were his friends and fellow students, and he, impassive, poorly dressed, threadbare, his clothes all stained, a mixture of ridicule and scorn for social conventions, indifferent, ill, sunk in the morass of neglect, committing suicide little by little perhaps because of the anemia of a brain that functions with a single goal, with a single aspiration: not to do a thing, to be useless, to sink in the mire little by little like a broken stick that the sea casts up on the beach in a belch of foam and flotsam.)

This is an impressively long and convoluted period, and it is indicative of the limits of the narrator's attempt to explain the causes of the unnamed protagonist's decline: perhaps he suffers from a "cerebral anemia"; he is possessed by an "aboulia" that prevents him from taking charge of his own life; he is dragged along by his impulses that prevent him from attending to his personal appearance, with the result that he is the object of ridicule; his self-absorption prevents him from any critical self-examination that would, by implication, lead to the betterment of his situation.

Elsewhere, the narrator speaks of the protagonist's disastrous involvement with a fallen woman, and his alcoholism is referred to on several occasions. In addition to what appears to be a catatonic schizophrenia that impels him to wander the streets aimlessly, totally divorced from reality, at the conclusion of the novel he is possessed by a manic-depressive reaction that results in a series of violent epileptic seizures. Podestá's narrator, although a physician like Podestá himself, does not use any of these scientific terms (except for epilepsy), and since the personality disorder of *el hombre de los imanes* is presented in only the most elliptic sort of way, they are only suggestions of what the author may have had in mind.[25] Concomitantly, it is difficult to ascertain the degree to which the protagonist's problems are the result of poor self-control or whether, in the true sense of the Naturalist's view of social dynamics, they are the result of blind forces he cannot control. In one passage of the

25. Ara writes: "The protagonist of *El hombre de los imanes* was without doubt a real being observed by him [Podestá] and placed in the center of a narrative whose interest resides precisely in the exposition of a hereditary disequilibrium that ruined him, from infancy, for the active life" (*La novela naturalista,* 24).

novel alone, both attributions are made, leading to a rather confused portrait for the reader (130–31).

It is significant that the protagonist of the novel remains nameless throughout. He is marked by the distinguishing characteristic of being obsessed by magnets; hence, his name as a metonym of the monomania that is referred to as accounting in part for his divorce from his social reality. Nevertheless, it is apparent that Podestá's novel conceives of the protagonist as a cipher for a range of social types who, although possessed by destructive psychoses, are immaterial as identifiable or personalized human individuals. As opposed to individuals who inhabit the real, material world, concerned with science and medicine, with the study of nature and an open-eyed scrutiny of reality, individuals like *el hombre de los imanes* are driven by philosophical ideas, by literary clichés, by vague and impractical dreams that, while alienating them from everyday reality, impel them along their path of self-destruction:

> Esa fantasía [de la vida política] tenía para él un atractivo irresistible, se sentía arrastrado a lo heroico, y hubiera pagado con un año de su vida, a falta de otra cosa, por tener ocasión de poner a prueba su decisión y su valor. (174)

> (That fantasy [of political life] held for him an irresistible attraction, and he felt himself drawn to the heroic, willing to pay with a year of his life if he had nothing else to offer the chance to put his decisiveness and his courage to the test.)

It is the determination to plunge himself into a romantic or idealized conception of political activity that leads to the epileptic fit of the protagonist, with the result that at the end of the novel he has been confined to an insane asylum as hopelessly lost to life in the real world.

The operative word in Podestá's exposition of the plight of *el hombre de los imanes* is *contraste.* Throughout, the protagonist is compared to and contrasted with, unremittingly unfavorably, the well-adjusted individuals who are productive members of society. One of the key scenes in the novel has the protagonist, after steeping himself in the reading of Zola, no less, deep in thought seated on a park bench. Around him move the cheerful denizens of a society committed to progress and well-being, newly arrived immigrants applied to the task of forging their personal and collective success in a world of limitless possibilities:

> Era una especie de marcha triunfal a las doce del día bajo los rayos del sol ardiente; parecía una ovación a este pedazo de la América, cuya fama corre hasta golpear las puertas de las aldeas más remotas, en busca de brazos vigorosos con la insignia de las mies y del arado. (94)

> (It was a sort of triumphal march at midday beneath the rays of the

burning sun; it seemed like an ovation for this piece of America, whose fame reached out to knock on the doors of the farthest villages in search of vigorous arms with the insignia of shafts of wheat and the plow.)[26]

Framed in these terms, it is of little consequence whether the protagonist is the victim of his own weak personality or an exponent of a truly Naturalist social dynamic of which he is essentially unaware and over which he can exert much less control. The fuzziness of Podestá's details in this regard is symptomatic of the main point: that *el hombre de los imanes* is the Other, the distorting mirror of a society brimming with enthusiastic self-confidence in the course of its social and economic progress. In the concluding sections of the novel, the narrator zeros in on the margination of the protagonist from this world, and the latter's fits of epilepsy confirm his status as an object of morbid fascination and repudiation by a society whose balanced order he belies in the degree of degradation of his unkempt and mentally diseased person (see especially pages 179, 199, and 219 in *Irresponsable*).

Irresponsable is a novel that cannot withstand a careful reading—either in terms of its adherence to the principles of European Naturalism or, more significantly, in terms of well-crafted narrative discourse. It is a significant work within the context of the Argentine Generation of 1880, however, to the extent that it reveals a coherent ideological posture. Far from being the scathing denunciation of a social dynamic that results in the inevitable destruction of marginal social types, as in the works of the paragons of Naturalism, Podestá's novel chooses instead to postulate a disjunctive image of a well-functioning and progressive society that is *threatened* by the negative and destructive example given by a dreamer like *el hombre de los imanes.* Condemned by his dreams and his inability (for whatever reason) to abide by the productive norms of his society, there can be no fate for him but to separate—exile—himself more and more from that society. As he himself realizes, in the narrator's postulation of this categorical disjunction, while the immigrant hordes will be successful in their determination to succeed in America, "—Yo estaré allí—dijo,—y extendió su brazo en dirección al cementerio" ("I will be there," he said, and he extended his arm in the direction of the cemetery; 96). In its overall coherence of meaning, *Irresponsable* may not be an encouraging example of Latin American Naturalism, but it is a singularly, if consciously, eloquent example of an ideologically determined vision of social margination.[27]

26. Compare chapter 9 of Blasi Brambilia, *Un novelista argentino del 80*.

27. Although Naturalism is not discussed, Angel Rama provides a fundamental essay on the problems of the imitation of European literary models in Latin America in *Transculturación narrativa en América latina*.

CHAPTER 4

The Failure of Control

The Limits of Power and Knowledge

It is not necessary to attribute to the cultural consciousness of the Generation of 1880 an overweening confidence in the ability to master nature and control society to admit the inevitability of texts that take exception to the confidence invested in power and knowledge. On the one hand, Naturalism permitted a scrutiny of the biological status of men and women and a metaphorical construal of society as a biological organism that could be studied and controlled. On the other hand, Naturalism in its many and often contradictory guises served to identify the multiple areas of nature that human knowledge had not yet been able to dominate.

Eduardo Wilde, as a physician and medical researcher, must have experienced both the promise of science to ameliorate suffering and the despair that can follow the realization that so much still lay beyond the mastery of science. The image of the doctor as a redeemer from physical suffering is countered by the representation of the failure of medicine in his famous story "Tini," in which a rhetoric of sentimentality and anguished expression highlights a subjective emotion upon contemplating the objective limits of science.

Wilde was one of the most prolific writers of the Generation of 1880, and it may seem unfortunate to reduce his contributions to the one short story examined here, no matter how frequently anthologized it may be. Through an evocation of the intensely emotional setting of physical suffering, "Tini" provides important clues as to how narrators and their audiences at that time viewed pain and death within the context of scientific possibilities and how they explained their feelings in the face of the failure of medical science. Since medical science was establishing itself in Argentina as one of the major accomplishments of the society brought about by the Generation of 1880, "Tini" cannot help but be viewed as a significant narrative in Wilde's vast oeuvre.

An identical medically incurable sickness, also visited upon an innocent child, is the basis of the narrative action of Eugenio Cambaceres's

Sin rumbo (Aimless), although that novel explores the broader issue of a typical Generation of 1880 clubman whose nonchalant confidence in the control he exercises on his world is undermined by his daughter's fatal illness. If Andrés is a paragon of the carefree good life permitted by Argentina's Golden Age, his destruction reveals the uncontrollable forces of nature that the facade of cheery hedonism of his privileged existence cannot, ultimately, contain.

In a sense, these narratives are correctives to the general spirit of optimism projected by the dominant ideology of the period. Where they differ from those optimistic narratives that highlight the social tensions produced by the policies and practices of the Generation of 1880 is in the identification of areas in which the goal of control through power and knowledge is undermined by the accidents of nature.

Seeing versus Doing: The Limitations of Verbal Representation and the Failure of Medicine in Eduardo Wilde's "Tini"

One of the truly remarkable aspects of late nineteenth-century culture in Buenos Aires is the growth of the medical arts and the incorporation of a wide array of medical theory, technology, and practice as provided by European professionals, who were themselves achieving quantum jumps in the advance of the scientific treatment of the ills of the human body.[1] Medicine addressed itself almost exclusively to remedying sickness, the definitions of which were expanding with the solidification of psychiatry and the incorporation within the mainstream of medicine of physical miseries not previously treated by a professionalized medicine.

Moreover, the social radius of treatment by medicine continued to reach out, as the services of medicine became available to ever larger spheres of the population. Indeed, some areas of medical treatment developed specifically for the treatment of classes or groups previously ignored by medicine, such as the diseases associated with marginated groups like prostitutes, the criminally insane, and the malnourished, mistreated, and exploited. Although their ailments (venereal diseases, drunkenness, tuberculosis, accidents in the workplace, industrial contamination, psychotic madness) were not restricted only to the masses, the social imperative to manage society at large as those masses flooded

1. "Medicine in Buenos Aires between 1880 and 1925 assimilates all of the techniques of leading countries. In the area of surgery anesthesia and asepsis are employed, and the laboratory becomes a part of diagnosis" (Argentino J. Landaburu, "La medicina en la capital federal de 1800 a 1925," 140).

into metropolitan areas to meet the needs of expanding industrialization translated into a wide role for medicine and related sciences.

Already by the latter half of the century, Buenos Aires had become a leading South American medical center in the training of medical personnel, in the establishment of a full spectrum of clinics, hospitals, and asylums, and in the importation of instruments, treatises, and specialists to enhance a level of training and practice that could hardly be surpassed anywhere else on the continent. This expansion of medicine, perhaps more than any other feature of nineteenth-century culture, attests so eloquently to the disparity between Buenos Aires and the rest of the country, where, with some spotty exceptions, medical services remained quite primitive by comparison to the brilliant display offered by the capital. Determined to provide themselves with state-of-the-art medical care and to use medicine as a powerful instrument in the elaboration of a modern society, the leaders of the period clearly recognized such advances in medicine, at least in Buenos Aires, as of paramount social and political importance. This fact was underscored by legislative and executive attention to medicine and related issues of health.

The medicine of the late nineteenth century was essentially curative, with prevention being an issue only in so far as it related to large-scale social projects such as the treatment of the breeding grounds of insects and the construction of sanitary works. The ethos of the profession, therefore, involved the confrontation between the significantly ill (that is, those sick enough to turn to a practice still quite expensive and still quite painful in its applications) and the complex knowledge, still often of a experimental nature, of the medical practitioner.

Eduardo Wilde (1844–1913) was one of the most outstanding of these practitioners. Having completed his course of studies brilliantly at the Universidad de Buenos Aires, Wilde distinguished himself for his selfless treatment of the victims of yellow fever during the terrible outbreak of that disease in Buenos Aires in the early 1870s. That epidemic changed radically the demographics of the city by inducing a mass migration of those with means from the decaying older south side to the expansive, newer residential areas of the northern edge bordering the Río de la Plata. Wilde's generosity and skill in dealing with the infirm of all social classes earned him considerable recognition, which embarked him on a public career that paralleled his devotion to science. He gained enormous prominence as a legislator, cabinet minister and presidential advisor, and diplomat. Wilde probably spent more time abroad than any of the other major figures of his generation, and his intellectual and literary production (his complete works fill nineteen volumes) attests to a very rich creative life.[2]

Among this diverse output, one of Wilde's texts that has achieved the status of a classic of Argentine literature is the short story "Tini." Originally published on the first page, and in the first six columns, of the inaugural issue of the Buenos Aires newspaper *El Diario* (September 19, 1881), "Tini" was later included in Wilde's 1889 collection of stories and sketches, *Prometeo y Cía.* Like any of the many texts written by doctors in South America, the United States, or Europe during this period, "Tini" is most immediately a documentary account of a fatal illness. The narrator speaks from the vantage point of a medical man, whether or not he is identified as a doctor (in this case, he is not, although he may as well be, since he speaks with the same idiom as does the doctor in the story), and one of the cultural functions of such texts was to provide the general reader with fictionalized information about the diseases medicine was engaged in treating.

"Medical narratives" popularized the details of medicine and provided a "human" setting for illness through the representation of characters and real-life interpersonal dramas associated with sickness and disease. By doing so, they may have served both to attenuate the anxiety of the general populace over the rapid growth of medicine and all of its discoveries in the form of treatment and illnesses to be treated and to monumentalize—and at times virtually to canonize—the person of the medical man. This circumstance accounts for the transition between the premodern image of the doctor as brutally satirized by Spain's Francisco de Quevedo or Peru's Juan del Valle y Caviedes and the later reverence for the doctor as a saintly father figure—at least until relatively recent desacralizations of the paternalistic physician.

Yet "Tini" is not, in fact, about the success of medical science. On the contrary, it deals, really quite sentimentally, with the pathetic conse-

2. The degree to which Wilde may be considered (like Mansilla) a key figure of the Generation of 1880 in his professional career, activities in politics, and intellectual and literary writings, is highlighted by Enrique Díaz Araujo, *Eduardo Wilde, el ideólogo argentino de ochenta;* and Enrique Pezzoni, "Eduardo Wilde: lo natural como distancia." The question is whether Wilde may properly be called an ideologue, in the absence of an explicitly formulated programmatic ideology. Nevertheless, a clearly defined ideology of intellectual and sociopolitical activism does emerge from the crowded agenda of his life. An excellent primer on Wilde and his multifaceted writing is provided by Guillermo Ara's "Introducción" to *Aguas abajo,* and an intellectual profile is provided by Belisario J. Montero, "La filosofía de Eduardo Wilde."

quences of a failure of treatment. *Crup,* English croup, was one of the most feared diseases of the pre-antibiotics era. It is defined by *Webster's Third International* as "a spasmodic laryngitis in infants and children characterized by episodes of difficult breathing and hoarse metallic cough that occur esp[ecially] at night and may be relieved by steam inhalations." What made croup particularly frightful was how it affected only small children, at a time when childhood had been ideologized as a time of innocence and extreme protective dependence: it usually led to fatal complications, and remedies available for its treatment were both few and imperfect. Moreover, one of the principal forms of treatment, at a time when anesthesia was still primitive, involved a painful tracheotomy and the insertion of a tube in order to overcome the swelling of the breathing passages, which became coated with a clogging membrane. When the eponymous protagonist of "Tini" is operated on in this fashion, the narrator describes him as a "mártir" (martyr) whose "débil cuerpecito se extendió de nuevo sobre su lecho de tortura" (small, weak body again stretched itself out on its bed of torture).[3]

Croup, therefore, may be considered a terrible symbol for the physical suffering visited by nature on young innocents, especially when viewed within the cultural context of both the preoccupation with curing of human suffering through medicine and the quite highly sentimentalized concern with the special privilege accorded to the newly discovered concept of childhood, given first a biological validity and then a social defense. As with other childhood diseases, the cultural "discovery" of croup, along with its inscription into the literature of Realism and Naturalism, is a sign both of the attention to the details of the biological cycle of human life and of the recognition of the handling of this cycle by medical science and technology. But, more specifically, croup is a sign of the abiding limitations of medicine, since all of the superior knowledge of the doctor, viewed as the repository of the specialized scientific knowledge known as medicine as well as the sort of highly trained individual who served the social elite of Buenos Aires, is useless in arresting the fatal course of Tini's affliction. Indeed, the doctor only serves to make him suffer more by subjecting him to the brutality of the futile tracheotomy, which may be viewed from the point of view of today's nonintrusive medicine as a form of physical rape, involving as it does the violent puncture or penetration of the boy's body by the breathing tube.

Wilde inaugurates his story by a far from subtle foreshadowing that

3. Eduardo Wilde, "Tini," p. 26. Hereafter cited parenthetically in the text by page number.

focuses the reader's attention on the chances for physical health as a question of the vagaries of nature rather than the benevolence of an almighty deity:

> —¡Será un famoso guardia nacional si la naturaleza lo permite!
> —Si Dios quiere, diga, doctor—objetó la dama.
> —Bien, si Dios quiere; en materia de creencias, tengo las de mis enfermas distinguidas.
> El doctor se retiró, y la madre del niño se quedó reflexionando en el correctivo puesto por su médico al augurio relativo al recién nacido. (18)

> ("He will be a famous National Guardsman, Nature permitting!"
> "You mean, God willing, doctor," the lady objected.
> "Fine, if God wills it. In matters of belief, I hold those of my distinguished female patients."
> The doctor withdrew, and the child's mother was left reflecting on the corrective given by the doctor to her hopes relative to the newborn.)

As a successful society doctor, Tini's medical guardian may parry suavely the religious formula of his wealthy client, but both she and the reader are sensitive to the fundamental disjunction between the strength of the newborn as a consequence of divine intervention or as a matter of the mysteries of physical nature. As a voyeur of physical nature and its manifestations in the legions of patients whose bodily narratives doctors had begun by the nineteenth century to record in detail (the Spanish for medical record is *historia clínica*), the practicing physician in his dual function as medical researcher was engaged in "reading" the human body and its miseries as part of the larger project of scientific knowledge and the use of the knowledge for the purpose of acting directly on material nature. In the case of medicine, this meant, of course, the prolonging of human life by remedying debilitating and incapacitating illness, as much as it also meant the direct manipulation of the body (with "mind" assimilated to the body as a constellation of physical manifestations) for the good of the dominant social practices.

If the ideologizing of childhood was part of a productive social economy, the imperative to safeguard childhood and to reduce suffering both to protect children and to suit them to systematized education (the slogan that the healthier children are, the better students they are) acquires considerable urgency for medicine. The physician of Wilde's story demonstrates his understanding of this relationship by linking Tini's prophesied career as a "famoso guardia nacional" with overcoming the odds of nature and, when the child does fall sick, by applying to his patient what procedures, no matter how desperate, he has at his disposal. His feelings of devastation at his failure to save Tini are profoundly human and presumably sincere. But it is also just as much a recognition at having been defeated by nature in the attempt to discharge his professional and social responsibilities to protect the child from, first, suffering (Tini's lethargy and his abandonment of his toys—learning, socializing instruments—are underscored) and, inevitably in the case of croup, death:

> Los médicos entraban, observaban, conversaban, ordenaban y salían silenciosos.
>
> Sólo uno, el de la casa, se quedaba más tiempo junto a la cama de Tini. Si jovialidad había desaparecido, su ciencia había medido el abismo y su corazón de hombre se impresiona ante aquella desolación inevitable.
>
> —¡Doctor, mi hijo se muere!—le decía la madre de Tini—. "Se muere", repercutía como un eco en el pecho del médico, pero sus labios no proferían una palabra. (30)

> (The doctors came in, observed, conversed, gave orders, and left silently.
>
> Only one, the family doctor, remained longer at the side of Tini's bed. If his joviality had disappeared, his science had taken the measure of the abyss, and his man's heart is overwhelmed in the face of that inevitable desolation.
>
> "Doctor, my son is dying!" Tini's mother told me. "He's dying" resounded like an echo in the breast of the doctor, but his lips had nothing to offer.)

Despite the ability to pay for the best medical attention available (and note the introduction of a phalanx of secondary physicians), Tini's parents are forced to face the truth of the doctor's foreshadowing of possible preadult mortality. Concomitantly, their sophisticated physician is obliged to accept yet one more incident of the limitations of his science, one more failure to decipher the text of horrible physical suffering in order to change its course.

Wilde cannot be said to stint in the marshaling of the sentimentality of the period surrounding the sacred trust of adults toward children, and the doctor's failure is a violation, no matter how unintentional and no matter how valiantly he struggles not to fail, of that trust. The clincher is the depiction of Tini's suffering and his separation, as part of the intuitive realization that he is going to die, from the world, the parents, the doctor pledged to protect him:

> Tini hizo un esfuerzo supremo para incorporarse: no pudo. Abrió sus grandes ojos, miró fijamente la luz de la lámpara, estiró los brazos hacia su mamá y los dejó caer de nuevo; la cánula dió su último ronquido y ... (31)

(Tini made a supreme effort to sit up, but he could not. He opened his large eyes, looked hard at the lamplight, stretched his arms out toward his mother, and let them fall again. The tube gave its last hoarse gasp and ...)

By sharing with the reader both the failure of the mother, whom the child cannot reach with his outstretched, weakened little arms, and the failure of the physician, whose *canícula* only serves to amplify the death rattle rather than to ward off death, Wilde's narrator appeals to the belief in the special privileges of childhood and the conviction that medicine must prevail to prevent pain from afflicting the innocents.

"Tini" is drenched with the sentimentality that flows from highlighting this unified failure, and the elements of pathetic fallacy that intersperse the final pages of the story are efficient rhetorical reinforcers of the dominant mood achieved by the narrator.[4] The narrator, in turn, individuates himself by alluding to his own grief over Tini's story and his inability ever to see a small, blond, curly-headed boy again without experiencing a renewed sense of that grief (32). Although contemporary readers may deride the steady trooping of such interlocking details of sentimentality, those details function to confirm the ideologizing of childhood and its often uncertain health aspects as an important part of the cultural context of the story. Moreover, in Wilde's "Tini" this dense sentimentality highlights unmistakably for the reader the extent of the contradiction of medical knowledge still provided by the facts of physical nature, despite society's monumentalization of the physician. Or, put differently, the story is built around the irresolvable tension between a sentimentalized image of the child and the inadequacies of medicine to sustain that image untouched by the realities of the bodily sickness:

¡Y qué bueno es vivir en un pueblo donde hay carruajes de todas clases y de todos precios; empresarios de diligencias, de ómnibus y de coches fúnebres; de coches fúnebres, sobre todo: para casados, para solteros, para viejos y para niños! (31)

(And how fine it is to live in a society where there are all kinds of carriages for every price; entrepreneurs of coaches, busses, funereal hearses: for married couples, for single men, and for children!)

Thus, medicine is unable to render obsolete the trade in children's coffins and hearses to carry them. As much as Wilde implies the con-

4. "Tini" is one of Wilde's texts that are discussed as exemplars of Modernismo by María Hortensia Lacau and Mabel Manacorda de Rosetti, "Eduardo Wilde y el modernismo." This identification is especially valid with reference to Wilde's approach to the representation of emotional states in the story, related to the "globalizing sentimentality" of the story.

tinued power of physical nature to frustrate our hopes for a long and painless existence, the story speaks, with all of the easy eloquence of its sentimentality, to the limitations of medicine as perceived by a man of science. Wilde's doctor may "correct" Tini's mother by suggesting that it is more a question of the designs of fickle nature than of divine providence whether the baby lives a healthy life, but Wilde's story also serves to "correct" the reader's uncritical belief in the miraculous efficacy of modern medicine. The story alludes to the grief of Tini's parents, but it focuses on the despair of both the physician and his narrator, a thinly transparent mask of Wilde the physician turned raconteur.

It is for this reason that the second major rhetorical aspect of Wilde's story may be viewed as an important correlative of a tale of failed medical art. Along with what we today may easily recognize as the stock rhetorical devices that confirm a sentimentalized view of human life, we may identify in "Tini" the less formulaic appeal to narrative inadequacy. If the story deals with the inadequacies of science, Wilde's narrator pursues his story while underscoring the inability of his narrative art to do full justice to what he wishes to relate.[5] The topos "words fail me" is, to be sure, a venerable formula of universal literature, and it is meant as much to allay any defects in the narration as it is to draw our attention to the relentless succession of deftly chosen words in the service of that narration. Such apologies are often nothing more than cleverly disingenuous appeals for the audience's applause for the success of the narrative, although on occasion they may attain a metanarrative function that attests to the breakdown of the pretensions of the narrative act, as in the case of incompetent or failed narrators in modern works like Augusto Roa Bastos's *Yo el Supremo* or José Donoso's *El obsceno pájaro de la noche.*

In the case of Wilde's story, the recourse to the topos of inadequate narration is metanarrative less because it may underscore a failure of fiction as knowledge through art than because it reinforces the limitations of knowledge as represented by medical science:

> Si hubiera palabras en algún idioma para describir el momento en que la madre de Tini volvió a ver a su hijo operado, yo intentaría bosquejar la escena. . . .

5. Wilde's many skeptical comments about literature and his own writing are discussed by Sylvia Molloy: "Wilde's texts, by their very construction, are the faithful reflection of the uncertainty that obsessed him" ("Lectura de Eduardo Wilde," 347). However, Wilde's reservations about the inadequacies of expression are no reason to echo comments by critics that there is no originality in his work; compare Juan Pablo Echagüe, "Eduardo Wilde."

Pero no hay tales palabras. La naturaleza ha puesto la expresión de los inmensos dolores fuera del alcance del lenguaje articulado, entregándosela a la música y a la pintura. Para sentir no basta entender, es necesario oír y ver. (26)

(If some language had words to describe the moment in which Tini's mother saw her son operated on again, I would attempt to sketch the scene. . . .

But there are no such words. Nature has placed the expression of immense suffering beyond the reach of spoken language, assigning it to music and painting. It is not enough to understand in order to feel; it is necessary to hear and see.)[6]

This passage contains the key expression of the rhetorical figure of the impossibility of expression. The *adynaton* (*impossibilia* in Latin) articulates the narrator's frustration in the face of capturing the emotional intensity of Tini's suffering and his mother's agitation in the face of that suffering. It serves, of course, to heighten the sentimental impact at this point in the narration, and it follows directly upon the description of the child's "torture" in the form of the tracheotomy at the hands of the doctor. There is earlier implied adynaton that comes at the beginning of the exposition of the first symptoms of Tini's illness, when the narrator states that, were he a painter, he would be able to portray the anxiety of human suffering in the form of a mother observing the sleep of her sick child (22).

The impossibility of putting into words the succession of feelings involved here—the mother's, the doctor's, the narrator's, and, in the first instance, Tini's—is counterbalanced by the superiority of an understanding predicated on seeing and hearing. That is, direct observation, whether in the course of daily life or in the exercise of scientific discovery, is preferable to the meager resources of the written word. One thing

6. The approximation between scientific and literary observation is underscored, with Wilde's typical humoristic irony, in the following aside from his famous essay on the distinguished Argentine medical man Ignacio Pirovano; the narrator is Wilde himself, in his identity as a physician: "Thus I, with that universal talent that characterizes me, took out my notebook and noted that prudent and scientific observation, so like many made by some of my colleagues and not a few augurers" ("Ignacio Pirovano," 66). One of the most commented upon aspects of Wilde's writing is his complex humorism, which is studied by Vergara de Bietti, *Humoristas del ochenta,* 19–38). Angela B. Dellepiane, "Eduardo Wilde y su 'gramática cerebral,' " probes in greater depth this aspect of Wilde's writing and his use of semantic paradoxes and various other rhetorical figures of irony, particularly with reference to his stand against social hypocrisy. She also surveys in detail the many comments on Wilde's humor and conflicting opinions as regards the unity of his creative writing.

this must mean is that experimental observation such as practiced by science, including medicine, is more effective than knowledge through literature. But what it also signifies, aside from the contest between art and science, is the notion that we are engaged in a process of "seeing" how things are. This may be our seeing through literature, or it may be the specialized forms of discovery promoted by the professionalized sciences of the late nineteenth century, or it may be the heightened perception of human experience promoted by knowledge whether gleaned through literature or science.

Wilde is, after all, promoting through the medium of fiction the notion of contemplating with understanding the pathos of the human circumstance, and, as we have seen, his story depicts very frankly the limitations of medical science in seeing, reading, and understanding the physical materiality of the body and its infirmities. A significant aspect of this gesture of contemplation is Tini's own self-observation in his suffering, which he is, of course, unable to understand (29). And, reinforcing the globalizing sentimentality of the narrator's depiction of the suffering to be seen, there is recourse to the pathetic fallacy of the lamppost, "que había mirado con su ojo amarillo durante toda la noche a través de las persianas el doliente cuadro" (which had contemplated with its yellow eye the painful picture throughout the entire night through the blinds; 29).

In view of the need to sentimentalize his narrative in order to intensify our grasp of the gap that still separates the full extent of human illnesses from what the doctor is able to do about them, the expression of adynaton and the insistent appeals to predicates like *ver, mirar,* and *observar* as related to patient, family, attendants, physician, and even inanimate nature underscore the narrator's frustration over the limitations of verbal expression as correlative with the limitations of scientific knowledge.

On the one hand there exists the need to know and the possibility of knowing through the process of scrutiny, and scientific observation is only a specialized form of scrutiny. Yet the representation of that scrutiny by both literature and medical practice is severely limited. Wilde's narrator effectively reinforces the controlling thesis of his story regarding the pathetic failures of a science whose efficacy society tends to overrate and, perhaps, to mythify. Hence the narrator makes a surprisingly contemporary accusation against the physician by implying that his procedures were "sosteniendo *artificialmente* una existencia que se extinguía" (artificially sustaining an existence that was fading; 31, emphasis added).

The Function of Suicide in Eugenio Cambaceres's *Sin rumbo*

¿Era un triste presagio lo que así lo conmovía, una de esas intuiciones misteriosas, la voz del corazón que no engaña, anunciándole alguna desgracia, alguna horrible desgracia? Pero ... ¿qué ... qué le podía suceder a él ... qué motivos tenía para alarmarse, para recelar del porvenir? ¿No vivía feliz, rico, a cubierto de la miseria por lo menos, tranquilo y contento al lado de su hija, gozando al verla crecer sana, fuerte, linda, ufano de sus encantos, soberbio, orgulloso de decirse padre de aquel ángel? ¡Sí, cierto ... era cierto todo eso ... pero ... podía dejar de serlo! ...[7]

(Was it a sad omen that moved him in that fashion, one of those mysterious intuitions, the voice of the heart that does not deceive, announcing to him some misfortune, some horrible misfortune? But ... What could happen to him? What reasons could he have to be alarmed, to distrust the future? ... Wasn't his life happy, he wealthy, protected from poverty at least, calm and content at his daughter's side, taking pleasure in seeing her grow up healthy, strong, attractive, proud of her charms and grand and proud of calling himself the father of that angel?)

It is widely maintained that within the novels of Eugenio Cambaceres (1843–1888) European Naturalism established a solid foothold in Argentina.[8] Certainly, the last two of Cambaceres's four novels, all written late in his life, manifest clearly the influence of this view of society and personal experience. *En la sangre* (In the blood; 1887) is almost a textbook example of the representation of the triumph of nature over culture, in this case the inevitable sway of poor genes at the expense of the attempts of an Italian immigrant to succeed in middle-class Argentine society. Customarily viewed as one of the prime examples of the use of Naturalism in the debate over the appropriateness of the official policy of attracting large numbers of immigrants to Argentina, most of whom could be said to have represented the outcast and marginal elements of European society, *En la sangre,* Cambaceres's last novel, was influential in arguing against the putative advantages of this policy.

Cambaceres sustained that, as a consequence of biological determinism, the "defective genes" of peasant immigrants would always prevail in leading them to corrupt or antisocial behavior, no matter what oppor tunities for integration into polite society were open to them in Argen-

7. Eugenio Cambaceres, *Sin rumbo,* 160–61. Hereafter cited parenthetically in the text by page number.

8. Ara, *La novela naturalista hispanoamericana,* 20–23; and Lichtblau, *The Argentine Novel,* 164–73.

tina. As a consequence, these elements could only serve to undermine the young health of the New World. What is striking about this ideological framework is the evident fact that Naturalism was being used not to criticize a status quo that led, with the implacable logic of a social and biological dynamic, to the degradation of unfortunate men and women, but to defend the status quo against elements, either native or foreign, that would threaten it.[9] It is on this basis that Naturalism in Argentina has been recognized as a cultural program that more often than not contributed to the cause of social control by a governing elite than to efforts at reform by an aroused minority. There is no need to dismiss *En la sangre* as an example of the willful misreading of the interests of Zola and other European Naturalists. Rather, the novel, which as fiction is hardly an example of a complex or subtle narrative effort, takes on an added dimension. Whereas it does not lend itself to any significant conclusions as regards the structural details of late nineteenth-century fiction, it assumes a new and curious dimension as a major example of the cultural ideology of a sort of "inverted" Argentine Naturalism.[10]

This circumstance is even more obvious in the case of Cambaceres's earlier novel, *Sin rumbo* (1885), the story of the decline and suicide of a wealthy landowning gentleman, a paragon of the elegant, clubman gentry that, by the Generation of 1880, moved easily between their prosperous ranches and farms, the café society of Buenos Aires, and the glittering capitals of their European models.[11] Andrés, in the best tradition of the fabled *droit du seigneur,* rapes the daughter of one of his ranch hands and enjoys an ennui-filled liaison with an Italian prima donna in Buenos Aires when evading the reality of having left the country girl pregnant. Bored by the demands of the operatic virago, as he is by most of the details of his comfortable life, Andrés decides to return to his ranch, suddenly enthralled by the idea of being a father. He learns that he is the father of a daughter, the mother having died in childbirth, and

9. Epple, "Eugenio Cambaceres."

10. Ara takes note of the apparent contradictions of Cambaceres's version of Naturalism: "In sum, in *Sin rumbo* Cambaceres approaches the experimental mode with a very sure instinct, although his determinism may at times look more like romantic 'adversity' than the fatality with which mechanical forces and biological inheritance work" (*La novela naturalista,* 23).

11. The authors of *El 80* insist on viewing Andrés as a figure of Cambaceres: "*Sin rumbo* is a novel with a closed structure in which suicide to a certain degree signals the disappearance of Cambaceres the person, who sacrifices himself on the altar of his group" (2:48). This observation is valuable in recognizing Cambaceres's identity with Andrés as exponent of a specific sector of Argentine society in the 1880s.

he devotes himself obsessively to raising the child. However, the little girl comes down with the croup and dies. As his farm buildings go up in flames, Andrés literally disembowels himself in easily the most melodramatic climax of an Argentine novel from the period, one certainly worthy of Esteban Echeverría's recently discovered "El matadero" (published in 1871, but probably written in the late 1830s) or Eduardo Gutiérrez's *folletines* on criminals and the Rosas era. Needless to say, this finale was widely criticized at the time, less because it portrayed a new example of physical violence to the Argentine reader (popular anecdotes regarding the activities of Rosas's Mazorca thugs offered even more gruesome tales of mutilation and death), but precisely because the post-Rosas social ethos pretended to offer a more ennobling view of human practices.[12]

It is in this detail of reader distaste that a fundamental ambivalence of Cambaceres's novel lies. If *En la sangre* provides support for the closed definitions maintained by the governing elite in the name of a vigorous and progressive material society, Cambaceres's less than flattering portrayal of the values of idle gentlemen in his first two novels, *Potpourri: silbidos de un vago* (1882) and *Música sentimental: silbidos de un vago* (1884), assumes conclusively pessimistic dimensions in *Sin rumbo*.[13] A cynical dandy has replaced the *vago* of the earlier novels. And it should be noted that it was unusual for Cambaceres to characterize in this fashion a member of the leisured class, since the term *vago* was usually used to characterize dismissively low-life vagrants like the figures of Fray

12. Giaconda Marún, in "Relectura de *Sin rumbo:* floración de la novela moderna," stresses Andrés as an example of modern nihilism and as the harbinger of the modern novel in Argentina dealing with the crisis of the modern man within capitalist society. Although I believe she overstresses this reading of Andrés at the expense of the latter third of the novel, I am in total agreement with her that seeing *Sin rumbo* as merely a rehashing of Naturalist hypotheses impoverishes it (p. 392). Although Marún and I are thus basically in agreement in not seeing *Sin rumbo* as an example of Zolaesque Naturalism, her reading of the novel looks toward the nihilistic vein of contemporary fiction, while my own is concerned with the interplay between Andrés's initial nihilism but subsequent euphoric optimism in the context of the social euphoria of the Generation of 1880. Epple has also taken exception to the practice of reading Cambaceres's works in terms of canonical European Naturalism, and he sees Andrés's crisis as that of a society undergoing a radical transformation: "Andrés's interior, 'existential' crisis is projected thus as the crisis of the dominant class in a period of transition when the old principles have lost their guiding efficacy and the new scale of values has not yet emerged clearly" ("Eugenio Cambaceres," 43). Epple's final conclusion is very close to my own, with the difference that the latter is demonstrated via a more specific examination of the plot structure of the text (p. 46).

13. Jitrik, "Cambaceres: adentro y afuera."

Mocho's stories. Moreover, the cynicism of Andrés, the paradigm of the landowning oligarchy, yields only to an obsessive monomania, the cherishing of his daughter at the expense of all else, and his self-destruction when he discovers that he cannot protect her from the laws of nature.

One might well argue that the sort of personal history represented by *Sin rumbo* has greater affinities with the novels of Thomas Hardy than with those of Émile Zola. This observation has less to do with the absence of Zola's emphasis on describing a degrading society in order to legitimize various forms of social reform than it has to do with echoes of Hardy's insistence on the implacable destruction of any and all forms of human aspiration as the result of natural forces inimical to the individual's enjoyment of existence. Hardy was basically concerned with a generalized hypocrisy of the genteel spokespersons of society that blinded them to the misery of the human lot. More specifically, his works demonstrate the inevitable tragedy arising from the conflict between noble ideals and overwhelming facts of life that had little to do with such ideals. Rather than a reformer, Hardy was simply a grim observer of the laws of nature that a character like Cambaceres's Andrés must inevitably confront. Moreover, like the Cambaceres of *Sin rumbo,* Hardy provided a masterful characterization of the decidedly nonromantic texture of rural life.

The purpose in referring to Hardy's writings is not to argue that, at least in the case of *Sin rumbo,* Cambaceres chose as his model for Naturalism the Englishman rather than Zola, with whom he is almost universally identified. It is doubtful that Hardy's works could have had any impact on Latin American writing at this early date, and, if they did, a decisive demonstration of influence would hardly help to make the novel any more important than is already recognized. True, in view of the possibility that Cambaceres and others restructured the priorities of Zolaesque Naturalism as part of their response to the conditions of Argentine cultural needs, it could be interesting to note that any adherence to the Hardy model was a more faithful reading of his view of the individual's fortunes in a hostile universe than it was of Zola's.

The major reason for thinking about other possible examples of Naturalism for *Sin rumbo* is the substantial question, once any adherence to the model of Zola can be set aside, as to what, precisely, is the problem of biological determinism at issue in Cambaceres's novel. What need for knowledge on the part of its readers is it answering on the basis of the principles, however understood, of Naturalism? And how does that knowledge and its need tabulate with the ideological forces at play within the cultural and literary horizons of the author and his readers?

Biological determinism does serve as an explicit if only parenthetical concern of Andrés and his narrator in chapter 34 (in a typical discourse mode of the period, Cambaceres's narrator, in an indirect, free style, assumes the task of speaking for the characters). Andrés, overjoyed at being given a meaning for his life in the form of his illegitimate daughter, wonders what sort of life he should plan for her. After reviewing a number of possibilities, he concludes that it is best to recognize the limitations of her inferior sex, even to the extent of praising those oriental societies in which women are totally subservient to the strong, guiding hand of wiser men:

> La limitación estrecha de sus facultades, los escasos alcances de su inteligencia incapaz de penetrar en el dominio profundo de la ciencia, rebelde a las concepciones sublimes de las artes; la pobreza de su ser moral, refractario a todas las altas nociones de justicia y de deber; el aspecto mismo de su cuerpo, su falta de nervio y de vigor, la molicie de sus formas, la delicadeza de sus líneas, la suavidad de su piel, la morbidez de sus carnes, ¿no revelaban claramente su destino, la misión que la naturaleza le había dado? ¿No estaban diciendo a gritos que era un ser consagrado al amor esencialmente, casi un simple instrumento de placer, creado en vista de la propagación sucesiva y creciente de la especie? ¡Ah! ¡Cuánto más sensatos y más sabios eran los pueblos de Oriente; cuánto mejor, más llevadera la suerte de la mujer bajo esas leyes, traducción fiel de las leyes naturales! (154–55)

> (The narrow limitation of her faculties, the short reach of her intelligence, incapable of penetrating the profound domain of science, resistant to the sublime conceptions of the arts; the poverty of her moral being, impervious to the lofty notions of justice and duty; the very appearance of her body, its lack of tone and vigor, the softness of its forms, the delicacy of its lines, the smoothness of her skin, the flush of her flesh. Did not these things reveal her destiny, the mission that nature had given her? Were they not shouting out that she was a being given over essentially to love, almost a simple instrument of pleasure, created with a view toward the successive and growing propagation of the species? Ah! How much more sensible and wise were the peoples of the Orient, how much more fortunate the fate of women under those laws, the faithful translation of natural laws!)

This is a rather glib translation of the ideas of the Spencerian determinism that enjoyed immense vogue among the late nineteenth-century Latin American social philosophers and statesmen who saw themselves charged with solving the problems of the multiple inferior elements of their society. As evidently useful as it is for assigning and holding social roles and for suggesting the possibility of a succession of tragic events if its basic truths are ignored, these meditations have little to do with either the death from croup of the female child involved or the gory suicide of her father. The girl does not live long enough to violate any of the laws presumed inherent in this analysis of woman's place nor does Andrés arrive at any conclusion other than respect for them.

The central narrative event in *Sin rumbo* is the rape of Donata, the girl's mother. Donata is claimed to have awakened to her own sexuality in the process: Argentine writers like Cambaceres, while they may have been insensitive to women's feelings about rape at the hands of masterful men as they indulged in what we may view as a brutal fantasy of the sexual education of women, were apparently more willing to acknowledge female sexual pleasure than was a writer like Thomas Hardy. That is, Cambaceres's sexual fantasy at least accords women a sexual role, even if it is ideologized lamentably in terms of a favor performed by the man. Tess gets raped like Donata but passes out rather than responding lustfully: "subyugada a pesar suyo por el ciego ascendiente de la carne en el contacto de ese otro cuerpo de hombre" (overwhelmed despite herself by the blind ascendance of her flesh in its contact with the other body of the man; 65). As a consequence of her forced sexual awakening, Donata is able to cooperate enthusiastically with Andrés's efforts to entertain his bored self with her body. Donata is devastated by Andrés's decision to abandon her for the attractions of Buenos Aires, and he is only in passing concerned that their intercourse has left her pregnant. The ensuing series of chapters describes Andrés's dalliance in Buenos Aires with the Italian opera singer, in whose opulent company he executes the commonplaces of Bacchanalian sensuality, only to end up just as bored with her as he is with everything else in his life. But it is at this point that he responds to a spark of joy at the prospect of returning to his property and assuming the role of dutiful father.

During his many meditations on the occasion of assuming his paternal responsibilities, Andrés wonders about a punishment from God for the irregular, extramarital nature of his daughter's conception. This undercurrent of regret, perhaps more than signifying a fossilized guilt complex in the man's upbringing, bespeaks the seriousness with which he takes being a father:

> Y ante la horrible amenaza un secreto sentimiento lo asaltaba, hecho de egoísmo, de debilidad, de cobardía, y queriendo creer y temiendo no llegar a conseguirlo, obstinadamente se empeñaba en cerrar los ojos a la importuna luz de su razón.
>
> Contra todo, a pesar de todo y porque sí, se esforzaba por remontarse en alas de una fe ficticia hasta la noción de Dios. . . .

> Pero como si entre las leyes ocultas que gobiernan el universo existiera una, bárbara, monstruosa, exclusivamente destinada a castigar por el delito de haber gozado alguna vez, el sueño acariciado por Andrés no debía tardar en disiparse convertido en una ironía sangrienta del destino. (158)

> (And in the face of the horrible threat a secret sentiment assaulted him, one formed of egotism, weakness, cowardliness, and wanting to believe and fearing not being able to, he insisted obstinately in closing his eyes to the annoying light of his reason.
>
> Against everything, in spite of everything, and because he wanted to, he made the effort to raise toward God himself on the wings of a fictitious faith. . . .
>
> But, as though among the hidden laws that govern the universe, there existed a barbarous, monstrous one destined to punish for the crime of having at one time felt pleasure, the dream nurtured by Andrés did not take long to dissipate, turned into a bloody irony of destiny.)

However, the wisdom of the French proverb, "A moment of pleasure, a lifetime of regret," is a rather curious point of reference for the central tragedy of a novel written in conformance with the tenets of Naturalism. The idea of divine punishment and of doomed fortunes as the consequence of the transgression of divine commandments is a plot formula of Romanticism and not of Naturalism. Only unless one equates God with the blind forces of biological determinism can an appeal to divine justice correspond to the Naturalists' world view. The idea that Andrea's agony is retribution for her mother's or for Andrés's lust is pointedly left to the father's fevered imagination, and it serves more to foreshadow the inevitability that something dreadful will befall the little girl than to explain why she ends up the propitiatory victim.

But Andrea is a propitiatory victim, and it is the impact of her terrible death that causes her father to disembowel himself. Thus, the point of reference is inevitably Andrés and his own particular place in the world. Concomitantly, whatever his tragedy is, whatever the point of Naturalism to be made in the representation of his existence, resides in that place in the world.

The very title of the novel, which we can understand as a hypogram of the text, signals Andrés's relationship with human existence. By contrast with the venerable Western, Christian topos of life as a road, a charted course that the individual pursues in the realization of human destiny and the fulfillment of God's design for mankind, Cambaceres's protagonist is a *homo viator,* a man wandering, *sin rumbo.* Certainly, Andrés is not aimless as a consequence of the lack of a proper education or the absence of adequate models for him to emulate in order to be a happy and well-adjusted member of his society (it must be remembered that it is during this period that psychiatry emerges as a powerful tool for the socialization and integration of individuals in the context of an increasingly complex modern urban existence). Rather, Andrés has chosen deliberately to repudiate the models of his privileged social status:

> Reñido a muerte con la sociedad cuyas puertas él mismo se había cerrado, con la sociedad de las mujeres llamadas decentes, decía, por rutina o porque sí, con una fe más que dudosa en la virtud, negando la posibilidad de dicha en el hogar y mirando el matrimonio con horror, buscaba un refugio, un lleno al vacío de su amarga misantropía, en los halagos de la vida ligera de soltero, en los clubes, en el juego, en los teatros, en los amores fáciles de entretelones, en el comercio de ese mundo aparte, heteróclito, mezcla de escorias humanas, donde el oficio se incrusta en la costumbre y donde la farsa vivida no es otra que una repetición grosera de la farsa representada. (87)

> (Mortally at odds with the society whose doors he had himself closed, with the society of decent women, he said, whether out of habit or because he meant it, with a more than doubtful faith in virtue and denying the possibility of happiness in the home and eying matrimony with horror, he sought a refuge, something to fill the void of his bitter misanthropy, in the delights of the easy life of a bachelor, in the clubs, in gambling, at the theater, in facile dalliances, in the commerce of the irregular world apart, a mixture of human flotsam where practice becomes routine and where the lived farce is nothing but a vulgar repetition of the farce acted out.)

This passage, which is in fact chapter 13 in its entirety, contains a number of semantic primes that require comment. In the first place, there is a binomial relationship between the antonyms *lleno* and *vacío.* Andrés turns, ultimately in vain, as we subsequently see in his relationship with the prima donna, to a form of hedonism in order to fill the void of his sense of an aimless existence. In terms of the road-of-life image, the individual's experience cannot help but be one of awe in the face of all the riches of life. This is the basic plot design of the Hispanic archetype on the subject, Cervantes's *Don Quijote,* where Quijote and Sancho are caught up in a maelstrom of onrushing adventures that more than adequately allay the tedium of existence from which they escape by taking to the byways of the world.

Yet Andrés, despite the privileges of his wealth and status, finds the world empty of meaning, and the substance of his life is the vain pursuit of something to occupy his time and to awaken his interest. In the process of describing this pursuit, both in Andrés's rape of Donata and his affair with the Italian opera singer, the narrator surveys some of the major points of reference of the demimonde of the fin-de-siècle clubman in a Buenos Aires of burgeoning prosperity. That this world is ultimately unsatisfactory for Andrés's needs echoes the cynical ennui of the common protagonist of Cambaceres's first two novels, both of which are set in the Paris of the Argentine landed gentry's seasonal recreation. Only in his fevered refuge in the concerns of paternity can Andrés find some respite from his boredom.

Also of importance in the structure of meaning of chapter 13 is Andrés's repudiation of polite or decent society. This repudiation must be seen as paralleling his interest in the philosophical speculation of writers such as Schopenhauer, whose image of human existence is decidedly at odds with the romantic idealism of the bourgeoisie during the height of late nineteenth-century capitalism. Called upon, as the local landowning baron, to lend his blessing to the dedication of a church altar, Andrés startles his neighbors with the following words, which break with the spirit of the ceremony:

> —Déjense de perder su tiempo en iglesias y en escuelas; es plata tirada a la calle. Dios no es nadie; la ciencia un cáncer para el alma. Saber es sufrir; ignorar, comer, dormir y no pensar, la solución exacta del problema, la única dicha de vivir. En vez de estar pensando en hacer de cada muchacho un hombre, hagan una bestia ... no pueden prestar a la humanidad mayor servicio. (74)

> ("Stop wasting your time in churches and schools—it's only money wasted. God is no one; science is a cancer for the soul. To know is to suffer; to be ignorant, to eat, to sleep, and not to think is the right solution for the problem, the only happiness in life. Instead of thinking about making a man out of every boy, make him a beast ... there is no greater service to humanity.")

Far from affirming the tenets of classical Naturalism, this *ex abrupto* echoes Andrés's reading in the canonical texts of radical pessimism of the period at direct odds with material progress. Moreover, the words underscore at this early juncture in the narrative his self-imposed separation from the dominant public values of his society. Throughout the novel, Andrés's aimlessness is tied, either by the narrator's references or by the gist of the protagonist's reflections, to these bleak premises that would justify his commitment to nihilistic extremism (again, one cannot help but recall the grim nihilism of Hardy's novels).

Finally, chapter 13 makes it clear that it is Andrés himself who has chosen to close the doors of decent society and that his situation as an outsider is self-imposed rather than the consequence of determining factors beyond his control. Andrés chooses to be a social outcast, and, as such, he is a victim neither of nature nor of society. If he is the victim of a particular set of beliefs that have come to "infect" him—that is, if he is the victim of an act of deliberate or accidental corruption—the narrator never gets around to saying, and, thus, this possible Naturalist formula cannot be adduced to explain Andrés's plight.

The only relief from deadening ennui for the protagonist of *Sin rumbo* comes in the form of his sudden and determined commitment to the joys of fatherhood. But it is an investment in an obsessive monomania that consumes him as much as a forbidden sexual passion or the crazed pursuit of philosophy might another (see *Sin rumbo,* 144). This emotional state and Andrés's feelings when finally his daughter is brought to him, the intensity of his involvement with her, his despair when she falls mortally ill, and his final impulse toward self-destruction as a form of expiation for what he cannot control: all are facets of the man's new-found response to the details of daily existence that he had formally disdained with such conviction. It is here where the basic conflict lies for Andrés: his inability, once he has made the unheard-of move of committing himself to something that gives meaning to his life, to control his destiny. One must remember that Cambaceres is portraying an individual accustomed to having his own way in life, whether as the master of prosperous landholdings or as a gentleman moving at ease in a society subordinate to his economic resources. Since the focus of the novel's narrative action is on Andrés's activities as a lover, in each of the relationships described—with Donata and with the Italian prima donna—he is able to dictate the conditions of the affair, to guide its course, and to decide when and how it will end.

The hubris of Andrés's control over his world and his personal destiny is what is challenged by the blind course of his daughter's fatal illness. Neither a punishment from heaven for her original sin in being the illegitimate child of an unsanctified liaison nor the consequence of the machinations of a defective social dynamic, Andrea's death brings her father face to face with a truth he had heretofore never been called upon to contemplate. There are pathetic circumstances of life this man of privilege cannot manipulate in conformance with his personal will. When Andrés is returning to his property to claim his child, his entourage is caught in a flash flood. As befits his status as the master, Andrés takes charge, even though it results in the death of one of his hands. When he is challenged by one of the men as to the wisdom of his order to forge ahead, he replies sharply to the effect that he knows what he is doing, and it is rewarded with the appropriate response: "—Como disponga, patrón, usted es el dueño" ("Just as you say, master, you're the boss"; 135).

Throughout Andrea's terrible illness, Andrés strives to prevail with the resources at the disposal of the master. He possesses his own will, the assistance of his household, the services of the medical profession, even his entire cultural heritage that he had rejected in the form of a Christian God of mercy. Nevertheless, "Yo todo fue en vao" (It was all in vain; 174). Thus, the essential conflict for Andrés lies in the limits on the power of his class to control the arbitrariness of nature. The impact of the circumstance described by *Sin rumbo* lies neither in the confused personality of Andrés nor in his skepticism and its replacement by a blind commitment to his daughter. Rather, it lies in the widening gulf between the arbitrariness of existence and the evidently unreliable promise of an organized and progressive society to offer ways to subjugate that arbitrariness. In this version of Naturalism, there is no original discovery as regards the arbitrariness of human destiny, the fragility of life, and the fickleness of human fortune; the entire Western literary tradition reveals a vast inventory of examples to confirm the odds against which human endeavor has always had to struggle. Instead, it is the underscoring of these odds as a counterpoint to the idea—and ideal—of control inherent to the social ideology of the masters of a progressive and civilized society. Not so much a reformist issue of the suffering of the common folk as victims of the implacable laws of a social dynamic wielded to the advantage of an economic and political elite, this version of Naturalism challenges the ingenuous confidence of this elite in controlling that dynamic.

Andrés is certainly not interested in the grandiose public questions that characterize the remaking of Argentine society by the leading thinkers and driving forces of the Generation of 1880. He is, however, from the point of view of culture as symptomatic of larger social questions, a synecdoche as far as Cambaceres is concerned of a specific dominant mentality. Andrés is able to live his life quite aimlessly, oblivious to the real suffering of the human condition, as evidenced by the way in which he is able to abandon the pregnant Donata, escape to Buenos Aires high society, and entertain himself with an opulent and sexually experienced opera singer. Moreover, he is able to do all of this with a supreme disdain for any significant versions of the meaning of life, versions that, despite whatever internal weakness they may have as definitive statements, are part of a Western cultural heritage that attempts to interpret the arbitrariness and fragility of human existence. When Andrés does finally turn his attention to his daughter, perhaps at first as simply another form of distraction from the tedium of life, he does so in the same spirit of obliviousness to the truth of existence. Thus, while he distracts himself with the meditation about what he will do with his daughter's life, fate, in the form of arbitrary nature, is about to take her from him with a chain of events that he cannot reverse, no matter how much masterful decisiveness he exercises.

Andrés's suicide could be viewed as a reassertion of control over his life: "¡Vida perra ... —rugió Andrés—yo te he de arrancar de cuajo! ... " ("A bitch of a life," Andrés howled, "I'll pull you up by the roots!"; 176). But it is a reassertion with a very high cost in the form of self-destruction that confirms the destruction of his world, the death of his daughter, and the burning of his property. In sum, it is the loss of all that Andrés had been led to believe that he controlled.

Naturalism of this variety in the context of a prevailing belief that one would do well to calmly despair over the fortunes of man serves to propose a cultural sign that is essentially confirmatory. Undoubtedly, this is the case with Hardy's writing within the context of generally wretched social conditions as texts signed by someone who held little hope for the improvement of individuals' lot in either nature or its extension as organized society. *Sin rumbo* may exemplify this same sort of Naturalism as a gesture of despair, but by contrast it functions as an exceptional sign within a cultural ideology that espoused boundless enthusiasm for the erection of a modern and progressive society ruled by men endowed with the power of scientific knowledge. No matter how insignificant a member the landowner and clubman Andrés may have been of this society, the aimless life he chooses to lead is in conformance with its principles and privileges. In the end, his destruction is a serious questioning of the ruling ideology, and it is only in this sense that Cambaceres's novel has any meaning as a social text.[14]

14. It is difficult to believe that many modern readers would share the enthusiasm over the crafting of the novel held by Nélida Salvador, "Cambaceres, Eugenio," 113. One critic who does concern himself with the narrative qualities of the novel is George D. Schade, "El arte narrativo en *Sin rumbo*."

CHAPTER 5

Rural Culture Revisited

The basis of Argentine wealth during the period of immense prosperity from 1880 to the Great Depression is to be found in the rural, agricultural sector. The conquest of the desert, the construction of a vast railway system, and a concerted immigration effort are all elements of the program related to this economic base. Yet prosperity meant the possibility of living in splendor in Buenos Aires, and, as for Andrés in Cambaceres's *Sin rumbo,* the metropolis rather than the farm or ranch came to represent status and well-being. The consequence in Argentine culture is the strong interest from this period forward in urban themes and the displacement by the city of issues related to the countryside, where the immigrants were originally intended to settle, all of which is symptomatic of the inevitability of the urban dominance.

Yet what happened in Buenos Aires affected rural society, if only to overlook, underestimate, and denigrate it. Political priorities set in Buenos Aires affected the countryside, quite often in a fashion judged to be detrimental. The need to enhance and expand the agricultural exploitation that had become the basis of national prosperity only served to restructure—sometimes violently—rural society, as, for example, in the subjugation of the nomadic gaucho to the role of steady ranch hand. Foreign immigration into rural areas stimulated by the social philosophy and political considerations of Buenos Aires ideologues led to inevitable cultural conflicts between the old Creole stock and the two largest groups of newcomers, Italians and Jews (the latter certainly quite alien to traditional Hispanic mores).

From one point of view, writers and intellectuals based in Buenos Aires recognized the value of the countryside by interpreting it in a process of mythification that culminates in Ricardo Güiraldes's famous gaucho novel, *Don Segundo Sombra* (1926). Two of the most interesting examples are by immigrants, both Spaniards. The play *Gauchos y gringos (bosquejo de costumbres argentinas en un acto y en verso)* (1884) by Justo S. López de Gomara (1858–1923) closes with the optimistic verses based on the joyous amalgamation of conflicting cultural patterns:

y del más alto al más bajo
el criollo y el inmigrante
formarán pueblo gigante
de progreso y de trabajo.[1]

(And from the highest to the lowest, the Creole and the immigrant will form a gigantic society of progress and work.)

The essay *Los inmigrantes prósperos* (first published in Spain in 1933, but written around 1902) is a series of vignettes by Francisco Grandmontagne (1866–1936) in which he delivers a paean to the prosperity of immigrant colonies, especially those of Spaniards, in the New World generally and Argentina in particular. Although more properly a member of Spain's Generation of 1898, Grandmontagne nevertheless represents an important "external" verification of the ideology of dynamic, assimilationist immigration in Argentina, one that in the case of the Spaniards will be undermined by the image of the impoverished urban *gallego* in early twentieth-century Argentine culture. But, as the texts examined in this chapter demonstrate, already within the scope of the writing of the Generation of 1880 there is the need to examine critically both accepted concepts of rural culture and the new mythopoesis it stimulated.

Gutiérrez's Juan Moreira figure, along with its subsequent dramatization by the popular Podestá theatrical group, represents undoubtedly, after José Hernández's *Martín Fierro* (1872 and 1879), the most enduring image of the Argentine countryside at this time. However, in addition to the gauchos and their culture, there is another historical reality, and that is the conflicts, so crucial in this time for the economic expansion of the country, relating to the domestication of the vast hinterland. This conflict involved the pitting of modernizing European society of Buenos Aires against traditional rural sectors. But it also brought into armed battle the survivors of the once dominant indigenous cultures and the whole array of European settlers and their descendants, anxious to stabilize their agricultural and ranching exploitation of the pampas. Although Garmendia's text can hardly be said to enjoy the stature of the canonical documents this study has concentrated on, it is an exemplar of an extensive bibliography of writing about the army and its role in the domestication of the countryside that is rarely examined by literary scholars.

1. Justo S. López de Gomara, *Gauchos y gringos (bosquejo de costumbres argentinas en un acto y en verso),* ll. 1210–13.

The Outlaw as Epic Hero: Eduardo Gutiérrez's *Juan Moreira*

. . . mire que ése es un hombre de mucha historia. . . .[2]

(Look, for this is a man of much history.)

The most immediate issue presented by a work like Eduardo Gutiérrez's *Juan Moreira* is that of ideological encrustation. It is not just that we are dealing with one of the seminal works of Argentine literature, one of the works that, during the period of the various projects of sociocultural definition that converge under the heading of the Generation of 1880, served to define a particular stance toward a cluster of significant ideological topics. Even more fundamental is the fact that *Juan Moreira* is part of a network of cultural texts that enjoy a unique resonance because they are concerned with one of the primary cultural myths of Argentina.[3]

While it is generally recognized that Gutiérrez's serialized novel is the origin of the Moreira myth in the sense that it was the first work to deal with the specific narrative associated with the eponymic figure of the story, it is important to recognize that Gutiérrez's narrative in reality participates in a wider network of related narrative and ideological strands.[4] There may be a particularly unique or specific narrative trajectory associated with the story of Juan Moreira. But one of the bases of its immediate repercussion among Gutiérrez's readers was that material dealing with gauchos had already circulated to some considerable extent among various segments of the Argentine reading public.

Gutiérrez began to publish *Juan Moreira* in 1879, when Hernández was completing the second part, the *Vuelta,* of *Martín Fierro.* Originally pub-

2. Eduardo Gutiérrez, *Juan Moreira,* 2d ed., 143. Hereafter cited parenthetically in the text by page number.

3. Rivera, in *Eduardo Gutiérrez,* and León Benarós, in "Eduardo Gutiérrez: un descuidado destino," are examples of critics who have sought to accord to Gutiérrez the literary importance that his own contemporaries were unwilling to recognize in his *folletines.* The latter tended to believe that the *folletines* exemplified appalling writing in both the carelessness of style and structure and in the marginal, "criminal" figures Gutiérrez dealt with and appeared to extol. As Benarós notes (pp. 21–22), it was Jorge Luis Borges who contributed to Gutiérrez's reevaluation by mentioning his preference for his *folletines* in his famous essay "La fruición literaria" (p. 101).

4. Angela B. Dellepiane, "Los folletines gauchescos de Eduardo Gutiérrez," discusses the features of Gutiérrez's gauchesque works as serialized composition in "Los folletines gauchescos." Section 5 of Benarós's essay is entitled "Los mitos"; chapter 7 of Rivera's monograph deals with " 'Los proyecciones' de la obra de Gutiérrez"; and María Bonatti, "Juan Moreira en un contexto modernista," discusses literary descendants. Adolfo Prieto, *El discurso criollista en la formación de la Argentina moderna,* provides a brilliant analysis of the *folletines* by Gutiérrez and others as a model of a national popular literature and its linguistic registers.

lished in 1872, Hernández's poem was an instant success and quickly became a cultural monument. Like Cervantes's reprise of *Don Quixote,* the *Vuelta* was necessary to protect the author's "product" from the diverse and often outrageous extensions built upon it both by enterprising imitators and the popular tradition. But aside from the folksy notion of a literary figure that resonates in the mind of readers such that they seem to assume an autonomous "real life" existence—the tradition of real life Quixotes and Uncle Remuses and Tom Sawyers who emerge as a testimonial to how readers enact the urge to correlate literature and other cultural artifacts to the everyday life—the enormous spread of the Martín Fierro type and its derivatives like Juan Moreira attests to the degree to which the texts that feature them strike a specific cultural note in great need, at a particular moment, of being sounded. The proliferation of gaucho or gauchesque material through the early nineteenth century, as part of a special Romantic adaptation of folk or popular material to the cause of the Independence movement (for example, the poems of Hidalgo and Lussich), is also part of the general field of cultural reference that Hernández's and Gutiérrez's narratives evoke.

However, to speak of the existence of a generalized field of reference, the "gaucho motifs," is not enough to indicate the extent of the response Gutiérrez's novel achieves at a particular moment in Argentine cultural history. The portrayal of the gaucho had emerged earlier in the century as part of a Latin American literary response to the Romantic interest in the culture of the people: the gaucho as embodying the lifestyle of an Arcadian idyll that may serve as an example for national identity, which is why Hernández's poem must first characterize this idyll and then chronicle its destruction in order to portray the plight and the destiny of Martín Fierro and his sons in the society of the Argentine Republic. But the gaucho as a figure of the destruction of the idyll has become for Gutiérrez the main point of departure.

Juan Moreira, therefore, is the synthesis of the *gaucho rebelde:* not the *gaucho malo* in Sarmiento's definition. The latter is an individual represented as cursed with a stigma of antisocial behavior that places him outside the range of idyllic features that Sarmiento is also at pains to detail; Facundo is the epigone of this sort of *antigaucho.*[5] Rather, Moreira creates the gaucho who has been forced into an antisocial role both as the consequence of the treatment to which he has been subjected and as the only path open to him to survive in a world he is unable to control.

Part of the general underpinnings of this conception of the gaucho's

5. Noé Jitrik, *Muerte y resurrección de "Facundo";* and C. A. Jones, *Sarmiento: "Facundo."*

plight, by the time of Gutiérrez's writing and its derivatives, is the Naturalist's conception of the conditioning forces of a society that define, inevitably and inexorably, a certain manner of being. There is much to be said, within the context of the rigidifying forces of the dominant social culture of the Generation of 1880, about literature and art around themes of criminal behavior, social misfits, immoral and abnormal conduct and the like; this is even more true in the case of works published in the 1890s. Surely this material reflects as much a normative concern for bringing all manner of lifestyles into conformity with a dominant mode, that of "polite society," as it does with various forms of "scientific" preoccupation with the residue of human behavior left behind by the forces of law and order, order and progress, in their dynamic drive to constitute one kind of social norm. In this sense, Juan Moreira as a figure of rebellion is not just a manifestation of the gaucho type, but of a larger social figure, one that will have considerable importance for the writing of the Generation of 1880. Of particular importance is how *Juan Moreira* plays upon the readership's interest in the gaucho figure as a social rebel, a criminal misfit whose conduct is the consequence of a conjunction of social forces that for complex reasons contradict the dominant pattern of law and order.

It would be easy to say that this interest is simply a morbid one: the more well-defined the social norm, the greater the interest inherent in the example of deviance from it. Hence, there is considerable mileage in the literature of the period to be derived from the figure of the prostitute.[6] But an assessment of interest based on a concept like morbidity is perhaps too affective to be of much analytical use. What must remain undeniable is that, as part of the project of sociocultural definition, with or without reference to the general principles called Naturalism, Gutiérrez appealed most successfully to his readers' interest in human situations on the margin of dominant social norms, which explains why he also wrote many other works on nongaucho criminal figures.[7]

The gaucho is on the margins of Gutiérrez's readers in a dimension

6. Domingo F. Casadevall, *El tema de la mala vida en el teatro nacional*.

7. "Gutiérrez's truculent pamphlets are conceived . . . on the principle of anecdotes that in the final analysis reflect the insecurity of the frontier world in the face of change. The illusion of factual reality arises from the temporal-spatial development of a typically novelistic conflict: the problematical opposition of *stability* (the hero in concert with his world) and *instability* (the hero in conflict with his world), as the revelation of a stage of rupture" (Rivera, *Gutiérrez,* 28). Dellepiane provides, furthermore, an inventory of how the social issues of his day were dealt with by Gutiérrez in his *folletines* ("Los folletines gauchescos," 491).

added to that of a social misfit like the prostitute. For where the latter is part of the urban scene that is continuous with the personal identity of Gutiérrez's readers, the gaucho is part of a rural setting that becomes a very powerful point of reference for a society whose controlling self-image is increasingly defined in urban terms. The gaucho is the Other in a double sense: the Other as the individual outside the law, and the Other as outside the controlling urban sector. If the criminal element provides one major defining feature of the writing of the Generation of 1880, so too will the dialectical relationship between urban and rural forces of Argentine identity whereby the latter will be seen both as a lost Arcadia and as the repository of a deleterious Hispanic past that must be swept away. One of the dominant images of the gaucho had, in effect, become the quintessence of the telluric primitive that must be assimilated to the dominant culture or, if not, destroyed. This imperative also includes the Indian and an entire range of social types that will, later, include the immigrant originally brought in to enrich the native stock.

These are the aspects of Gutiérrez's novel that constitute facets of its ideological encrustation, from the point of view of readers in 1879 as well as for readers one hundred years later. While *Juan Moreira* may not be as artistically "primitive" a novel as criticism is wont to assert, there can be no avoiding the fact that it is this sort of encrustation that makes it such a centerpiece in a characterization of the cultural writing of the Generation of 1880.

Although the appeal to historical fact may be one of the hoariest devices of narrative fiction, it is of special importance in the case of a novel like *Juan Moreira.* During a cultural period that witnessed the attempt to ground explanation—"narrative" in the largest sense—in an appeal to scientific fact, methodology, and reasoning, the appeal to real events by Gutiérrez may be taken as a rhetorical guarantee of the legitimacy of his story. Certainly, the novel is called upon to justify its continued existence in the face of the rise of a formal historiography dedicated to charting the ways in which it is different from narrative fiction. Both the emphasis on what can generally be called the fantastic and the utilization of historical motifs by fictional writers during the Romantic period provided an ample basis of contrast for positivistic historiographers to trace where such poetry left off and scientific knowledge began.

The formal discipline of late-nineteenth-century historiography might not have been possible—or even necessary—if it had not been for the Romantic aesthetic, which provided a rather neat though extreme point of reference for the difference that the academic historians sought to promote and prize. The concern for seeking the mysterious or hidden bases of human motivation and conduct that led to what were later considered the outrageous plots of Romantic fiction meant a concern for what lay beyond the verifiable, the reasonable, or the natural. Often the quest for the unknown and the supernatural led to an interest in historical materials, to the so-called Romantic Revival that is an integral part of the writing of that period. Such a revival of historical materials—presented to the reader by a narrator who claims to have had privileged access to them, the ploy of the documents found forgotten in a customhouse—contributed to the dwelling on the supernatural or on what lay beyond the ken of everyday life.

The historical writing that emerges in the late nineteenth century is determined to base its appeal on the sort of explicit documentary evidence and logical reasoning that were argued to be the antithesis of the plot structure and narrative strategies of the historical novel. And, precisely, much of the new historical writing dealt with the themes and materials of the novel it sought to preempt: chronicles of antiquity, biographies of great men (that is, the Romantic hero revised), the ebb and flow of historical events as determinants in the formation of a national character, and the concern for the texture and details of daily life that will lead to the rise of the anthropological and sociological disciplines as adjuncts of scientific historiography.

Such intellectual thrusts must necessarily displace, if only because they have the attractive patina of the new, the conventions of an earlier historical fiction. Certainly in all of the European nations undergoing national redefinitions during the latter part of the nineteenth century, there is a primacy accorded to the interpretations offered by the academic historians, and it is all too easy to see today how they served the ideology of these processes rather than being merely the detached objective observers they claimed to be. This process was even more true in Latin America, where the period beginning roughly in 1880 is crucial in the implantation of a Liberal society that will, in the view of its proponents, solve once and for all the independent non-Hispanic destiny of the several republics.

It is within the context of these priorities that Gutiérrez's appeal to the availability of facts to support his story of Juan Moreira's career assumes a special importance as one basis for a reading of the text. At two points close to midway in his narrative, Gutiérrez asserts the privilege of fact. The first quotation is used to allay presumed skepticism on the part of the reader as regards the veracity of the events and feats attributed to Moreira:

> No hacemos novela, narramos los hechos que pueden atestiguar el señor Correa Morales, el señor Marañón, el señor Casanova, juez de paz de

entonces, y otras muchas personas que conocen todos estos hechos. Hacemos esta salvedad, porque hay tales sucesos en la vida de Juan Moreira, que dejan atrás a cualquier novela o narración fantástica, escrita con el solo objeto de entretener el espíritu del lector. (83)

(We are not writing a novel, we are narrating the fact to which Mr. Correa Morales, Mr. Marañón, Mr. Casanova can attest to, the latter the justice of the peace at that time, as well as many other persons familiar with these facts. We make this caveat because there are so many events in Juan Moreira's life that they leave far behind any novel or fantastic narrative written with the sole object of entertaining the spirit of the reader.)

It must be noted that an affirmation of this sort occurs in tandem with a variety of qualifiers that occur throughout the novel to the effect that "parece imposible que" (it seems impossible that), "parece increíble que" (it seems incredible that), and so on. Such qualifiers are used to head assertions that support Gutiérrez's presentation of Moreira as both a paradigm of the noble gaucho and as a superior exemplum of the virtuous individual, both as a model of Christian charity and as a fearless avenger of wrongs done to him and his family, immediate and extended.

Since, in the course of the novel, Moreira repeatedly triumphs against the fatal destiny that has befallen him and the hostile forces that persecute him, the appeal to historical fact serves to frame the uniformity of these triumphs and the ease with which Moreira appears able to overcome the odds ranged against him by circumstance and society. Were he not to prevail at the conclusion of each of the episodes that provide the major narrative nuclei of the novel, Gutiérrez would be left without a story to tell and a particular point to be made about what Moreira must represent for the reader. In view of how the pattern of events by which Moreira wins with such ease the armed contests that challenge his survival—the terms taken from Propp's morphology of the folk tale is deliberate here—Gutiérrez is constrained to condition his narrative with the reminder that it is not to be read in terms of the conventions of the simply *novelesco,* by which it is reasonable to assume Gutiérrez means the outrageously fictional considered to be the lowest common denominator of Romantic epics:

Esa misma noche vino al rancho un paisano, amigo de Santiago, con una novedad bastante grave para otro que no hubiera sido Juan Moreira; y que vino a sentar su reputación de valiente en Cañuelas, con un hecho que no nos atreveríamos a narrar, si el señor Nicolás González, juez de paz en aquella época, no pudiera atestiguar este hecho novelesco, digno de los espíritus fuertes que figuraron en la Edad Media. (112)

(That same night a country man came to the cabin, a friend of Santiago's, with some news that would be serious for anyone other than Juan Moreira, who staked his reputation as a brave man on Cañuelas with a deed that we would not dare to narrate if Mr. Nicolás González, the justice of the peace at that time, were not able to testify to this novel-like deed, worthy of the strong spirits that peopled the Middle Ages.)

Obviously, no one expects readers to avail themselves of the sources the narrator specifies. What is at issue is not the existence of such sources but the illusion of fact that reference to them provides to the narrative.

This illusion of the appeal to fact extends to the narrator's overall stance toward his story and the mediating role he assigns himself between it and the reader. In addition to assertions of factual or documentary sources, the narrator repeatedly affirms that his information is based on personal contacts with the places of the story and with surviving witnesses of the events chronicled:

> Hemos hablado una sola vez con Moreira, el año 74, y el timbre de su voz ha quedado grabado en nuestra memoria. (18)
>
> Hemos hecho un viaje ex profeso a recoger datos en los partidos que este gaucho habitó primero y aterrorizó después. . . . (19)
>
> Hemos hablado con los empleados de policía que han combatido con Moreira, inválidos todos, y que figurarán a su tiempo en esta narración, y hemos conversado largamente con el capitán de las partidas de plaza de Lobos y Navarro, inválidos también, y todos ellos nos han relatado la honda impresión que producía la mirada de Moreira en el combate. (36)
>
> (We have spoken only once with Moreira, in the year 1874, and the pitch of his voice is engraved in our memory.
>
> We have made a trip for the sole purpose of gathering data in the townships that this gaucho first inhabited and then later terrorized. . . .
>
> We have spoken with the police personnel who fought against Moreira, all of them incapacitated, who will figure in due course in this narrative, and we have spoken at length with the captain of the force in Lobos and Navarro. They were all incapacitated, and they have all spoken of the deep impression produced by the look on Moreira's face during battle.)

These references are from the early portions of the novel, and their strategic location may be taken as part of a need felt by the narrator to confirm the legitimacy of what he is relating.

It is customary to speak of the narrator of the late nineteenth-century novel as "omniscient" and as wont to control the narrative in a deus ex machina fashion toward making sure that events conform to a preconceived plan or design. Gutiérrez presents no substantial or innovative deviation from this pattern, and it is clear that his narrative of the criminal career of Juan Moreira is meant to support an unambiguous thesis. This thesis comes at the very end of the story, and it confirms the extent to which the novel appeals to a reformist sentiment that is a central concern in the period for the transition from the Hispanic feudal past to a more enlightened Liberal society. It also confirms the need to underscore the extent to which the structure of daily national life continued to deviate from such an ideal:

> ¡He aquí los graves defectos de que adolece nuestra célebre Justicia de Paz!
>
> De un hombre nacido para el bien y para ser útil a sus semejantes, hacen una especie de fiera que, para salvar la cabeza del sable de las partidas, tiene que echarse al camino y defenderse con la daga y el trabuco. (226)

> (Here you have the grave defects that our celebrated Justice of the Peace system suffers from!
>
> They take a man born to be good and useful to his neighbors, and they turn him into a kind of a beast that, in order to save his head from the sabers of the police, must take to the highway and defend himself with dagger and gun.)

A good case could be made for how Gutiérrez's interest lies in recording the vestiges of the feudal Hispanic past rather than in underscoring defects of the emerging Liberal structures. In either case, he stands as the mediator between the reader to whom rhetorical appeals of understanding must be made and the story of an individual who, by any definition of antisocial behavior, ends up engaging in unbridled lawlessness as the result of injustices of which he has been victim.[8]

Juan Moreira exhibits an unambiguous and uncomplicated story line: Juan Moreira is a fine specimen of a gaucho, a model citizen and worker, and an exemplary friend to his neighbors. Because of his popularity and his success with a woman whom he marries and by whom he has a son, he attracts the enmity of the local police authority, the *teniente alcalde.* As every Argentine knows, Moreira, after various episodes of mistreatment at the hands of the *teniente alcalde,* who exercises virtually absolute authority over the gauchos of his jurisdiction, kills the *gringo* store owner Sardetti in a quarrel over money that Moreira has loaned him and that Sardetti refuses to repay. Sardetti, who is a caricature in the novel of the hated immigrants that native Argentines felt were usurping their econ-

8. Carlos A. Egan, in "Peripheralization and Cultural Change: Argentina, 1880–1910," discusses antisocial behavior in Argentina and its reflection in cultural materials as the consequence of an integrated series of sociocultural forces.

omy, is egged on by the *teniente alcalde* in refusing to honor his debt to Moreira. Moreira subsequently must kill the *teniente alcalde* in order to escape justice for the death of Sardetti. Moreira's words, "—Ahora, que se cumpla mi sino" ("Now, let my destiny be fulfilled"; 34), initiate the main trajectory of the story, Moreira's flight from justice until his final treacherous capture and assassination.

This trajectory is appropriately episodic, as Gutiérrez strings together a series of approximately a dozen narrative nuclei that demonstrate repeatedly Moreira's attempt to hang onto a shred of decency, self-respect, and virtuous feelings against the odds of the accumulating case against him as a common criminal to be hunted down and killed like a wild animal. The principal thrust of these episodes involves situations in which Moreira finds himself obliged to defend his honor against what seem to be legions of evil men, "bad" gauchos, who are ironically the epitome of the unthinking violence and random brutality attributed to Moreira. Each time Moreira must defend himself against these aggressors, his persecutors are provided with one more justification for hunting him down. For purposes of the narrative's coherence and cohesion, Moreira sees these circumstances as confirmation of the fatal destiny that he must fulfill, and his weary observations to this effect punctuate the narrative:

> —¡Maldita sea mi suerte!—continuó, dirigiéndose a la puerte y llevando aún la daga en la mano—. ¡Que no puedo pisar un sitio sin tener que matar a un hombre! (105)
>
> —¡Está de Dios que no puedo luchar con mi sino! (145)
>
> ("Damn my luck," he went on, addressing the door and still carrying the dagger in his hands. "I can't go anywhere without having to kill a man!"
>
> "It is God's will that I not struggle against my destiny!")

These are only two examples of the epiphonemic phrases by which the narrator has Moreira characterize the fateful circumstances in which he finds himself entrapped, circumstances that constitute a trap of both happenstance and social design from which he cannot escape.

For purposes of the heightened characterization of his narrative, Gutiérrez organizes his material in such a way that the fundamental circumstance, provided by the unjust persecution Moreira experiences in protecting his good name, against the *teniente alcalde*'s interest in his wife, and his property, against Sardetti's fraud, is reinforced by, to use once again an allusion to the morphology of the folk tale, the dragons placed in his path that he must slay in order to remain free. For Gutiérrez's narrative, the irony is that these dragons are *both* embodiments of the evil that the noble gaucho's value system is ranged against *and* images of law and authority. Either his victims are ignoble officials or their death simply adds to the weight of evidence against Moreira by which official authorities are empowered to persecute him. When either these "dragons" or the authorities they represent turn out, in fact, to be figures of noble virtue consonant with Moreira's ideals, he is allowed to spare them and they become champions of his cause, much in the sense of the figure of Cruz in *Martín Fierro.* Significantly, although these individuals may go forth to proclaim how Moreira is an innocent victim of injustice, that they are unable to assuage the forces pursuing him adds to the case the narrator makes against a specific system of authority.

The trajectory of Moreira's flight from justice reaches a high point in the chapter "El nido de desventuras" (Nest of misfortunes). It is here he learns what has happened to his wife and son, "sumido en una meditación extraña, hundido en el abismo de sus penas" (deep in a strange meditation, sunk in the abyss of his suffering; 126). If up to this point Moreira's concern has been to return to his wife and son and to protect them from being persecuted in his absence, he now knows that there can be no turning back. Although neither his words as a character nor the narrator's as the controlling point of view in the narrative allude to a code of morality or to the effect that, once having been possessed by another man, Vicenta can never be taken back by or return to Moreira, it is obvious that this sort of standard is taken for granted by the characters (Moreira and his *compadre* Giménez, who is the bearer of the terrible story), narrator, and implied reader. That the modern reader may find this circumstance unreal is beside the point, since accepting it is clearly required as a fundamental point in order for Gutiérrez's novel to proceed.

It is because Moreira realizes that he cannot now turn back that his purpose in life shifts from returning to rescue and protect his family to avenging the wrong that has been done to him. He does return, but it is to kill the *teniente alcalde* in the bed that he now shares with Moreira's wife, Vicenta. Significantly, this is Moreira's first failure, and a subsequent attempt to kill the *teniente alcalde* also fails. Moreira's third and conclusive failure occurs when he is finally killed, the victim of the treachery of another gaucho who points him out—references to the Judas figure are explicitly used—to the military squadron pursuing Moreira. Moreira's need to kill the *teniente alcalde* and then to die himself becomes a ruling passion, and in the hands of another author a decade or so later, the story might have become a study in the psychopathology of the criminal mind. However, Gutiérrez remains faithful to his intention to portray the misfortunes of a good gaucho forced to pursue a life of violence. Toward this end, it is important that the narrative be circumscribed in terms of the iterative nuclei that underscore the futility of any attempt by Moreira to defend himself, to vindicate himself, or to prevail against the system of oppression and persecution that closes in around him.

In terms of the failure of the noble gaucho forced to go bad, the narrator supplements the juxtaposition of Moreira's inherent nobility the circumstances of violence thrust upon him with a major example of literary intertextuality. One might argue that the image of the wandering gaucho, meeting with one adventure after another on the open road, is in some sense an allusion to the Quijote model or even the figure of the wandering Jew. However, Gutiérrez has special emphasis for the model of the Cid, the Medieval Spanish warrior who rebels against an unjust liege lord, only to regain his confidence and to vindicate his nobility through the agency of his own superior virtue as an eloquent embodiment of the feudal ideal.

Juan Moreira's intertextuality with the Cid narrative is based on an echo of one of the poem's key opening lines: "Dios, qué buen vassallo, si oviesse buen señore!" (God, what a good vassal, if only he had a good lord!; l. 20). Compare the following aside by both the narrator and other characters in Gutiérrez's narrative: "Ya lo hemos dicho, [Moreira] hubiera hecho una figura gloriosa" (We've already said that Moreira would have made a glorious figure; 15). This echo is rounded out by one of the supplementary chapters added by Gutiérrez to *Juan Moreira* when it was published in book form, "La daga de Moreira": "La daga de Moreira is digna de figurar en un museo al lado de la espada del Cid" (Moreira's dagger is worthy to figure in a museum alongside the Cid's sword; 228). This sort of intertextuality adds a specifically literary dimension to the characterization of Moreira's inherent nobility and virtue as the ideal gaucho—a sort of Argentine "natural man"—corrupted and perverted into a life of violence at the hands of a corrupt and perverted official authority.

Of course, it is the primacy of this opposition that provides the plot impetus for Gutiérrez's narrative: the image of the lost Eden, of the trammeled Adam whose fall is the result of an external agency, and of the struggle against an implacable fate, not an impersonal and unknown fate, but one that is the specific correlative of a degraded social circumstance. This opposition provides the fundamental ideological configuration of Gutiérrez's novel and the point of reference both for the terms chosen to characterize Moreira and his misadventures and for the interpretation of their general sense of meaning. It is on the basis of this controlling ideology that we understand the irony of some of the chapter titles: "La pendiente del crimen" (The slope of crime)—Moreira's "crimes" are defined by the greater crime of his unjust persecution; or "La fuerza del sino" (The force of destiny)—Moreira's destiny is dictated by a corrupt social system and not by the secret forces of the universe as evoked by this title taken from the Duque de Rivas's famous romantic drama and Verdi's opera based on it.

The role that the narrator assumes as a mediating consciousness for Moreira's situation as the propitiatory victim of a corrupt social system is directly related to the generic ambiguity of Gutiérrez's work. Clearly, no pretense is made to be writing either history or biography: the simple absence of any of the normal apparatus of those emerging disciplines would allow the reader to accept the fact that *Juan Moreira* is basically a literary work, if only by default. The author goes to great length to confirm the historical or documentary accuracy of the general outlines of the story being presented. Yet there is an essential ambiguity arising from this appeal to fact on the one hand and the novelistic licenses that the author takes as a matter of course in characterizing Moreira's personal attitudes toward the fate that has befallen him.

If the narrator mediates between the story and the reader to the extent that a particular social thesis is being promoted and the rhetoric of the story points toward the highlighting of that thesis, Gutiérrez's narrator does not "crowd out" Moreira's own consciousness. That is, where one usually associates with the novel of Naturalism a narrator who must assume the entire burden of speaking for the characters, since, in their degraded circumstances, they are unable to speak or think for themselves, Gutiérrez, as part of his image of Moreira as an Adam unjustly denied the Edenic existence his noble spirit entitles him to, is careful to authenticate this image of the gaucho by having him speak in his own voice.

Moreira is able to verbalize his value system and the priority it accords to both defending one's person and respecting others. He is also able to reflect on his destiny, his sense of frustration and rage, his drive for revenge, and, ultimately, his death wish—all in order to escape a dead-end existence. These features of Gutiérrez's image of Moreira are particularly evident at the turning point in the narrative, the moment when Moreira's friend Julián informs him of the evil that has befallen his family. Although there is no way to verify the narrator's record of Moreira's words and reactions within a historiographic norm of documentary authentication, the foregrounding of Moreira as an individual reacting to his personal tragedy is crucial to the ideological position whereby the gaucho as epitomized by Moreira is an Adam brought down by a nefarious social system.

Audience Competence and the Theatrical Version of *Juan Moreira*

A reading of the dramatic version of *Juan Moreira,* written by Gutiérrez himself and first performed in 1886 in two acts by the troupe of the Uruguayan actor José J. Podestá, gives the impression of a work that is distinctly naive and unaccomplished artistically. The scenes—five in the first act and six plus a *Mutación* in the second—seem to skip from one episode to another in the description of the unjust persecution and eventual death of the "good gaucho" Juan Moreira. There is no apparent psychological development, at least as we associate it with Realist-Naturalist drama, and little in the way of a clear development of dramatic events from proposition to complication and denouement. In sum, the play seems to have only the barest of dramatic tension and to possess only an archaeological interest. A charitable if patronizing attitude would conclude that it was more attractive as the theatricalization of the Podestá troupe than as the literary text we read.

There is a unanimous recognition of *Juan Moreira* as the inaugural work of a national Argentine theater.[9] But legitimate questions can be raised concerning its artistic importance, particularly when read today or compared with European drama of the 1880s. While it is possible to attribute the fragmentary or episodic nature of *Juan Moreira* to the dramatic immaturity of the author and the primitiveness of the pre-Sánchez Argentine stage, it is possible to understand—if not justify aesthetically—this feature in terms of the reception of a work by its contemplated audience.

All literary works embody an implicit identification of their immedi-

9. The importance of the figure of Juan Moreira in the development of a national theater in Argentina and its enthusiastic reception are discussed by Raúl H. Castagnino, *Literatura dramática argentina,* 81–82. See also his *Sociología del teatro argentino.* Concerning audience reception of *Juan Moreira,* see Juan Carlos Ghiano's introduction in *Teatro gauchescho primitivo,* 13–16. Ghiano recognizes, in his opening paragraph, the limited nature of the Gauchesque theater alongside the poetry or the novel on the same themes (p. 5). Documentary information concerning the original pantomime version and the important decision to perform a spoken version of the play is presented by Rubén A. Benítez, *Una histórica función de circo,* and Oscar R. Beltrán, "Eduardo Gutiérrez y su pantomima *Juan Moreira.*"

ate audience and of the literary competence of that audience. In the case of *Juan Moreira* one can state that, in general terms, its audience could be counted on to have had a relatively limited experience with traditional, spoken theater, although it may have been extensively familiar with the contemporary pantomimes of the Podestá company and, indeed, *Juan Moreira* was first presented as a pantomime. Thus, it is possible to identify certain tendencies and overtheatricalizations designed to ensure and reinforce audience comprehension of the conventions of the dramatic enactment. On the other hand, the audience can be assumed to have had extensive familiarity with the Juan Moreira legend to the extent that that story jibed with the personal experiences of the audience or of friends and relatives who may have suffered similarly arbitrary treatment at the hands of the agents of law and order that is the main point of Gutiérrez's novel.

Roland Barthes has noted, in his extensive commentaries on reader competence and how works of literature are structured in terms of that competence, that, among other codes, all works depend on a reader knowledge of a specific *referential* or *cultural code.* This code, whose components are hierarchical and go from the universal to the cabalistic, from the internalized referential knowledge of all mankind to that of limited in-groups, means that it is not always necessary for authors to "fill in all the gaps." They can depend on the assumed competence of readers with this code or a subset of it to complete the story or grasp its implications. Allusions in classical literature or topical references in contemporary writings, songs, and jokes are all basic examples of the "shorthand" of the referential code. Barthes speaks of complex examples in nineteenth-century fiction, and it is true that when a realistic or a symbolist-psychological literature deals with the unknown or the unusual or deals with the familiar from unexpected perspectives the referential code becomes less reliable and can even constitute an ironic antiphony between popular wisdom and the true sense of the text.

In the case of *Juan Moreira*—as in most *costumbrista* fiction, or in early allegorical narratives based on established Christian stories, or in the *romance histórico* and *fronterizo*—there is little question of unexpected interpretation. The work may be seen simply as the dramatization of the familiar. The episodic nature of the play, rather than a lamentable defect of structural coherence when the work is analyzed in intrinsic isolation, becomes a completely justifiable structural openness when we see *Juan Moreira* in terms of the audience competence it implicitly anticipated. In short, there is no need either to give the complete details of the Moreira story either as specific legend or as a sociological type or to provide a texture of logical action and transition. Both are part of the audience competence and may, as a consequence, be comfortably dispensed with. It is only for modern readers that a problem of confusing fragmentation may occur, and thus it behooves us to "recover" from the structure of the work the historically conditioned competence we are expected to have. This may not necessarily increase the artistic value of *Juan Moreira,* but it does enable us to understand the principles underlying its structural configuration.

We may see the structural principle by which the discourse of a text is a function of the presumed reader-audience competence in several aspects of the drama *Juan Moreira.* For example, much of the language of the text is stereotyped, and we may say that such a language reinforces or supports the presumption that the popular audience will want to encounter in the play everyday speech with which it is familiar. A familiar linguistic pattern, therefore, seems to substantiate the premise that the audience competence implied by *Juan Moreira* will demand, as an adjunct of a story with which it is familiar, a language that likewise does not deviate from a colloquial norm. Conversely, both the highly concentrated expression of Romantic drama, with its emphasis on a language (and, of course, on a theme) that is pregnant with symbolic nuances, and the pseudodocumentary expression of Realist and Naturalist drama that attempts, in its turning away from Romantic symbolism, to convey faithfully the sociolinguistic texture of daily speech, are inappropriate to *Juan Moreira* as pre-Realist but post-Romantic theater. That is to say, the language of the play is neither symbolic in a Romantic fashion nor documentary in the often exaggeratedly verist sense of Realist-Naturalist theater. Rather, the language reflects a conception of speech that is a mixture of colloquial, daily expression and an expression that, still on a colloquial level, passes for the poetic or the symbolic. In this sense the language suggests a documentary verism without actually attaining it: it is a literary language that is "paracolloquial." It should be noted that many of the best plays of the major Latin American playwright of the period, the Uruguayan Florencio Sánchez (1875–1910), whatever Realist-Naturalist pretensions he may have had, are likewise characterized by this same register of linguistic expression—*La gringa* or *Barranca abajo,* for example.

Three features of linguistic expression in *Juan Moreira* may be adduced in support of the foregoing contention concerning a paracolloquialism demanded by a presumed audience competence: (1) language forms that capture an audience's linguistic self-image—the Argentine *voseo,* phonologic phenomena like *pensao* or *verdá,* lexical items like *juepucha* or *tata,* figures of speech like *¿Qué vientos lo traen por aquí, amigo?* or *Largue todo el rollo, amigo Julián;* (2) metaphors of the sort to be found in foregrounded popular speech where an effort is made to be "poetic" and to go beyond the cliché-ridden formulas of most colloquial expressions—"Sí, han creído que soy vaca que se ordeña sin manear" (Yes, they think I'm a cow who can be milked without having to be hobbled),[10] "tanto se baraja el naipe que al fin se gasta" (you shuffle the cards so much they wear out; 413), "... Yo no soy mancarrón patrio pa que me hagan parar a mano, ni soy candil pa que así no más me priendan" (I'm no local nag you can stop with one hand, nor a lantern you can light so easily; 422); (3) "reasoning" that reflects the attempt of the humble individual to give some sort of coherent account of his circumstance and his experiences, a reasoning that is, moreover, a repository of recognizable folk wisdom (accurate or otherwise), popular values, and the cunning of the individual obliged constantly to protect his meager interests from the rapacious. Reasoning of this kind forms the very basis of the work and on it rests the definition of Moreira's plight and his subsequent destiny. Although issues of semantic content and narrative development are involved, the structures of this reasoning involve a particular verbal texture. In the opening scene of the play, special attention is paid to questions (erotesis) and to the entailments in the last speech of Moreira:

ALCALDE.—Señor Sardetti. Usted ha sido llamado porque dice Moreira que usted le debe diez mil pesos.

SARDETTI.—Señor, eso es falso, yo no le debo ni un solo peso.

ALCALDE.—¿Y a qué viene entonces tanta mentira? ¿Por qué vienes a cobrar un dinero que no es tuyo?

MOREIRA.—Señor, yo cobro mi plata que he prestao y la cobro porque la necesito, este hombre quiere robarme si dice que no me debe, y yo entonces, señor Alcalde, vengo a pedir justicia.

ALCALDE.—La justicia que yo te he de dar es una barra de grillos, ladrón, que vienes a contar bolazos.

MOREIRA.—¿Quiere decir que no me debes nada?

SARDETTI.—Nada.

MOREIRA.—Y usted, ¿no quiere hacer que me pague?

ALCALDE.—Es claro, puesto que nada te debe, y que tú has venido a jugar sucio.

MOREIRA.—Está bueno, amigo. Usted me ha negao la deuda para cuyo pago le di tantas esperas, pero yo me la he de cobrar dándole una puñalada por cada mil pesos. Y usted, don Francisco, que me ha echao al

10. Eduardo Gutiérrez, *Juan Moreira,* in *Los clásicos del teatro hispanoamericano.* Hereafter cited parenthetically in the text by page number.

medio de puro vicio, guárdese de mí porque ha de ser mi perdición en esta vida, y de su justicia tengo bastante. (408–9)

(MAYOR.—Mr. Sardetti. You have been called because Moreira says you owe him 10,000 pesos.

SARDETTI.—Sir, that's a lie, I don't owe him a single peso.

MAYOR.—Why all this lying, then? Why do you sue for money that isn't yours?

MOREIRA.—Sir, I'm here to collect money that I've loaned because I need it. This man intends to rob me if he says that he doesn't owe me, and I, Mr. Mayor, have come to demand justice.

MAYOR.—The justice you'll get from me is a leg iron, thief, coming here telling lies.

MOREIRA.—You mean you owe me nothing?

SARDETTI.—Nothing.

MOREIRA.—And you won't make him pay me?

MAYOR.—That's right, because he doesn't owe you anything, and you've come here to play him dirty.

MOREIRA.—That's fine, friend. You have denied what's owed me after I gave you so much time to pay. But I'll collect by stabbing you once for each thousand pesos. And you, Don Francisco, who's cast me aside out of pure nastiness, be on guard against me because it'll be my ruin yet. I've had enough of your justice.)

In the fifth scene, Moreira and the Alcalde, now identified as Don Francisco, have another exchange; once again questions of "reasoning" are at issue:

DON FRANCISCO.—Pues sí, amigo, en cuanto Moreira caiga en mis manos no va a contar el cuento.

UN VECINO.—Pero, señor, el amigo Moreira era un buen criollo y lo que él ha hecho, lo hubiera hecho usted mismo, Don Francisco, y cuando un hombre como él se halla en la mala, es preciso darle algún alivio, que demasiado tiene con andar huido del pago.

DON FRANCISCO.—No, lo he de perseguir hasta encontrarlo y cuando lo encuentre lo he de matar como a un perro, pero antes de matarlo lo he de hacer sufrir alzándome con su mujer que me ha robado, porque yo me iba a casar con ella, y ya que no ha querido ser mi mujer, será mi gaucha. *(Moreira da un puntapié a la puerta, y cuando entra, todos se paran.)*

MOREIRA.—Quien va a matar de esta hecha, y a matar como matan los hombres, soy yo don Francisco que lo vengo a pelear, pa tener el gusto de levantarlo en la punta de mi daga, como quien mata a un perro. *(Don Francisco saca el revólver y le tira un tiro.)* Así matan ustedes, de lejos y sin riesgo ... (416)

(DON FRANCISCO.—Well, yes, friend, as soon as Moreira falls into my hands, that'll be the end of him.

A NEIGHBOR.—But, sir, my friend Moreira was a good neighbor, and what he has done you would've also, Don Francisco. And when a man like him finds himself down and out, it is necessary to give him some relief, since it's bad enough to be on the run.

DON FRANCISCO.—No, I'll go after him until I find him, and when I find him I'll kill him like a dog, but before I kill him, I'll make him suffer by running off with his wife who he stole from me, because I was going to marry her, and since she didn't want to be my wife, she'll be my woman. [*Moreira kicks the door, and when he enters, everybody stands up.*]

MOREIRA.—I'm the one who's going to do any killing around here, Don Francisco, for I'm here to fight, to have the pleasure of lifting you up with the tip of my dagger, just like you kill a dog. [*Don Francisco takes out his revolver and fires at him.*] That's the way your kind kills, from a distance and without taking any risks.)

A final example is Moreira's self-explanation when his motives are questioned by a political boss whose life he has just saved. This time, Moreira's account of his reasons establishes a counterpoint between the nobility of his act and the degradation of his lot in life:

MARAÑON.—Yo agradezco lo que usted ha hecho amigo Moreira y si alguna vez puedo serle útil en alguna cosa, acuda a mí, porque desde este momento soy su amigo.

MOREIRA.—No me agradezca nada, señor. Lo que yo he hecho, lo hubiera hecho cualquiera. Yo lo quiero a usted porque necesito querer a alguno y usted se me figura que es algo mío, que es mi hijo o que es mi hermano. Yo soy un hombre maldito, que he nacido para penar y pa andar huyendo de los hombres, que han sido mi perdición, y he querido a usted porque siento que al quererlo puedo respirar con más franqueza, y esto es tan dulce para mí, que si usted me mandase entregar a la partida, ahora mismo iba y me presentaba.

MARAÑON.—¿Y por qué anda usted, así, errante, retando a la justicia con sus actos que son malos? ¿Por qué no trabaja usted como antes y deja esa mala vida?

MOREIRA *(muy triste)*.—Con las penas que yo tengo en el corazón habría que llorar un año. Yo era feliz al lao de mi mujer y de mi hijo, y jamás hice a un hombre ninguna maldad. Pero yo habré nacido con algún sino fatal porque la suerte se me dio güelta y de repente me vi perseguido al extremo de pelear pa defender mi cabeza; usted ya sabe todo cuanto ha pasao, patrón. (418)

(MARAÑON.—I'm grateful for what you've done, friend Moreira, and if there's ever anything I can do for you, just let me know, for I'm your friend from now on.

MOREIRA.—Don't thank me for a thing, sir. What I've done, anyone would've done. I love you because I need to love someone, and you seem to me to like myself, as though you were my son or my brother. I am a damned man who has been born to suffer and to flee from men, who have been my downfall, and I have felt love for you because I feel that by loving you I can breath easier, and that is so sweet to me that, even if you were to order me to turn myself in to the police, I would go and do it.

MARAÑON.—And why are you always on the run, sir, defying justice with your deeds which are evil? Why don't you work as before and abandon this evil life?

MOREIRA [*very sad*].—There's enough suffering in my heart to cry a year. I was happy at the side of my wife and son, and I never did any man wrong. But I must have been born under a fatal sign because my luck turned and I suddenly saw myself persecuted to the extent of fighting to defend my head. You know everything that happened, boss.)

In addition to these linguistic features, all of which, it is maintained, reinforce the audience's sense of familiarity with what is going on and thus permit the episodic nature that marks the text, we have in the first act a mingling of prose and poetry, the latter in the form of a *payada* that gives further credence to the assertion that the language of the play is not simply documentarily colloquial in its reliance on an identification with the audience's linguistic self-image. The text of the *payada,* although undoubtedly faithful to the tenor and rhetoric of such popular diversions, is only tangentially colloquial. Rather, it seems to "give the tone" of the setting for the work and, in the closing strophes, to articulate the *vox populi* embodied in the characters of the play and, homologously, in the audience of the latter (see *Juan Moreira*, 411).

In these ways, and despite the fact that *Juan Moreira* is "weak" on plot development and "logical" representation, it is possible to see how a texture of familiarity is established for the audience in which two fundamental aspects of its competence in the face of cultural-literary artifacts are brought into play: first, the identification of a well-known legend associated either generally or specifically with the figure of Juan Moreira; second, the "acceptance" of the familiarity of the representation offered to it because of the particular linguistic registers of the work that may be called paracolloquial in their ability to be textually foregrounded. At the same time, these apparently familiar registers may be reassuring to the audience, an audience whose competence could not accept a thorough-going linguistic defamiliarization. In summary, to call *Juan Moreira* "primitive" or "unaccomplished" because of its episodic nature is not altogether justified. While it may not be an outstanding example of dramatic art, its fragmentariness may be seen less as the result of artistic naiveté on the part of Gutiérrez-Podestá and more as a question of a type of literary structure permitted by the sort of audience competence it implicitly envisioned.

Human Feelings and Military Discipline in José Ignacio Garmendia's *Cuentos de tropa*

> Estas digresiones me dominan de tal modo, que me escapo inconsciente á cada momento de mi título, es imposible corregirme; porque escribo con mi corazon y él ejerce despóticamente la influencia de los recuerdos, domina la cabeza y embarulla la lista con ese desaliño que ya en mi modo de escribir es natural y perdonable, porque demasiado se hace en salvar del olvido (sin pretension literaria alguna) tipos de otros tiempos de los cuales hoy ni remotamente se tiene idea.[11]

> (These digressions control me to such an extent that I escape at any moment from my title, and it is impossible to correct me. For I write with my heart, and it exercises the despotic influence of memory, ruling my head and messing up the list with that disorder that is already natural and excusable in my way of writing, because there is too much to do in rescuing from oblivion [without any literary pretenses] types from other times about which today one hasn't the remotest idea.)

The prominence of military activity during the nineteenth century in Latin America is a widely acknowledged fact. The struggle for independence from Spain, the rivalry between competing power factions, the ambitions of individual strongmen and their followers, the conflicts between central and federal models of government, and various campaigns of pacification and domination involved the military in many of the founding activities of the Latin American republics, an involvement that has often been used to explain the willingness of the military to assume direct governing responsibility in the twentieth century.

In Argentina, the overthrow of Rosas and the subsequent period of national reorganization involved considerable military activity, especially the subjugation of provincial caudillos and the imposition of a centralized government based in Buenos Aires, which, in order to consolidate federal power, was separated as a federal district from the province of Buenos Aires. The consolidation of a strong central government based in Buenos Aires was achieved in 1880, and this date also marks the achievement of a national order of peace and tranquility in which the army is increasingly less active in armed campaigns. Before 1880, the Argentine army, subsequent to the expeditions against provincial caudi-

11. José María Garmendia, *Cuentos de tropa (entre indios y milicos)*, 277–78. Hereafter cited parenthetically in the text by page number.

llos who held out against central control, was involved in the Expedición al Desierto to contain nomadic Indians and to defeat those who fought against the economic organization of the Pampa (1879) and the Guerra de la Triple Alianza (1865–1869) against Paraguay. The mobilization of a large army for the latter war, which pitted Argentina, Brazil, and Uruguay against scrappy Paraguay, made possible the concentrated effort of the Expedición, an operation so vital to the expansion of a landed oligarchy and political control over the central countryside.[12]

All of this resulted in a dramatic transition from the volunteer, citizen militia of the war for independence to the professional army that, by the turn of the century, Argentina had installed along strict Prussian lines. The multiple aspects of this evolution served as the basis for a body of writing in late nineteenth-century Argentina concerning army life and military operations. In conformance with the memorialist strand of the writing of the period, a number of texts are the personal accounts of individuals who participated in military campaigns and who witnessed the evolution of the army. José Ignacio Garmendia (1812–1925), writing under the pseudonym Fortún de Vera, provides one interpretation of the role of the army in his *Cuentos de tropa (entre indios y milicos)* (Troop stories [among Indians and soldiers], 1891; it should be noted that the text of *Cuentos de tropa* is marked by very erratic orthography and an almost chaotic use of the accent mark, lending it the surely unintentional appearance of unedited entries in a campaign diary).

A loosely structured series of commentaries about what a professional army ought to be like, based on historical examples and European models, and a collection of anecdotes that illustrate his beliefs, *Cuentos de tropa* provides both a nostalgic version of life among the troops and a declaration of principles for the modernization of what had historically been a raggle-taggle organization. Concomitantly, Garmendia recalls what the army had been in his youth (he would have been in his early thirties when he served as a major in the war with Paraguay) while also speaking programmatically as regards the role and character of a professional army.

Garmendia's evocation of the army of his youth is unabashedly nostalgic, and his comments are underlain by an ubi sunt lament for what has become an institution of the past. Curiously enough, his comments also speak of the passing of the indigenous population with which the first settlers of the Pampa cohabitated precariously and whose safety the army was supposed to defend, often not to any appreciable degree. "En

12. Viñas, *Indios, ejército y fronteras*.

la pampa" is a series of vignettes that Garmendia published pseudonymously in the newspaper *El Tribuno;* neither the pseudonym nor the inclusive dates of these fragments is given, although the section is dated January 1876. The author speaks of a way of life that has now disappeared:

> Mi afan tendrá su recompensa, no todo el querido panorama desaparece entre el espeso vapor de la bruma de la distancia, algo salvaremos de ese naufragio de la memoria, aquella dura vida de soldado medio indio, austera, miserable, corajosa, astuta y empedernida en los trabajos y en los peligros, amagada sin cesar por el sobresalto, á caballo, siempre á caballo, veloz, rápida sobre la marcha, sin tiempo para nada, ya sea combatiendo por la vida, ya sea esquivando receloso la persecucion, ó la sorpresa artera, teniendo por techo el firmamento con sus eternos guías, y por suelo la ondulosa llanura con sus hermosos lagos, que parecen mirajes de plata que marcan la etapa con el rastro imperceptible, ha de reflejar sus tintes, que aunque pálidos, dejarán siempre un bosquejo de esa pintoresca época que ya pasó. (330)
>
> ¿Qué queda? (333)
>
> (My interest will have its recompense, and not all of the beloved panorama will disappear in the dense vapor of fog of distance. We will salvage something from that shipwreck of memory, that harsh life of the half-Indian soldier, austere, miserable, brave, astute, and devoted to the tasks and the dangers, constantly threatened by surprise, on horseback, always on horseback, swift, rapid at march, with no time for anything, whether fighting for their lives or apprehensively dodging being pursued or the clever attack, having as the roof over their heads the firmament with its eternal guides and the uneven ground as a floor, with its beautiful lakes that look like silvery mirages that mark the way with an imperceptible trace, reflecting their colors which, although pale, will always be a sketch of that picturesque bygone time.
>
> Is there anything left?)

This bit of nostalgia for a way of life, of both the frontier army and the Indian populations destroyed or subjugated by the Expedición, comes quite late in *Cuentos de tropa,* and Garmendia's opening discussion on the nature of modern army life is unquestionably that of an older man intent on echoing the principles of organized discipline integral to institutionalized life in Argentina near the end of the century. The first segment of *Cuentos de tropa* is entitled "Cómo se cumple una orden," and in it Garmendia states his own military philosophy: greater discipline, less theory about war in the safety of the city, and more experience in the execution of military operations in the actual field of battle.

Undoubtedly, a subtext of *Cuentos de tropa* is the transition from a personalist army built on the venerable principles of a caudillo surrounded by loyal followers and a modern army in which demonstrated accomplishment must be the criterion of authority and for promotion. The references to other ways of achieving rank and the disclaimers of any personal attack are traces of this subtext:

> Soy partidario decidido de la juventud, porque ella en los ejércitos tiene el rol mas brillante y hermoso, el entusiasmo patriótico del combate; pero creo, que el mayor mal que se le hace, es demostrarle que la escala de los ascensos en la carrera militar argentina, no tiene dificultad ninguna; ni importa un sacrificio el adquirirla, y que es tan fácil como subir cualquier escala cómoda, cuyos peldaños se remontan con mucho descanso, y que lo mismo tiene para el favoritismo los distinguidos servicios de cuarenta años, como los insignificantes que puedan representar la tercera parte.
>
> Estas son verdades amargas pero oportunas, para enseñar que se exponen aquí sin la intención de herir a nadie, sino hacer notar un grave error cuyo remedio se tiene á la mano, siempre que nos demos cuenta de lo que es y será un buen ejército, y no se haga juego de niño de la primera institución del país, que está encargada nada menos que de la salvaguardia de la patria. (11–12)

> (I am a decided partisan of youth, because youth has the most brilliant and beautiful role in armies, that of the patriotic enthusiasm of combat. But I believe that the greatest evil done to youth is to show it that the scale of ranks in the Argentine military career presents no difficulty, that sacrifice in acquiring rank is not important and that it is as easy as climbing an easy flight of stairs, whose steps allow for a lot of breathers, and that favoritism and forty years of service are the same thing, as insignificant as the service of a third party.
>
> These are bitter but opportune truths, in order to show that they are put forth here without the slightest intention of hurting anyone, but rather to underscore a grave error whose remedy is within reach, as long as we realize what a good army is and will be and leave off playing children's games with the country's primary institution, one charged with nothing less than safeguarding the fatherland.)

The ringing tone with which this passage closes establishes the didactic intent of Garmendia's book, and the nostalgia of "En la pampa," with its earlier date, can be viewed as a contrasting parenthesis in the overall panorama of what the army in Argentina has been and what it has become and must continue to become so that, as the "country's primary institution" it can "safeguard the fatherland."

However, it becomes clear that the bulk of Garmendia's text is not a propaedeutic of the new, professional military, but, precisely as the title states, a series of stories concerning troops—that is, Garmendia's personal recollections of major events during his life as a soldier. While these stories are appended as exempla to his general comments on the need for order and discipline in the army, the personal note and an appreciation for individual differences is what makes them interesting as narratives of the period. The most interesting, and the longest, story in *Cuentos de tropa* is "El miliciano Rojas" (Rojas the Recruit). It is the description of a loyal soldier, of the sort evoked nostalgically in the quotation from "En la pampa," who is unfortunately a recalcitrant drunkard who subscribes only infrequently to the exigencies of military protocol. Garmendia evokes him in fond detail, underscoring Rojas's personal attachment to him and his courage and commitment as a soldier. Yet Rojas is unable to adapt himself to wartime discipline, and his constant refrain revolves around the indignities to an "hombre libre" (free man) occasioned by the structure of authority, principally as it relates to the prohibition against his getting drunk.

Rojas is thus a counterparadigm of the professional soldier Garmendia has ostensibly undertaken to promote, and, years after their relationship during the war against Paraguay, it is clear that Rojas continues to exercise a fascination over his former superior. Rojas is presented with all of the descriptors usually reserved for the "natural" man: his impulsiveness, his emotional outbursts, the disorderliness of his person and conduct, his resistance to authority and to anything remotely resembling discipline, his inability to "appreciate" the niceties of civilization, and so on. Yet it is evident that Garmendia hardly saw him as stupid and ignorant; Rojas is repeatedly praised for his native intelligence, for his ingenious resourcefulness (particularly with respect to bootlegging drink), and for his quick wit in defending himself against the demands of authority. For Garmendia, Rojas is an assemblage of contradictions, between his inability to adjust to military discipline and his commitment as a soldier, and it is this contradictory nature that fascinates the narrator against the backdrop of his repeated defense of the Prussian professionalization of the army. Garmendia appreciates the conflict between Rojas as a free spirit and the need for authority that he, as an officer, embodies. Yet, his narrative is marked by repeated gestures of defense of Rojas's conduct: "Fuera de esto, Rojas era un buen muchacho" (except for this, Rojas was a good boy; 153).

The characterization of Rojas as a "un muchacho grande" (an overgrown child; 153) assumes fuller narrative proportions when Garmendia recounts the execution of Gómez, Rojas's close companion in arms. Gómez, like Rojas, was often drunk, but, unlike Rojas, who was a happy drunk, Gómez would become ugly and combative. During one drunk, Gómez kills another man and is executed for it. Rojas is devastated, and Garmendia's descriptions of the pathos of the man's loss confirms his attachment to the spirited soldier.

From one point of view, the account of Gómez's execution returns the narrative to the seriousness of military discipline, not just the general social need for punishment for murder, but rather the question of authority associated with the ban on drinking in order to maintain discipline. Yet the narrator eschews the opportunity to drive this point home with any explicitness, and his story ends with praise for Rojas's human qualities instead: "¡Ah! siquiera ese buen amigo podía llorar" (Ah, this good friend could even cry; 248).

"Rojas el miliciano" is the portrait of an interesting and charming individual, a man whose free spirit is the basis of his attraction for the narrator, not his qualities as a paragon of the military discipline Garmendia sets out determinedly to champion. True, Rojas is a loyal soldier and an effective combatant, but more out of his personal commitments than out of professionalism as a soldier. As a consequence, there is an underlying and very obvious conflict in *Cuentos de tropa.* On the one hand, it is marked throughout by the narrator's adherence to a particular development of the Argentine army in order for it to serve as the "salvaguardia de la patria." But on the other hand, and from a far more interesting point of view, the digressions for which the narrator apologizes repeatedly are the opportunity for the characterization of the glories of a preprofessional army and of "natural" but undisciplined soldiers like Rojas:

> ¿Pero á dónde me he ido á parar? más no es tiempo perdido cuando se habla de las glorias nacionales; es bueno de cuando en cuando en esta época herir las imaginaciones jóvenes, negligentes que navegan alegres y contentos en el mar de la molicie, con los recuerdos sagrados de las grandes cosas que han hecho los argentinos. (119–20)

> (But where has my friend gone? Yet it is not a waste of time to speak of national glories. It is good now and then at this time to wound the imagination of the young, navigating carefree, happy and content in their sea of the soft life, with the sacred memories of the great deeds performed by the Argentines.)

Conclusion

Three types of documents have been examined in this study. The principal group consists of the major narrative works of writers associated with the Generation of 1880. These works—*La gran aldea, La Bolsa, Sin rumbo, Memorias de un vigilante*—are integral to our information concerning the period. Indeed, it is so frequent for historians and other social scientists to quote from these works that one often has the impression that they are less literary texts than they are primary sources. But this circumstance is precisely one of the principal motives for the present study and the question that it has posed: To what extent can these works, while still being considered novels, with all of the rhetorical trappings of narrative fiction of the late nineteenth century that their authors took such pains to absorb from their European models, be read primarily as ideological documents? Of course, the European and American parallels of these novels have also frequently served as major sources for social scientists, and both Realism and Naturalism were movements founded to a large part on principles that the social scientists were to crystallize as dominant methodologies.

The readings I have proposed of these novels go, however, beyond the historian's interest in the surface data they present. Such data, rhetorical manipulation aside, may be taken as a reliable index of the issues of interest to authors and their readers at the time of composition, like the descriptions of nouveaux riches trappings in *La Bolsa,* the machinations of the political process in *La gran aldea,* or emerging underworld types in Fray Mocho's *Memorias de un vigilante.* Numerous works cited in the Bibliography, signed by both historians and literary critics, have surveyed the content of the writings of the Generation of 1880 for these data, and Jitrik, Campanella, and the authors of *El 80* have done an excellent job of providing a composite portrait of Argentine society as it is represented in the writings of the period.

Where this study has sought to provide an original contribution to the role of literature in the Generation of 1880 has been to examine texts in terms of the underlying structuring principles of their organization as defined by ideological parameters. These parameters are complex and must be identified on several levels. Some of the questions that have been asked have to do with the very notion of narrative fiction and how it can pretend to provide an interpretation of social, political, and cultural movements of the day. These Argentine writers have little to add to the principles and priorities inherited from their European models, and in fact it has been customary to wish to demonstrate the serious defects of their novelistic design and execution. Nevertheless, if we accept the axiom that all writing is an ideological statement, we can leave aside the thorny question of authorial talent to address the various ways in which ideologizing inevitably takes place.

By the same token, there is little need to wonder whether such ideologizing was conscious, but whether the parameters that the critic's reading identifies are borne out by the features of the text, in conformance with prevailing analytical protocols. Concomitantly, whether those parameters matched the horizons of understanding of readers during the 1880s and 1890s or whether they are attributes of the reader a century later is not of essential concern. Certainly, contemporary critics can only read within the structures of their own ideologies, a circumstance that is further complicated when the critic has been formed outside the culture he is studying.

It is less than satisfactory merely to correlate critical interpretations with historical information, drawn either from the period (or parallel texts) or from subsequent historical analyses, since this information too is a function of ideological processes. It is for this reason that one cannot speak of the critic as simply engaged in "recovering" the originative meaning of cultural texts, and perhaps even less so in the case of complex literary narratives. There is a rich bibliography of contemporary ideological readings of Hardy, Zola, Howells, and other major and minor figures. What characterizes these readings is the recognition that the critic is not striving to restore the "meaning that the author intended for his works." Rather, ideological interpretation is designed to show us how we can continue today to read past texts as part of our cumulative process of acquiring knowledge about human society. Put differently, the Argentine Generation of 1880 only exists for us today to the extent that we can continue to read its texts within our own sociocultural horizons.

I said in the Introduction that the major extrinsic justification for this study is that the Generation of 1880 laid the bases for Argentine society during its greatest consolidation and that those bases continue to have validity for many of the ways, active and reactive, in which Argentina thinks about itself as a nation. The simplest confirmation of the importance of these cultural documents is that they continue to be read in Argentina as founding literary documents, a status accorded them because they belong to such an important period in that country's past. Yet one of the characteristics of the sustained reading of founding documents is that they tend to become encrusted with abiding interpretations. In the case of the works examined in this study, it has meant mostly the attention to the surface data that are of most interest to historians and opinions concerning the stylistic and formal relationships between them and their presumed European models.

What an ideological reading of the sort offered here hopes to be able to accomplish is to maintain the historical affiliation of the texts, while at the same time opening them up, so to speak, in terms of analytical strategies provided by contemporary critical practices. This has meant, in this study, focusing on a few details of a text and proceeding to explore what the ideological meanings of those details are. No pretense is made that the original readers of the texts might have seen those details as important or, if they did, that they would have attributed the same significance to them that this study has.

Rather, the significance that is attributed to them is a function of the contemporary critic's understanding—his contemporary ideological horizons—with respect to the importance of the period being dealt with and the social and cultural texts it generated. The identification of patriarchal absence in *La gran aldea* during a period in which patrimony is understood to have been an organizing principle of society, the creation of a role of social witness in *Memorias de un vigilante* in a period in which social analysis is a function of the need to control an ever more complex community, the justification of suicide in *Sin rumbo* at a time when the body is, first of all, perceived as a capital that cannot be squandered and, second, when the problems of life are optimistically viewed as solvable by science are all the results of a textual reading that correlates details of narrative structure with an understanding of the role of cultural texts as forms of social interpretation within original and successive contexts of a sociopolitical consciousness.

What we have come to recognize as a conventional literary history would either focus on only the consensually accepted major texts by prominent authors or create a series of tiers that would hold texts in place in terms of their perceived relative merit. Several such conventional sources exist in Spanish for the study in these terms of the literature of the Generation of 1880. By contrast, the practice of according an expansive ideological interpretation to selected textual details leads to a justification of the second type of text examined in this study. These secondary texts are all works of major figures—Cané, Mansilla, González. They are not clearly literary, however, either by our contemporary classifications or by the even more rigid classifications of one hundred years ago, when the proliferation of cultural practices and intellectual disciplines required the energetic dividing up of corpora and the zealous guarding of distinctions.

Autobiographical memoirs, travel books, and sociological disquisitions were not usually valued as literary documents, and the library subject classifications that emerged at the same time have routinely assigned them to nonliterary compartments, which is where one must look for them even in libraries today. In matter of fact, however, Argentine literary histories have usually considered them alongside more "clearly" literary works, and my analysis of them here has simply been to confirm that practice.

But rather than admit them to the study as ancillary literary works of value because of their influence on the literary tradition or stylistic features that echo the literary practices of the day, the inclusion of such texts in this study corresponds less to a desire to confirm that they are "literary" than to assert for them, in the context of an ideological reading of cultural texts, a sociocultural influence coextensive with, if not in some cases greater than, the prominence of conventional novels.

The third group of texts represents more of an overt defiance of conventional literary history. By taking works of Wilde and Ramos Mejía that are not their most famous or, in the case of Wilde, by evoking all of his multifaceted writing in terms only of one short story, I am rejecting the literary historian's need to discuss each writer comprehensively in terms of a putatively organic *oeuvre* that constitutes his place in Argentine cultural history. Although these analyses are meant to be contributions to Argentine cultural history, the emphasis is rather with some guiding themes as seen in the works discussed rather than through the overall symbolic meaning of Argentine society in 1880 viewed through the writing of Wilde, or through the writing of Gutiérrez, or through the writing of Fray Mocho. Some will complain that the result is neither a recognizable literary history nor the sort of unified cultural history that the Generation of 1880 deserves. The most appropriate response, it seems to me, is to plea for the greater depth of analysis of selected works placed in a mosaic pattern as a valid alternative to a more thorough, and considerably lengthier, historiography.

The critical bibliography on the literary writing of the Generation of 1880 is surprisingly thin, given the repeated general attestations to the significance of writers and texts, and the bulk of existing criticism has focused on either sociohistoric data or on some structural details like narrative voice or plot organization. To read these works in terms of their ideological parameters is to engage in a form of critical practice that is based on a tension between sociohistorical contexts and rhetorical strategies. I do not know if this makes the works more complex in terms of the sort of metric our literary tradition has grown to prize so insistently. It does, however, have the advantage of interfacing specific textual features, viewed as literary or otherwise, with hypotheses concerning the ways in which we may continue to read past cultural documents. Nor do I know if any of the specific conclusions my analyses have reached are surprising. But their principal merit lies in the intent to attest to the material specificity and independence of texts, while at the same time demonstrating how they can only be meaningful when read against a dense network of other sociocultural texts.

It is in this sense that we speak of verbal texts as rewritings of the social texts, and specific texts as rewritings of other texts together with which they constitute a continuum of textual practices. Thus, texts are not intrinsically meaningful: their meaning, rather, is a function of the place the critic can identify for them in the dense network of a culture's textual production. It has been easy to choose the texts discussed in this study because of the century of accumulated esteem attached to a particular author and particular works. It has also been easy to know where to begin with them, since there is also one hundred years of accumulated discussion of them. The major problem has been how to demonstrate, and to validate within the parameters of accepted critical protocols, the specific ideological dynamics that in conjunction with identifiable textual strategies account for one or another way of reading a particular text within the context of the Argentine Generation of 1880. Thus, this study must finally stand on the processes of determining meaning for each text as one facet of how the members, central and peripheral, of the Generation of 1880 were able to write about the dramatically changing society of their particular moment in Argentine history.

Appendix: Chronology

1852 Battle of Caseros in which Rosas is overthrown; founding of the Club del Progreso.

1853 A new national constitution approved by the Constitutional Congress held in Santa Fe.

1854 Construction begun on first Argentine railroad, the Ferrocarril del Oeste.

1857 Construction of the original Teatro Colón (on the site now occupied by the Banco de la Nación), the first building in Argentina to make use of iron.

1859 The forces of Buenos Aires defeated in a conflict with those of the national Confederation.

1860 Mitre's assumption of the governorship of Buenos Aires; beginning of final thrust in the conflict over the role of Buenos Aires in national unity, with Mitre supporting the dominance of the province and its capital city; founding of the Club del Plata.

1861 The forces of the Confederation defeated by those of Buenos Aires (under the direction of General Bartolomé Mitre), thereby paving the way for national unification under the leadership of the Province of Buenos Aires.

1862 Mitre proclaimed national president by an electoral college representing the provinces; Mitré elected the first president of the República Argentina.

1863 Construction begun on the railway link between Rosario and Córdoba, the first British railway venture in Argentina.

1865–1870 War waged against Paraguay in concert with Brazil and Uruguay.

1868 Domingo Faustino Sarmiento inaugurated as president; defeat of Mitre's handpicked successor.

1869 First national census.

1870 Newspaper *La Nación* founded by Mitre; *Una excursión a los indios ranqueles* published by Lucio V. Mansilla.

1870–1871 Franco-Prussian War prompts first Argentine foreign investment crisis.

1871 Yellow fever epidemic, claiming more than 7,000 victims, prompting migration of monied class from the colonial southside to the sparsely settled northside and leading to creation of aristocratic Barrio Norte; selfless care for the sick by the young physician Eduardo Wilde.

1872 First part of *Martín Fierro* published by José Hernández.

1873 Argentine Academy of Sciences and Letters founded.

1874 Nicolás Avellaneda inaugurated as president; defeat of Mitre's handpicked candidate; creation of the Jardines de Palermo (today, the vast Parque Palermo) on the site of Rosas's estate.

1875 Authorization of construction of the Puerto de Buenos Aires.

1876 Founding of the Sociedad Hipódromo Argentino; promulgation of the Ley de Inmigración y Colonización.

1877 The first industrial exposition in Buenos Aires featuring exclusively national materials.

1878 Publication of first volume of José M. Ramos Mejía's *Las neurosis de los hombres célebres en la historia argentina;* second volume published in 1882.

1879 General Julio A. Roca's Expedition into the Desert to undertake the definitive subjugation of the Indians, with 8.5 million hectares of land passing into the hands of 381 persons on the basis of prior land sales to finance the military venture; second part of Hernández's *Martín Fierro* published; publication in serial form of Eduardo Gutiérrez's *Juan Moreira;* inauguration of the Politeama theater, which features many foreign artists.

1880 Carlos Tejedor leads revolution against the national government; Buenos Aires declared national capital, thereby separating it from the Province of Buenos Aires (the new capital of which becomes La Plata); Roca inaugurated as president.

1881 Reimposition by Roca's administration of the gold standard, which had been abandoned in 1876 because of the financial crises of the period; stimulation by official policies of Jewish immigration to Argentina in response to Russian pogroms; publication of Eduardo Wilde's "Tini."

1882 Publication of Eduardo Gutiérrez's *Juan Manuel de Rosas: los dramas del terror;* founding of the Jockey Club by future president Carlos Pellegrini; authorization of construction of sanitary works for Buenos Aires.

1883 Authorization of construction of the first Hotel de Inmigrantes in the Buenos Aires port area.

1884 Declaration of the laws mandating civil marriage and lay education, the fruit of an effort led by Eduardo Wilde as

Ministro de Justicia, Culto e Instrucción Pública; publication as a *folletín* of Lucio V. López's *La gran aldea;* publication of Miguel Cané's *Juvenilia;* publication of Antonio Argerich's *¿Inocentes o culpables?*

1885 Publication of Eugenio Cambaceres's *Sin rumbo.*

1886 Miguel Juárez Celman inaugurated as president; presentation of dramatic version of Eduardo Gutiérrez's *Juan Moreira* by Podestá theatrical troupe; Sarah Bernhardt's appearance at the Teatro Politeama, one of the city's major cultural centers.

1887 Founding of the Centro Científico Literario and its publication, *La revista científica literaria;* founding of the Sociedad del Cuarteto.

1888 Inauguration of the present Teatro Colón; inauguration in Buenos Aires of the Teatro de la Opera, one of the major cultural centers of the city; Adelina Patti Nicolini's appearance at the Teatro Politeama.

1889 Publication of Miguel T. Podestá's *Irresponsable.*

1890 Severe stock market crisis and depression, the culmination of financial events of mid–1889 (land values plunge by 50 percent in a twelve-month period); Leandro N. Alem leads revolution, prompting Celman's resignation and the inauguration of Carlos Pellegrini as president in 1891; the Ferrocarril del Oeste sold to British interests, which now control all major Argentine railways; publication of Carlos María Ocantos's *Quilito.*

1891 Publication in serial form in *La Nación* of Julián Martel's *La Bolsa* (not published in book form until 1898); publication of José Ignacio Garmendia's *Cuentos de tropa (entre indios y milicos);* renegotiation of Argentine national debt with British interests as part of attempt to recover from the financial disaster of 1890; debt renegotiated in 1893, with subsequent deferments; full financial recovery by 1896; foundation of the Jewish Colonization Society with funding from the Baron de Hirsch.

1892 Luis Sáenz Peña inaugurated as president. Founding in the home of the poet Rafael Obligado of El Ateneo, a literary and artistic circle that brought together the most outstanding elements of Argentine intelligentsia.

1893 Arrival in Buenos Aires of the Nicaraguan poet Rubén Darío, considered the major figure of Spanish-American Modernism; Darío will remain in Argentina, the center of the Spanish-

American literary world, until 1898; publication of Joaquín V. González's *Mis montañas.*

1895 Resignation as president of Sáenz Peña and inauguration of José E. Uriburu.

1897 Founding of the general interest magazine *Caras y caretas;* recognition by a constitutional convention of the new demographic realities of the country brought about by massive immigration; publication of José Sixto Alvarez's *Memorias de un vigilante.*

Bibliography

Primary Sources

Alvarez, José Sixto [pseud., Fray Mocho]. *Cuentos de Fray Mocho.* Con ilustraciones de Basaldúa. Buenos Aires: Editorial de la Universidad de Buenos Aires, 1963.

———. *Memorias de un vigilante.* Buenos Aires: Hyspamérica, 1985.

Argerich, Antonio. *¿Inocentes o culpables?* Buenos Aires: Hyspamérica, 1984.

Cambaceres, Eugenio. *Sin rumbo.* Buenos Aires: Plus Ultra, 1986.

Cané, Miguel. *Juvenilia.* 6th ed. Buenos Aires: Editorial Universitaria de Buenos Aires, 1976.

Garmendia, José María. *Cuentos de tropa (entre indios y milicos).* Buenos Aires: Jacobo Peuser, 1891.

González, Joaquín V. *Mis montañas.* In *Tres clásicos argentinos,* 165–412. Prólogo de Julio Molina Aguirre. Madrid: Aguilar, 1953.

———. *La tradición nacional.* Buenos Aires: Hachette, 1926.

Grandmontagne, Francisco. *Los inmigrantes prósperos.* Madrid: M. Aguilar, 1944.

Gutiérrez, Eduardo. *Juan Manuel de Rosas: los dramas del terror.* Buenos Aires: Harpón, 1944.

———. *Juan Moreira.* In *Los clásicos del teatro hispanoamericano,* edited by Gerardo Luzuriaga and Richard Reeve, 408–23. Mexico City: Fondo de Cultura Económica, 1975.

———. *Juan Moreira.* 2d ed. Buenos Aires: Editorial Universitaria de Buenos Aires, 1965.

López, Lucio V. *La gran aldea: costumbres bonaerenses.* Buenos Aires: Plus Ultra, 1965.

López de Gomara, Justo S. *Gauchos y gringos (bosquejo de costumbres argentinas en un acto y en verso).* Buenos Aires: Universidad de Buenos Aires, Facultad de Filosofía y Letras, Instituto de Literatura Argentina "Ricardo Rojas," 1963.

Mansilla, Lucio V. *Cuentos del fogón (Excursión a los indios ranqueles).* Buenos Aires: Editorial Nova, n.d.

———. *Entre-nos: causeries del jueves.* Buenos Aires: Hachette, 1963.

———. *Una excursión a los indios ranqueles.* Edición, prólogo y notas de Julio Caillet-Bois. Mexico City: Fondo de Cultura Económica, 1947.

———. *Narraciones de un porteño.* Buenos Aires: "Argentina Libre," 1943.

Miró, José María [pseud., Julián Martel]. *La Bolsa: la diputación de Alberto.* Buenos Aires: Plus Ultra, 1975.

Podestá, Manuel T. *Irresponsable: recuerdos de la Universidad; novela argentina.* Buenos Aires: Minerva, 1924.

Ramos Mejía, José M. *Las neurosis de los hombres célebres en la historia argentina.* Edición completa en 1 volumen con un prólogo de José Ingenieros. Buenos Aires: Acaconda, 1936.

Villafañe, Segundo I. *Horas de fiebre.* Buenos Aires: Universidad de Buenos Aires, Facultad de Filosofía y Letras, 1960.

Wilde, Eduardo. "Ignacio Pirovano." In *Tini y otros relatos,* 63–76. Buenos Aires: Editorial Universitaria de Buenos Aires, 1960.

———. "Tini." In *Tini y otros relatos,* 17–33. Buenos Aires: Editorial Universitaria de Buenos Aires, 1960.

Secondary Sources

Anderson Imbert, Enrique. "La Generación del 80." In *On the Centennial of the Argentine Generation of 1880,* edited by Hugo Rodríguez Alcalá, 1–10. Latin American Studies Program, no. 4. Riverside: University of California, 1980.

———. "La literatura argentina de 1880–1910." In *La Argentina del ochenta al centenario,* edited by Gustavo Ferrari and Ezequiel Gallo, 725–43. Buenos Aires: Sudamericana, 1980.

Andreetto, Miguel Angel. "Temas de las *Memorias de un vigilante* de José S. Alvarez." *Presencia* 3 (1966): 93–99.

Ankersmit, F. R. *Narrative Logic: A Semantic Analysis of the Historian's Language.* The Hague: Martinus Nijhoff, 1983.

Ara, Guillermo. *Fray Mocho: estudio y antología.* Buenos Aires: Ediciones Culturales Argentinas, 1983.

———. "Introducción." In *Aguas abajo,* by Eduardo Wilde, 5–43. Buenos Aires: Huemul, 1964.

———. *La novela naturalista hispanoamericana.* Buenos Aires: Editorial Universitaria de Buenos Aires, 1965.

La Argentina del ochenta al centenario. Edited by Gustavo Ferrari and Ezequiel Gallo. Buenos Aires: Sudamericana, 1980.

Argentina, la otra patria de los italianos. General editor Manrique Zago. Buenos Aires: Manrique Zago, 1983.

Avellaneda, Andrés. "Contra su época: una lectura de la poesía del ochenta." In *On the Centennial of the Argentine Generation of 1880,* edited by Hugo Rodríguez Alcalá, 191–213. Latin American Studies Program, no. 4. Riverside: University of California, 1980.

———. *El habla de la ideología: modos de réplica literaria en la Argentina contemporánea.* Buenos Aires: Sudamericana, 1983.

———. "El proceso de la centura y la centura del 'Proceso': Argentina, 1976–1983." Unpublished.

Azeves, Angel Héctor. "La ascendencia romántica de los poemas gauchescos." *Revista de educación,* n.s. 3, no. 12 (1958): 434–46.

Bakhtin, Mikhail. *Rabelais and His World.* Cambridge: The M.I.T. Press, 1968. Orig. published in Russian in 1965.

Barthes, Roland. *S/Z.* Translated by Richard Miller. New York: Hill and Wang, 1974.

Beltrán, Oscar R. "Eduardo Gutiérrez y su pantomima *Juan Moreira.*" In *Los orígenes del teatro argentino,* 129–56. Buenos Aires: Luján, 1934.

Benarós, León. "Eduardo Gutiérrez: un descuidado destino." In *El Chaco,* by Eduardo Gutiérrez, 7–68. Buenos Aires: Hachette, 1960.

Benítez, Rubén A. *Una histórica función de circo.* Buenos Aires: Universidad de Buenos Aires, Departamento Editorial, 1956.

Biagini, Hugo Edgardo. *Cómo fue la generación del 80.* Buenos Aires: Plus Ultra, 1980.

Blasi, Alberto. "Dos narradores del 80: Fray Mocho y Manuel T. Podestá." In *On the Centennial of the Argentine Generation of 1880,* edited by Hugo Rodríguez Alcalá, 68–95. Latin American Studies Program, no. 4. Riverside: University of California, 1980.

———. "Manuel T. Podestá." *Boletín de la Academia Argentina de Letras* 159–60 (1976): 55–89.

———. "El médico novelista Manuel T. Podestá." *Chasqui* 12, nos. 2–3 (1984): 10–18.

Blasi, Alberto Oscar. "Las crisis del noventa y sus imágenes en la narrativa argentina." In *Actas de las Terceras Jornadas de Investigación de la Historia y Literatura Rioplatense y de los Estados Unidos,* 31–40. Mendoza: Universidad Nacional de Cuyo, Facultad de Filosofía y Letras, 1968.

———. *Los fundadores: Cambaceres, Martel, Sicardi.* Buenos Aires: Ediciones Culturales Argentinas, 1962.

———. *Introducción a Lucio V. López.* Buenos Aires: Huemul, 1965.

Blasi Brambilla, Alberto. *Un novelista argentino del 80: Manuel T. Podestá.* Buenos Aires: Huemul, 1980.

Blasi Brambilla, Alberto Oscar. "Fray Mocho y su versión de la transición finisecular." *Revista de educación,* n.s. 5, nos. 5–6 (1960): 256–66.

Bonatti, María. "Juan Moreira en un contexto modernista." *Revista iberoamericana* 104–5 (1978): 557–65.

Borello, Rodolfo A. "Los escritores del 80." *Revista de literatura argentina e iberoamericana* 1 (1959): 32–46.

———. "Habla y lengua literaria en la narrativa: 1880–1910." In *Actas de las Terceras Jornadas de Investigación de la Historia y Literatura Rioplatense y de los Estados Unidos,* 41–46. Mendoza: Universidad Nacional de Cuyo,

Facultad de Filosofía y Letras, 1968. Also in his *Habla y literatura en la Argentina,* 73–101. Tucumán: Universidad Nacional de Tucumán, Facultad de Filosofía y Letras, 1974.

Borges, Jorge Luis. "La fruición literaria." *El idioma de los argentinos,* 101–9. Buenos Aires: M. Gleizer, 1928.

Brown, Jonathan C. "The Bondage of Old Habits in Nineteenth-Century Argentina." *Latin American Research Review* 21, no. 2 (1986): 3–31.

Burgos, Fernando. "Planos ideológicos de la modernidad en *Sin rumbo.*" *Megafón* 14 (1984): 135–40.

Burns, E. Bradford. *The Poverty of Progress: Latin America in the Nineteenth Century.* Berkeley: University of California Press, 1980.

Butler, Christopher. *Interpretation, Deconstruction, and Ideology: An Introduction to Some Current Issues in Literary Theory.* Oxford: Clarendon Press, 1984.

Cambours Ocampo, Arturo. "Los escritores argentinos en 1880." In his *Indagaciones sobre literatura argentina,* 73–88. Buenos Aires: Albatros, 1952.

Campanella, Hebe N. "La atmósfera literaria." *El movimiento positivista argentino,* edited by Hugo Edgardo Biagini, 38–77. Buenos Aires: Belgrano, 1985.

———. *La generación del 80: su influencia en la vida cultural argentina.* Buenos Aires: Tekné, 1983.

Carilla, Emilio. *Literatura argentina, 1800–1950 (esquema generacional).* Buenos Aires: Ministerio de Educación de la Nación, Universidad Nacional de Tucumán, Facultad de Filosofía y Letras, 1954.

———. "El 80 y el concepto de generación." In *On the Centennial of the Argentine Generation of 1880,* edited by Hugo Rodríguez Alcalá, 46–67. Latin American Studies Program, no. 4. Riverside: University of California, 1980.

Casadevall, Domingo F. *El tema de la mala vida en el teatro nacional.* Buenos Aires: Guillermo Kraft, 1957.

Castagnaro, R. Anthony. "The Novel in Nineteenth-Century Argentina." In his *The Early Spanish American Novel,* 69–183. New York: Las Américas, 1971.

Castagnino, Raúl H. *Literatura dramática argentina.* Buenos Aires: Pleamar, 1968.

———. *Miguel Cané: cronista del ochenta porteño.* Buenos Aires: Oeste, 1952.

———. *Sociología del teatro argentino.* Buenos Aires: Nova, 1963.

Castellanos, Luis Arturo. "Situaciones conflictivas en la historia y literatura argentina entre 1880 y 1910." In *Actas de las Terceras Jornadas de Investigación de la Historia y Literatura Rioplatense y de los Estados Unidos,*

75–83. Mendoza: Universidad Nacional de Cuyo, Facultad de Filosofía y Letras, 1968.

Castillo, Homero. "Procedimientos dramáticos en *La gringa.*" *Duquesne Hispanic Review* 6.1 (1967): 31–36.

Castiñeiras, Julio R. *Algunos aspectos de la obra de Joaquín V. González.* La Plata: Universidad Nacional de La Plata, 1938.

Clark, Priscilla B. P. "Literature and Sociology." In *Interrelations of Literature,* edited by Jean-Pierre Barricelli and Joseph Gibaldi, 107–22. New York: The Modern Language Association of America, 1982.

Clementi, Hebe. "José María Ramos Mejía (1849–1914)." In *El movimiento positivista argentina,* edited by Hugo Edgardo Biagini, 388–98. Buenos Aires: Belgrano, 1985.

Crawford, William Rex. "Independence and Nationhood [Argentina]." In his *A Century of Latin American Thought,* 12–51. Rev. ed. New York: Frederick A. Praeger, 1961.

———. "Positivism and Idealism in Argentina." In his *A Century of Latin American Thought,* 95–169. Rev. ed. New York: Frederick A. Praeger, 1961.

Cúneo, Dardo. "Esquema interpretativo del 80." In *Actas de las Terceras Jornadas de Investigación de la Historia y Literatura Rioplatense y de los Estados Unidos,* 113–16. Mendoza: Universidad Nacional de Cuyo, Facultad de Filosofía y Letras, 1968.

Dellepiane, Angela B. "Eduardo Wilde y su 'gramática cerebral.'" In *On the Centennial of the Argentine Generation of 1880,* edited by Hugo Rodríguez Alcalá, 115–60. Latin American Studies Program, no. 4. Riverside: University of California, 1980.

———. "Los folletines gauchescos de Eduardo Gutiérrez." *Revista iberoamericana* 104–5 (1978): 487–506.

Díaz Araujo, Enrique. *Eduardo Wilde, el ideólogo argentino de ochenta.* Mendoza: Universidad de Mendoza, Facultad de Ciencias Jurídicas y Sociales, Centro de Estudiantes de Derecho, 1976.

Dowling, William C. *Jameson, Althusser, Marx: An Introduction to the Political Unconscious.* Ithaca: Cornell University Press, 1984.

Duhalde, Eduardo Luis. *El estado terrorista argentino.* Barcelona: Argos Vergara, 1983.

Duncan, Tim. "La prensa política: 'Sud-América', 1884–1892." In *La Argentina del ochenta al centenario,* edited by Gustavo Ferrari and Ezequiel Gallo, 761–83. Buenos Aires: Sudamericana, 1980.

Eagleton, Terry. *Literary Theory: An Introduction.* Minneapolis: University of Minnesota Press, 1983.

Echagüe, Juan Pablo. "Eduardo Wilde." In *Páginas selectas,* 281–94. Buenos Aires: Ediciones Argentinas, 1945. Also, in his *Escritores de la Argentina,* 109–35. Buenos Aires: Emecé, 1945.

Egan, Carlos A. "Peripheralization and Cultural Change: Argentina, 1880–1910." *Proceedings of the Pacific Coast Council on Latin American Studies* 10 (1982–1983): 11–28.

Enciclopedia de la literatura argentina. Compiled by Pedro Orgambide and Roberto Yahni. Buenos Aires: Sudamericana, 1970.

Epple, Juan. "Eugenio Cambaceres y el naturalismo en Argentina." *I&L: Ideologies and Literature* 14 (1980): 16–50.

Estrada, José Manuel. *La política liberal bajo la tiranía de Rosas.* Buenos Aires: Estrada, 1942.

Ferns, H. S. *Argentina.* London: Ernest Benn, 1969.

Fishburn, Evelyn. *The Portrayal of Immigration in XIXth Century Argentine Fiction (1845–1902).* Berlin: Colloquium Verlag, 1981.

Foster, David William. "*Amalia* como novela gótica." *Anales de literatura hispanoamericana* 6 (1977): 223–28.

———. "David Viñas: lecturas reconstructivistas de la historia nacional." *I&L: Ideologies and Literature,* forthcoming.

———. "Elementos de literaturización en un *diálogo* de Bartolomé Hidalgo." *Anuario de letras* 21 (1983): 237–82. Also in *Estudios de literatura argentina,* 85–95. Buenos Aires: Universidad de Buenos Aires, Facultad de Filosofía y Letras, Instituto de Literatura Argentina "Ricardo Rojas," 1982.

———. *Para una lectura semiótica del ensayo latinoamericano.* Madrid: José Porrúa Turanzas, 1983.

Fraser, Howard. *Magazines and Masks: "Caras y caretas."* Tempe: Arizona State University, Center for Latin American Studies, 1987.

Gallo, Ezequiel, and Roberto Cortés Conde. *Argentina: la república conservadora.* Vol. 5 of *Colección Historia argentina,* edited by Tulio Halperín Donghi. Buenos Aires: Paidós, 1987.

Gandía, Enrique de. "Introducción." In *La política liberal bajo la tiranía de Rosas,* by José Manuel Estrada. Buenos Aires: Estrada, 1942.

Garrels, Elizabeth. "El 'espíritu de la familia' en *La novia del hereje* de Vicente Fidel López." *Hispamérica* 46–47 (1988): 3–24.

Ghiano, Juan Carlos. "Estudio preliminar." In *Entre-nos: causeries del lueves,* by Lucio V. Mansilla, 7–33. Buenos Aires: Hachette, 1963.

———. "Miguel Cané y su tiempo." In *Constantes de la literatura argentina,* 65–80. Buenos Aires: Raigal, 1953.

———. *Teatro gauchesco primitivo.* Buenos Aires: Losange, 1957.

Giusti, Roberto F. "Fray Mocho." *Cursos y conferencias,* July-September 1953, pp. 231–34.

———. "La prosa de 1852 a 1900." In *Historia de la literatura argentina,* edited by Rafael Alberto Arrieta, 3:359–438. Buenos Aires: Peuser, 1958–1960.

González, Julio V. "Prólogo." In *El juicio del siglo, o cien años de historia argentina,* by Joaquín V. González, ix-xxi. Buenos Aires: Editorial Rosario, 1945.

González Arrili, Bernardo. "Lucio Vicente López." *Journal of Inter-American Studies* 5.2 (1963): 161–68.

González, Santiago. *Miguel Cané.* Buenos Aires: Centro Editor de América Latina, 1968.

Graña, María Cecilia. "Buenos Aires en la imaginación del 80. El teatro como paradigma." *Letterature d'America* 4, 16 (1983): 89–121.

Halperín Donghi, Tulio. "La historiografía: treinta años en busca de un rumbo." In *La Argentina del ochenta al centenario,* edited by Gustavo Ferrari and Ezequiel Galloc, 829–40. Buenos Aires: Sudamericana, 1980.

———. "Una nación para el desierto argentino." In *Proyecto y construcción de una nación (Argentina 1846–1880),* ix-ci. Caracas: Biblioteca Ayacucho, 1980.

Ingenieros, José. "La personalidad intelectual de José M. Ramos Mejía." In *Las neurosis de los hombres célebres en la historia argentina,* by José M. Ramos Mejía, 9–67. Buenos Aires: Anaconda, 1936.

Jameson, Fredric. *The Political Unconscious: Narrative as a Socially Symbolic Act.* Ithaca: Cornell University Press, 1981.

Jitrik, Noé. "Cambaceres: adentro y afuera." In *Ensayos y estudios de literatura argentina,* 35–54. Buenos Aires: Galerna, 1970.

———. *Muerte y resurrección de "Facundo."* Buenos Aires: Centro Editor de América Latina, 1968.

———. *El 80 y su mundo.* Buenos Aires: Jorge Alvarez, 1968.

———. *La revolución del 90.* Buenos Aires: Centro Editor de América Latina, 1970.

Jones, C. A. *Sarmiento: "Facundo."* London: Grant & Cutler, in association with Tamesis Books, 1974.

King, Harry Lee, Jr. "Juan Manuel de Rosas and His Epoch as Portrayed in Argentine Fiction." Ph.D. dissertation, University of Colorado, 1962.

Kohn Loncarica, Alfredo G., and Abel L. Agüero. "El contexto médico." In *El movimiento positivista argentino,* edited by Hugo Edgardo Biagini, 119–40. Buenos Aires: Belgrano, 1985.

Lacau, María Hortensia, and Mabel Manacorda de Rosetti. "Eduardo Wilde y el modernismo." *Expresión* 4 (1947): 16–29.

Lafleur, Héctor René, Sergio D. Provenzano, and Fernando P. Alonso.

Las revistas literarias argentinas, 1893–1967. Buenos Aires: Centro Editor de América Latina, 1968.

Landaburu, Argentino J. "La medicina en la capital federal de 1880 a 1925." Seminario de Historia de la Medicina Argentina, *Historia general de la medicina argentina,* 135–41. Córdoba: Universidad Nacional de Córdoba, Dirección General de Publicaciones, 1976.

Lanuza, José Luis. *Genio y figura de Lucio V. Mansilla.* Buenos Aires: Editorial Universitaria de Buenos Aires, 1965.

Leal, Luis. "El cuento de la generación del ochenta." In *On the Centennial of the Argentine Generation of 1880,* edited by Hugo Rodríguez Alcalá, 25–45. Latin American Studies Program, no. 4. Riverside: University of California, 1980.

Lebedinsky, Mauricio. *La década del 80: una encrucijada histórica.* Buenos Aires: Siglo Veinte, 1967.

Lescano, Luis R. "[Resúmenes históricos, etc.]." In *La Bolsa: la diputación de Alberto,* by José María Miró [pseud., Julián Martel], 7–45. Buenos Aires: Plus Ultra, 1975.

Levene, Ricardo. *Ideas sociales directrices de Joaquín V. González.* Buenos Aires, [1935].

Lewald, H. Ernest. "Aim and Function of Costumbrismo Porteño." *Hispania* 46 (1963): 525–29.

Lichtblau, Myron I. *The Argentine Novel in the Nineteenth Century.* New York: Hispanic Institute in the United States, 1959.

Linares, Carlos Alberto. "La generación de 1880." *Gaceta literaria* 20 (1960): 6–7.

Literatura, ideología y lenguaje. Edited by Mario Monteforte Toledo. Mexico City: Instituto de Investigaciones Sociales, Universidad Nacional Autónoma de México; Grijalbo, 1976.

Lynch, John. *Argentine Dictator: Juan Manuel de Rosas, 1829–1852.* Oxford: Clarendon Press, 1981.

Marasso, Arturo. "Joaquín V. González, el artista y el hombre." *Boletín de la Academia Argentina de Letras* 18 (1937): 181–211.

Marín, Marta. *Fray Mocho.* Buenos Aires: Centro Editor de América Latina, 1967.

Markiewicz, Henry. "Ideología y obra literaria." *Texto crítico* 26–27 (1983): 32–44.

Marún, Giaconda. "Relectura de *Sin rumbo:* floración de la novela moderna." *Revista iberoamericana* 135–36 (1986): 379–92.

Mastronardi, Carlos. "Fray Mocho, espejo de criollos." In *Formas de la realidad nacional,* 99–108. Buenos Aires: Ediciones Culturales Argentinas, Ministerio de Educación y Justicia, 1961.

Megenney, William W. "*La gran aldea* de Lucio V. López: novela integral." *Letras de Buenos Aires* 6 (1982): 21–34.

Molloy, Sylvia. "Imagen de Mansilla." In *La Argentina del ochenta al centenario,* edited by Gustavo Ferrari and Ezequiel Gallo, 745–59. Buenos Aires: Sudamericana, 1980.

———. "Lectura de Eduardo Wilde." *Nueva revista de filología hispánica* 22 (1973): 337–48.

Montero, Belisario J. "La filosofía de Eduardo Wilde." *Revista de filosofía, cultura, ciencias, educación* 6 (1921): 365–89.

Morales, Ernesto. *Fray Mocho.* Buenos Aires: Emecé, 1948.

Morando, Horacio C. "Eduardo Gutiérrez: populismo y fama literaria." *Foro literario* 9–10 (1981): 27–31.

El movimiento positivista argentino. Edited by Hugo Edgardo Biagini. Buenos Aires: Belgrano, 1985.

Nallim, Carlos Orlando. "La visión del indio en Lucio V. Mansilla: testimonio y literatura en *Una excursión a los indios ranqueles.*" *Latino América* 7 (1974): 101–33.

Nobile, Beatriz de. *Análisis de "La Bolsa."* Buenos Aires: Centro Editor de América Latina, 1986.

El 80. Buenos Aires: Centro Editor de América Latina, 1968–1969.

Olaso, Ezequiel de. "Notas para una discusión sobre la cultura de ochenta." In *La Argentina del ochenta al centenario,* edited by Gustavo Ferrari and Ezequiel Gallo, 697–705. Buenos Aires: Sudamericana, 1980.

On the Centennial of the Argentine Generation of 1880. Edited by Hugo Rodríguez Alcalá. Latin American Studies Program, no. 4. Riverside: University of California, 1980.

Onega, Gladys. *La inmigración en la literatura argentina, 1880–1910.* Buenos Aires: Galerna, 1969.

Operativité des méthodes sociocritiques. Edited by Ralph Heyndels and Edmond Cros. Montepellier: Centre d'Etudes et Recherches Sociocritiques, 1984. *Actes,* Symposium de l'Université Libre de Bruxelles, Juin 1980.

Pagés Larraya, Antonio. "Del legado literario del 80: la crítica." In *On the Centennial of the Argentine Generation of 1880,* edited by Hugo Rodríguez Alcalá, 11–24. Latin American Studies Program, no. 4. Riverside: University of California, 1980.

———. "Estudio preliminar." In *Horas de fiebre,* by Segundo I. Villafañe, vii-li. Buenos Aires: Universidad de Buenos Aires, Facultad de Filosofía y Letras, 1960.

———. " 'Juvenilia': un título y una actitud en nuestra literatura." In *Sala Groussac,* 41–53. Buenos Aires: Guillermo Kraft, 1965.

Pérez Amuchástegui, A. J. *Mentalidades argentinas (1860–1930).* 6th ed. Buenos Aires: Editorial Universitaria de Buenos Aires, 1984.

Pezzoni, Enrique. "Eduardo Wilde: lo natural como distancia." In *La Argentina del ochenta al centenario,* edited by Gustavo Ferrari and Ezequiel Gallo, 707–24. Buenos Aires: Sudamericana, 1980.

Piccirilli, Ricardo. *Los López, una dinastía intelectual: ensayo histórico literario, 1810–1852.* Buenos Aires: Editorial Universitaria de Buenos Aires, 1972.

Ponce, Aníbal. "Lucio V. López." In *La vejez de Sarmiento,* 117–93. Buenos Aires: L. J. Rosso, 1927.

Popolizio, Enrique. *Vida de Lucio V. Mansilla.* Buenos Aires: Pomaire, 1985.

Prieto, Adolfo. *El discurso criollista en la formación de la Argentina moderna.* Buenos Aires: Editorial Sudamericana, 1988.

———. *La literatura autobiográfica argentina.* Buenos Aires: Jorge Alvarez, 1966.

Pró, Diego F. "Joaquín V. González (1863–1923)." In *El movimiento positivista argentino,* edited by Hugo Edgardo Biagini, 463–75. Buenos Aires: Belgrano, 1985.

Propp, Vladimir. *The Morphology of the Folktale.* Edited with an introduction by Svatava Pirkova-Jakobson; translated by Laurence Scott. Bloomington: Indiana University Research Center in Anthropology, Folklore and Linguistics, 1958. Orig. published in Russian in 1928.

Quesada, Ernesto. *Dos novelas sociológicas—"La Bolsa" y "Quilito."* La Plata: J. Peuser, 1892.

Rama, Angel. *Transculturación narrativa en América latina.* Mexico City: Siglo XXI, 1982.

Ramos, Julio. "Entre otros: *Una excursión a los indios ranqueles* de Lucio V. Mansilla." *Filología* 21 (1986): 143–71.

Rebollo Paz, León. "Miguel Cané a través de su archivo inédito: el hombre privado, el artista, el argentino cabal." *Boletín de la Academia Argentina Nacional de la Historia* 43 (1970): 77–90.

Reis, Roberto. "O recato da escritura." *Rocky Mountain Review* 35 (1981): 13–26.

Rivera, Jorge B. *Eduardo Gutiérrez.* Buenos Aires: Centro Editor de América Latina, 1967.

Rock, David. *Argentina, 1516–1982: From Spanish Colonization to the Falklands War.* Berkeley: University of California Press, 1985.

Rodríguez Alcalá, Hugo. "En el 'centenario' de la generación del 80: releyendo *Juvenilia.*" In *On the Centennial of the Argentine Generation of 1880,* edited by Hugo Rodríguez Alcalá, 177–90. Latin American Studies Program, no. 4. Riverside: University of California, 1980.

Roig, A. A. "A. Jacques, un ecléctico francés en el Río de la Plata: un capítulo de la influencia del pensamiento francés en América Latina." *Caravelle* 19 (1972): 143–56.

Rojas, Ricardo. *Elogio de Joaquín V. González.* Buenos Aires: Universidad de Buenos Aires, Facultad de Filosofía y Letras, Instituto de Literatura Argentina, 1925.

———. "Los prosistas fragmentarios." In *Obras completas,* 8:426–73. Buenos Aires: Losada, 1948. Orig. in his *Historia de la literatura argentina.*

Romano, Eduardo. *Análisis de "Don Segundo Sombra."* Buenos Aires: Centro Editor de América Latina, 1967.

Romero, José Luis. "La era aluvial." In *Las ideas políticas en la Argentina,* 167–83. Mexico City: Fondo de Cultura Económica, 1946.

Rozitchner, León. *Perón: entre la sangre y el tiempo; lo inconsciente y la política.* Buenos Aires: Centro Editor de América Latina, 1985.

Ruffinelli, Jorge. *La revista "Caras y caretas."* Buenos Aires: Galerna, 1968.

Russich, Luciano G. *El inmigrante italiano en la novela argentina del 80.* Madrid: Plaza Mayor, 1974. Introduction published as "El inmigrante italiano en la novela argentina del 80." *Chasqui* 12, nos. 2–3 (1983): 42–49.

Salvador, Nélida. "Cambaceres, Eugenio." In *Enciclopedia de la literatura argentina,* compiled by Pedro Orgambide and Roberto Yahni, 111–15. Buenos Aires: Sudamericana, 1970.

Scalavini, Jorge M. "La literatura crítica del Unicato. 1880–1890." In *Actas de las Terceras Jornadas de Investigación de la Historia y Literatura Rioplatense y de los Estados Unidos,* 263–75. Mendoza: Universidad Nacional de Cuyo, Facultad de Filosofía y Letras, 1968.

Schade, George D. "El arte narrativo en *Sin rumbo.*" *Revista iberoamericana* 102–3 (1978): 17–29.

———. "Los viajeros argentinos del ochenta." *Texto crítico* 28 (1984): 82–103.

Schwarz, Roberto. *Ao vencedor as batatas: forma literária e proceso social nos inícios do romance brasileiro.* Sao Paulo: Duas Cidades, 1977.

Scobie, James R. *Buenos Aires: Plaza to Suburb, 1870–1910.* New York: Oxford University Press, 1974.

Senkman, Leonardo. *La identidad judía en la literatura argentina.* Buenos Aires: Pardés, 1983.

Shapiro, Michael J. "Literary Production as a Politicizing Practice." In *Form, Genre, and the Study of Political Discourse,* edited by Herbert W. Simons and Aram A. Aghazarian, 159–94. Columbia: University of South Carolina Press, 1986.

Solá, Graciela de. "El fragmentarismo en los escritores del 80. 'Entre-nos' de Lucio V. Mansilla." *Universidad* 66 (1965): 131–58.

———. "Reivindicación de un escritor." *Revista argentina e iberoamericana* 3 (1961): 117–22.

Solari, Antonio. "Lucio V. López: el escritor, el catedrático, el hombre público." *Tellus* 13–14 (1949): 49–75. Republished as *Lucio V. López, el hombre: su vida y su obra.* Buenos Aires, 1949.

Szuchman, Mark D. *Order, Family, and Community in Buenos Aires, 1810–1860.* Stanford: Stanford University Press, 1988.

Tanner, Roy L. *The Humor of Irony and Satire in the "Tradiciones peruanas."* Columbia: University of Missouri Press, 1985.

Tiempo, César. "Joaquín V. González." *Cuadernos del Congreso por la Libertad de la Cultura* 81 (1964): 45–61.

Verdugo, Iber H. "Estudio preliminar." *La gran aldea,* by Lucio V. López, xi-xlvi. Buenos Aires: Kapelusz, 1965.

Vergara de Bietti, Noemí. *Humoristas del ochenta: Eduardo Wilde, Eugenio Cambaceres, Lucio López, Bartolomé Mitre y Vedia y José S. Alvarez (Fray Mocho).* Buenos Aires: Plus Ultra, 1976. Essay on Alvarez published orig. as "Fray Mocho en el Buenos Aires del 900." *Boletín de la Academia Argentina de Letras* 38 (1973): 77–91.

Vidal, Hernán. *Sentido y práctica de la crítica literaria socio-histórica: panfleto para la proposición de una arqueología acotada.* Minneapolis: Institute for the Study of Ideologies and Literatures, 1984.

Villaverde, Aníbal. "Ideas sociales de José María Ramos Mejía." *Boletín del Instituto de Sociología* 3 (1944): 189–204.

Viñas, David. "Biología, escepticismo y repliegue: Cambaceres y los naturalistas." In his *Literatura argentina y realidad política: de Sarmiento a Cortázar,* 37–41. Buenos Aires: Siglo Veinte, 1971.

———. "Cané: miedo y estilo." In his *Literatura argentina y realidad política: apogeo de la oligarquía,* 57–70. Buenos Aires: Ediciones Siglo Veinte, 1975.

———. *Indios, ejército y fronteras.* Mexico City: Siglo XXI, 1982.

———. *Literatura argentina y realidad política: apogeo de la oligarquía.* Buenos Aires: Ediciones Siglo Veinte, 1975. First published as *Del apogeo de la oligarquía a la crisis de la ciudad liberal: Laferrère.* Buenos Aires: Jorge Alvarez, 1965 and 1967.

———. *Literatura argentina y realidad política: de Sarmiento a Cortázar.* Buenos Aires: Siglo Veinte, 1971.

———. "Mansilla: clase, público y clientela." In his *Literatura argentina y realidad política: apogeo de la oligarquía,* 9–55. Buenos Aires: Ediciones Siglo Veinte, 1975.

———. "Martel y los culpables del 90." In his *Literatura argentina y reali-*

dad política: apogeo de la oligarquía, 70–93. Buenos Aires: Ediciones Siglo Veinte, 1975.

Viola, Miguel Angel. "Fray Mocho y la incomunicación argentina." *Gaceta literaria* 17 (1959): 3, 12.

Volek, Emil. "La carnavalización y la alegoría en *El mundo alucinante*, de Reinaldo Arenas." *Revista iberoamericana* 130–31 (1985): 125–48.

Wapnir, Salomón. "Joaquín V. González, el soñador." *Universidad* 39 (1959): 29–35.

Whitaker, Arthur P. *Argentina*. Englewood Cliffs, N.J.: Prentice-Hall, 1964.

White, Hayden. *The Content of the Form: Narrative Discourse and Historical Representation*. Baltimore: The Johns Hopkins University Press, 1987.

Williams, Raymond. *Marxism and Literature*. Oxford: Oxford University Press, 1977.

Wright, Ione S., and Lisa M. Nekham. *Historical Dictionary of Argentina*. Metuchen, N.J.: Scarecrow Press, 1978.

Yunque, Alvaro. *Fray Mocho, precursor del lunfardo: Versos rantes*. Buenos Aires: Metrópolis, 1971.

Zalazar, Daniel E. "Alejandro Korn y la generación del ochenta." In *On the Centennial of the Argentine Generation of 1880*, edited by Hugo Rodríguez Alcalá, 96–114. Latin American Studies Program, no. 4. Riverside: University of California, 1980.

Zárate, Armando. *Facundo Quiroga, Barranca Yaco: juicios y testimonios*. Buenos Aires: Plus Ultra, 1985.

Zima, Peter V. "Towards Sociological Semiotics." *Sociocriticism* 2 (1985): 113–28.

Index

Acculturation, 41
Alberdi, Juan Bautista, 3
Alem, Leandro N., 185
Alencar, José de, 102
Alonso, Fernando P., 45
Alvarez, José Sixto, 15, 44–56, 141–42, 178, 181; *Memorias de un vigilante,* 44–56, 178, 180, 186; *Vida de los ladrones célebres de Buenos Aires y sus maneras de robar,* 46
Andreetto, Miguel Angel, 54
Ankersmit, F. R., 74
Ara, Guillermo, 47, 118, 123, 131, 139
Arcos, Santiago, 18
Argerich, Antonio, 115, 117–22; *¿Inocentes o culpables?,* 115, 117–22
Artigas, José G., 36, 39
Audience competence, 166–67, 171–72
Autobiographical writing, 32, 95–96, 181
Avellaneda, Andrés, 107
Avellaneda, Nicolás, 3

Bakhtin, Mikhail, 77
Barbarie. See *Civilización/barbarie*
Barthes, Roland, 166
Belgrano, Manuel, 81
Beltrán, Oscar R., 165
Benarós, León, 153
Benítez, Rubén A., 165
Bernhardt, Sarah, 185
Biagini, Hugo Edgardo, 4, 18
Biographical studies, 9–10
Biological determinism, 88, 115, 119, 122, 142, 143, 145
Blasi Brambilla, Alberto Oscar, 4, 44, 105, 123, 127
Bonatti, María, 153
Borges, Jorge Luis, 153
Brown, Guillermo, 85
Burns, E. Bradford, 2, 4, 58, 86

Cambaceres, Eugenio, 106, 115, 116, 117, 119, 123, 128, 139–50; *En la sangre,* 115, 139, 140; *Música sentimental: silbidos de un vago,* 141; *Pot-pourri: silbidos de un vago,* 31, 141; *Sin rumbo,* 117, 129, 139–50, 151, 178, 180, 185
Campanella, Hebe Noemí, 94, 105, 178
Cané, Miguel, 6, 15, 31–48, 181; *En viaje,* 32; *Juvenilia,* 31–48, 185
Canon, 9, 11, 116
Caras y caretas, 45, 186
Carilla, Emilio, 22
Carnivalization, 77–81, 84
Casadevall, Domingo F., 155
Castagnino, Raúl H., 34, 165
Castellanos, Luis Arturo, 4
Castiñeiras, Julio R., 58
Caudillos, 63–64, 68, 172
Cervantes Saavedra, Miguel de, 146, 154
César, Julio, 36
Civilización/barbarie, 37, 39, 60
Clark, Priscilla B. P., 1
Clementi, Hebe, 86
Comparative analysis, 11
Costumbrismo, 44–46, 53, 92, 96, 104, 165
Crawford, William Rex, 64
Cultural code, 166
Cultural documents, 180, 182
Cultural formation, 41
Cultural text, 10, 13, 26, 60, 101, 153, 179, 181

Darío, Rubén, 185
Deconstructive reading, 11, 74
Dellepiane, Angela B., 137, 153, 155
Díaz Araujo, Enrique, 131
Dickens, Charles, 35, 92
Donoso, José, 136
Dowling, William C., 12
Duhalde, Eduardo Luis, 83
Duncan, Tim, 95
Duque de Rivas. *See* Saavedra Ramírez de Baquedano, Angel de, duque de Rivas

Echagüe, Juan Pablo, 136
Erheverría, Esteban: "El matadero," 80, 141
Egan, Carlos A., 160
Epple, Juan, 123, 140, 142
Estrada, José Manuel, 84–85

Ferns, H. S., 4, 5

Folletín, 71, 141, 153, 155, 185
Foster, David William, 17, 60, 73
Francia, Dr. (José Rodríguez Gaspar de Francia), 85
Fraser, Howard, 45
Fray Mocho. *See* Alvarez, José Sixto
Frederick the Great, 36

Gamboa, Dr., 82–83
Gandía, Enrique de, 85
Garmendía, José Ignacio, 152, 172–77; *Cuentos de tropa*, 172–77, 185
Garrels, Elizabeth, 102
Ghiano, Juan Carlos, 17, 32, 165
Giusti, Roberto F., 45, 94, 123
González, Joaquín V., 15, 57–67, 181; *El juicio del siglo, o cien años de historia argentina*, 58; *Mis montañas*, 57–67, 186; *La tradición nacional*, 58, 60, 64; *La universidad de la Plata*, 58; *Universidades y colegios*, 58
González, Julio V., 58
González, Santiago, 34
González Arrili, Bernardo, 94
Grandmontagne, Francisco: *Los inmigrantes prósperos*, 152
Groussac, Paul, 95
Güemes, Martín Miguel, 36, 39
Güiraldes, Ricardo, 151; *Don Segundo Sombra*, 60, 66
Gutiérrez, Eduardo, 68, 69–84, 86, 87, 141, 152, 153–72, 181; *El Chacho*, 71; *Juan Manuel de Rosas: los dramas del terror*, 68, 69–84, 86, 184; *Juan Moreira* (novel), 70, 152, 153–65, 184; *Juan Moreira* (play), 165–72, 185; *Los montoneros*, 71
Gutiérrez, Juan María, 80

Halperín Donghi, Tulio, 68, 77
Hardy, Thomas, 109, 119, 142, 144, 147, 150, 179
Hernández, José, 154; *Martín Fierro*, 152, 153, 162, 184
Hidalgo, 154
Historical analysis, 12
Historiography, 68, 74, 156, 157, 181
Howells, William Dean, 179

Ideologeme, 7
Ideological approach, 10, 11, 13, 76–77, 178–82
Ingenieros, José, 86, 87, 90
Intertextuality, 86, 163

Jacques, Amédée, 33, 35–39, 42
Jitrik, Noé, 2, 38, 78, 95, 141, 154, 178
Jones, C. A., 154
Juárez Celman, Miguel, 113, 114

Lacau, María Hortensia, 135
Lafleur, Héctor R., 45
Landaburu, Argentino J., 129
Landscape as a poetic text, 60–62, 67
Lanuza, José Luis, 16
Larra, Mariano de, 93, 96
Lebedinsky, Mauricio, 4
Lee King, Harry, Jr., 70
Levene, Ricardo, 61
Lewald, H. Ernest, 93
Liberal ideology, 7, 33, 46, 65, 68, 77, 78, 85, 91, 157, 160
Lichtblau, Myron I., 94, 99, 105, 118, 123, 139
Literary response, 11
Literaturization, 63, 67
López, Lucio V., 92; *La gran aldea*, 92, 178, 180, 185
López, Vicente Fidel, 102
López de Gomara, Justo S.: *Gauchos y gringos*, 151
Lunfardo, 54–56
Lussich, Antonio D., 154
Lynch, John, 70, 85

Machado de Assis, Joaquim Maria, 102
Manacorda de Rosetti, Mabel, 135
Mansilla, Lucio V., 6, 15, 16–31, 131, 181; *Entre-nos: causeries del jueves*, 17; *Una excursión a los indios ranqueles*, 16–31; *Narraciones de un porteño*, 17
Marasso, Arturo, 57
Marín, Marta, 54, 56
Markiewicz, Henry, 4
Mármol, José: *Amalia*, 73
Martel, Julián. *See* Miró, José María
Marún, Giaconda, 141
Mastronardi, Carlos, 45
Mayol, Emilio, 45
Maza, 82–83
Megenney, William W., 94
Metaphors of representation, 10, 74
Miró, José María, 104–17; *La Bolsa*, 104–17, 178, 185
Mitre, Bartolomé, 3, 33, 70, 97, 105, 183–84
Modernism, 62, 135, 185
Molloy, Silvia, 18, 136
Montero, Belisario J., 131

Morales, 54
Morando, Horacio C., 68
Moreno, José María, 81
Mythopoesis, 152

Nallim, Carlos Orlando, 16
Narrative processes, 115
Narrative strategy, 72–73
Narrative texture, 29, 116
Naturalism, 8, 78, 88, 91, 92, 93, 105, 115, 116, 117, 119, 121, 122, 123, 124, 127, 128, 132, 139, 140, 142, 145, 147, 149, 150, 155, 164, 167, 178
Naturalization of myths, 66
Nobile, Beatriz de, 106

Obligado, Rafael, 57, 185
Ocantos, Carlos María: *Quilito,* 185
Olaso, Ezequiel de, 4
Onega, Gladys, 107
Otherness, 17, 28, 127, 156

Páez, 36, 39
Pagés Larraya, Antonio, 31, 185
Palma, Ricardo, 93
Paternalism, 102
Patriarchalism, 102
Pellegrini, Carlos, 3, 95, 184, 185
Pellicer, Eustaquio, 45
Pérez, Santos, 79
Pérez Amuchástegui, A. J., 8, 102
Pezzoni, Enrique, 131
Piccirilli, Ricardo, 94
Pirovano, Ignacio, 137
Podestá, Manuel T., 115, 119, 122–27, 123, 152, 165, 166; *Irresponsable,* 115, 122–27, 185
Ponce, Aníbal, 95
Popolizio, Enrique, 16
Positivism, 7, 64
Prieto, Adolfo, 31, 153
Pró, Diego F., 57
Propp, Vladimir, 158
Provenzano, Sergio D., 45

Quesada, Ernesto, 106
Quevedo, Francisco de, 131
Quiroga, Facundo, 57, 65, 72, 79

Rabelais, François, 77
Rama, Angel, 127
Ramos Mejía, José M., 68, 69, 85–90, 181, 184; *Las neurosis de los hombres celebres en la historia argentina,* 68–69, 85–90, 184; *Rosas y su tiempo,* 85
Realism, 53, 74, 92, 93, 96, 117, 132, 167, 178
Rebollo Paz, León, 32
Referential code, 166
Reis, Roberto, 102
Reynafé family, 72, 75, 79–80, 83–84
Rivadavia, Bernardino, 81
Rivera, Jorge B., 70, 153, 155
Roa Bastos, Augusto, 136
Roca, Julio A., 3, 7, 16, 17, 31, 114, 184
Rodó, José Enrique, 42
Rodríguez Alcalá, Hugo, 32
Roig, A. A., 33
Rojas, Ricardo, 32, 58
Romance fronterizo, 166
Romance histórico, 166
Romano, Eduardo, 60
Romanticism, 14, 61, 92, 122, 145, 147, 154, 156, 158
Romero, José Luis, 3
Rosas, Juan Manuel de, 1, 2, 3, 7, 16, 30, 37, 39, 42, 43, 58, 63–64, 68–90, 96, 97, 141, 172, 183, 184
Rozitchner, León, 90
Ruffinelli, Jorge, 45
Russich, Luciano G., 118

Saavedra Ramírez de Baquedano, Angel de, duque de Rivas, 164
Sáenz Peña, Luis, 185, 186
Salvador, Nélida, 150
Sánchez, Florencio, 167
Sarmiento, Domingo Faustino, 3, 39, 60, 72, 154; *Facundo,* 72, 154, 183; *Recuerdos de provincia,* 60
Scalavini, Jorge M., 4
Schade, George D., 19, 32, 150
Schwarz, Roberto, 102
Semiotic, 12
Senkman, Leonardo, 107
Shakespeare, William, 35
Shapiro, Michael J., 42
Solá, Graciela de, 17
Solari, Antonio, 94
Spanish American Modernism. *See* Modernism
Stock Market Cycle, 9, 91, 105–6
Szuchman, Mark D., 102

Tanner, Roy L., 93
Tejedor, Carlos, 184

Textual coherence, 10
Textual power, 15, 30
Textual production, 13, 77, 182
Textual strategies, 11, 60, 182
Thematic studies, 9–10
Tiempo, César, 61

Uriburu, José E., 186
Urquiza, Justo José de, 3

Validation, 29
Valle y Caviedes, Juan del, 131
Verdi, Giuseppe, 164
Verdugo, Iber H., 95
Vergara de Bietti, Noemí, 44, 137
Villafañe, Segundo I., 105
Villaverde, Aníbal, 86
Viñas, David, 4, 5, 17, 18, 31, 106, 173
Viola, Miguel Angel, 53
Volek, Emil, 77

Wapnir, Salomón, 57
Whitaker, Arthur, 58
White, Hayden, 74
Wilde, Eduardo, 6, 128, 129–38, 181, 184; "Tini," 128, 129–38, 184
Williams, Raymond, 1, 11
Wright, Ione S., 33

Yunque, Alvaro, 54

Zárate, Armando, 72
Zola, Émile, 109, 119, 140, 142, 179